The Golden Book of
BAKING

The Golden Book of

BAKING

BARRON'S

First English language edition
for the United States and Canada
published in 2009 by Barron's Educational Series, Inc.

Originally published under the title *The Golden Book of Pâtisserie*
Copyright © McRae Books Srl 2008

The Golden Book of Pâtisserie
was created and produced by McRae Books Srl
Via del Salviatino, 1 – 50016 Fiesole, Florence, Italy
info@mcraebooks.com
www.mcraebooks.com
Publishers: Anne McRae, Marco Nardi

Project Director Anne McRae
Art Director Marco Nardi
Photography Brent Parker Jones (R&R Publications)
Photographic Art Direction Neil Hargreaves
Introduction Carla Bardi
Texts Rachel Lane, Ting Morris, Carla Bardi
Editing Helen Farrell, Anne McRae
Food Styling Lee Blaylock, Neil Hargreaves
Layouts Aurora Granata
Pre-press Filippo Delle Monache, Davide Gasparri

All inquiries should be addressed to:
Barron's Educational Series, Inc.
250 Wireless Boulevard
Hauppauge, New York 11788
www.barronseduc.com

ISBN-13: 978-0-7641-6272-5
ISBN-10: 0-7641-6272-1

Library of Congress Control Number: 2009920838

Printed in China
9 8 7 6 5 4 3 2 1

The level of difficulty for each recipe is given on a scale from
1 (easy) to 3 (complicated).

CONTENTS

INTRODUCTION

For me, the French word *pâtisserie* will forever conjure up the pastry shops of Paris where as a student I would splurge on cakes, pastries, and all manner of "baked things" that I could ill afford but never resist. Row upon row of tantalizing choux pastry vol-au-vents and eclairs, tarts, pies, strudels, mille-feuilles, palmiers, roulades and layer cakes, along with savory quiches, tartlets, and pies were beautifully displayed in the bakery windows.

Many of those pastry shops sold the freshest, tastiest, most delicious food I've ever eaten, but there were disappointments too, especially after I left "the City of Light." The same artfully arranged, seemingly perfect pastries in bakery windows would turn out to be soggy, or heavy, or only half-warmed in a micro-wave, or even taste like a revival of yesterday's offerings. So I decided that the only possible solution was to learn to bake these delicious things at home.

The recipes in this book were developed by Rachel Lane, Ting Morris, and myself. We selected more than 300 classic and modern cookies, bars, brownies, cakes, pies, tarts, pastries, yeast cakes, and savories—all of which can easily be prepared at home. We have graded each recipe 1, 2, or 3 for level of difficulty, with most falling into the first or second categories. There are a few more challenging recipes, for those of you who want to test your skills! These include the Almond Berry Supreme (see page 370), Red Fruit Dacquoise (see page 394), and Chocolate Eclairs (see page 526), among others.

With a well-stocked pantry and some basic kitchen equipment you can tackle all the recipes in this book.

INGREDIENTS: We have specified large eggs throughout. Large eggs weigh about 2 ounces (60 g) each. We have used all-purpose (plain) flour throughout since that is what most people have in their pantries. We found the results more than satisfactory. When the recipes list sugar, we mean ordinary granulated sugar; all other sugars are indicated by name—superfine (caster) sugar, confectioners' (icing) sugar, light brown sugar, and dark brown sugar. While not specified in the recipes, you should use whole milk for best results.

METHOD: Always use softened butter at room temperature when creaming with sugar. Beat by hand or with an electric mixer until pale and creamy. Eggs should also be at room temperature; cold eggs can curdle the batter. Take them out of the refrigerator an hour or two before you start. Modern flour is all pre-sifted, so there is no need to sift it before adding to the batter. Cocoa powder will often benefit from sifting—to remove the lumps rather than to add air. Solid ingredients such as chocolate chips should always be added last. Stir in by hand or use a mixer on low speed.

EQUIPMENT: Standard baking equipment should include baking sheets (trays), loaf pans, round cake pans (8- and 9-inch/20- and 23-cm), springform pans, tart pans, pie plates, standard muffins pans, electric mixer, food processor, handheld mixer, measuring cups and spoons, kitchen scales, rolling pin, whisks, pastry bag, parchment paper, and plastic wrap (cling film).
Happy baking!   Carla Bardi

COOKIES, BARS, AND BROWNIES

ANZAC COOKIES

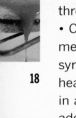

Preheat the oven to 350°F (180°C/gas 4). • Line three large cookie sheets with parchment paper. • Combine the oats, flour, coconut, and sugar in a medium bowl, stirring to combine. • Melt the corn syrup and butter in a small saucepan over medium heat. • Combine the baking soda and boiling water in a cup or small bowl, stirring until dissolved and add to the melted butter mixture. It will froth up a little. • Pour the butter mixture into the dry ingredients, stirring until combined. • Roll walnut-size balls of the dough and place on the prepared cookie sheets, flattening slightly with the back of a fork. Leave 1 inch (2.5 cm) space between each cookie as they will spread a little during baking. • Bake for 15 minutes, or until golden. • Let cool on the baking sheet for a few minutes. Transfer to a rack and let cool completely.

1   cup (150 g) old
    fashioned rolled oats
1   cup (150 g) all-purpose
    (plain) flour
¾   cup (90 g) shredded
    (desiccated) coconut
¾   cup (150 g) sugar
3   tablespoons light corn
    (golden) syrup
½   cup (125 g) butter
1   teaspoon baking soda
    (bicarbonate of soda)
2   tablespoons boiling
    water

Makes: about 30 cookies
Preparation: 15 minutes
Cooking: 15 minutes
Level: 1

■ ■ ■ *This is a New Zealand cookie, named after the Australian and New Zealand Army Corps (ANZAC) that fought in World War I at Gallipoli (1915). Since they were baked in New Zealand and shipped to the other side of the world they had to contain ingredients that wouldn't easily spoil. Whatever their origins, they still taste great today!*

YO YO'S

Cookies: Preheat the oven to 350°F (180°C/gas 4).
• Line two large cookie sheets with parchment
paper. • Beat the butter, sugar, and vanilla using an
electric mixer on medium-high speed until pale and
creamy. • Combine the flour, baking powder, and
custard powder in a medium bowl. • With mixer on
low speed, gradually beat into the butter mixture
until well incorporated. • Roll thirty small balls and
place on the prepared cookie sheets, spacing 1 inch
(2.5 cm) apart. Flatten slightly with the back of a
fork to create a pattern. • Bake for 15–20 minutes,
or until firm and light golden brown. • Let cool on
the cookie sheets for a few minutes. Transfer to a
rack and let cool completely. • Vanilla Butter Filling:
Beat all the filling ingredients using an electric
mixer on medium-high speed until pale and creamy.
• Turn half of the cooled cookies over flat-side up
and spread the filling evenly over the top. Place
the remaining cookies on top and gently
sandwich together.

Cookies

¾ cup (180 g) butter, softened

⅓ cup (50 g) confectioners' (icing) sugar

½ teaspoon vanilla extract (essence)

1 ½ cups (225 g) all-purpose (plain) flour

1 teaspoon baking powder

⅓ cup (50 g) custard powder

Vanilla Butter Filling

¼ cup (60 g) butter, softened

½ cup (75 g) confectioners' (icing) sugar

⅛ teaspoon vanilla extract (essence)

2 tablespoons custard powder

Makes: 15 filled cookies
Preparation: 20 minutes
Cooking: 15–20 minutes
Level: 1

MONTE CARLOS

Cookies: Preheat the oven to 350°F (180°C/gas 4).
• Line three large cookie sheets with parchment paper. • Combine the flour, baking powder, custard powder, and coconut in a medium bowl. • Beat the butter and sugar with an electric mixer on medium-high speed until pale and creamy. • With mixer on low speed, gradually add the mixed dry ingredients and milk, beating until well mixed. • Roll forty small balls and place on the prepared cookie sheets, spacing 1 inch (2.5 cm) apart. Flatten slightly with the back of a fork to create a pattern. • Bake for 15–20 minutes, or until firm and light golden brown. • Let cool on the cookie sheets for a few minutes. Transfer to a rack and let cool completely. •
Coconut Butter Filling: Beat the butter and confectioners' sugar using an electric mixer on medium-high speed until pale and creamy. • Stir in the milk and coconut. • Turn half of the cooled cookies over flat-side up and spread the filling evenly on the cookies. Turn the remaining cookies over and spread with raspberry preserves. Sandwich the two halves together.

Cookies

1½ cups (225 g) all-purpose (plain) flour

1 teaspoon baking powder

¼ cup (30 g) custard powder

⅓ cup (50 g) shredded (desiccated) coconut

½ cup (125 g) butter, softened

½ cup (100 g) superfine (caster) sugar

¼ cup (60 ml) milk

Coconut Butter Filling

⅓ cup (90 g) butter, softened

⅔ cup (100 g) confectioners' (icing) sugar

3 teaspoons milk

2 tablespoons shredded (desiccated) coconut

⅓ cup (110 g) raspberry preserves (jam)

Makes: 20 filled cookies
Preparation: 20 minutes
Cooking: 15–20 minutes
Level: 1

COFFEE AND HAZELNUT CREAMS

Cookies: Beat the butter and sugar using an electric mixer on medium-high speed until pale and creamy. • Add the egg yolk and beat until just combined. • Dissolve the coffee in the boiling water in a cup or small bowl. • With mixer on low speed, gradually add the flour, baking powder, ground hazelnuts, and coffee mixture, beating until well combined. • Roll the dough into an 8-inch (20-cm) long log, wrap in plastic wrap (cling film), and place in the freezer for 30 minutes, or until firm enough to cut without flattening. • Preheat the oven to 350°F (180°C/gas 4). • Line three large cookie sheets with parchment paper. • Remove the cookie dough from the freezer and cut into forty rounds, using a sharp knife. • Place the rounds on the prepared cookie sheets, spacing 1 inch (2.5 cm) apart. • Bake for 10 minutes, or until light golden brown. • Let cool on the baking sheet for a few minutes. Transfer to a rack and let cool completely. • Coffee Filling: Dissolve the coffee in the boiling water in a cup or small bowl. • Add the butter and confectioners' sugar and beat well using a wooden spoon. • Turn half of the cooled cookies over flat-side up. Spread the filling evenly over the cookies, reserving 4 tablespoons for decorating the tops. • Place the remaining cookies on top and gently sandwich together. • Put a small dollop of the remaining filling on top of each cookie sandwich and press a hazelnut halve into it.

Cookies

- ¼ cup (60 g) butter, softened
- ¼ cup (50 g) superfine (caster) sugar
- 1 large egg yolk
- 2 teaspoons freeze-dried coffee granules
- 2 teaspoons boiling water
- ¾ cup (125 g) all-purpose (plain) flour
- ½ teaspoon baking powder
- ¼ cup (25 g) finely ground hazelnuts
- 10 whole hazelnuts, halved

Coffee Filling

- 1½ teaspoons freeze-dried coffee granules
- 1½ teaspoons boiling water + extra, as required
- 2 tablespoons butter, softened
- 1 cup (150 g) confectioners' (icing) sugar

Makes: 20 filled cookies
Preparation: 20 minutes
   + 30 minutes to chill
Cooking: 15 minutes
Level: 1

BLACK PEPPER SHORTBREAD COOKIES

Combine the flour, baking powder, baking soda, cinnamon, allspice, and salt in a medium bowl.
• Beat the butter and sugar in a large bowl with an electric mixer at high speed until pale and creamy.
• With mixer on low speed, beat in the cream, mixed dry ingredients, and black pepper to form a smooth dough. • Form the dough into a log about 2¹/₂ inches (6 cm) in diameter. Wrap in plastic wrap (cling film) and refrigerate for 30 minutes. • Preheat the oven to 375°F (190°C/gas 5). • Butter four large cookie sheets. • Slice the dough ¹/₄ inch (5 mm) thick and place the cookies 1 inch (2.5 cm) apart on the prepared cookie sheets. • Bake for 5–7 minutes, or until just golden. • Transfer to racks and let cool completely.

3   cups (450 g) all-purpose (plain) flour

1   teaspoon baking powder

1   teaspoon baking soda (bicarbonate of soda)

1   teaspoon ground cinnamon

1   teaspoon ground allspice

¹/₄   teaspoon salt

1   cup (250 g) butter

1   cup (200 g) sugar

¹/₄   cup (60 ml) heavy (double) cream

1   teaspoon freshly ground black pepper

Makes: about 55 cookies
Preparation: 40 minutes
  + 30 minutes to chill
Cooking: 5–7 minutes
Level of difficulty: 1

COCONUT AND CHERRY COOKIES

Preheat the oven to 400°F (200°C/gas 6). • Line three large cookie sheets with parchment paper.
• Beat the butter and confectioners' sugar with an electric mixer on medium-high speed until pale and creamy. • Add the egg and beat until just combined.
• With mixer on low speed, add the flour, coconut, and finely chopped cherries, mixing to combine.
• Place 36 small spoonfuls of batter onto the prepared cookie sheets, spacing 1 inch (2.5 cm) apart. Top each one with a piece of cherry. • Bake for 10–15 minutes, or until light golden brown. • Let cool on the cookie sheets for a few minutes. Transfer to a rack and let cool completely.

½ cup (125 g) butter, softened

1 cup (150 g) confectioners' (icing) sugar

1 large egg

1¼ cups (180 g) all-purpose (plain) flour

1 teaspoon baking powder

½ cup (60 g) shredded (desiccated) coconut

½ cup (90 g) candied (glacé) cherries, finely chopped

9 whole candied (glacé) cherries, quartered

Makes: 36 cookies
Preparation: 15 minutes
Cooking: 10–15 minutes
Level: 1

BELGIUM COOKIES

Spiced Cookies: Preheat the oven to 350°F
(180°C/gas 4). • Line three large cookie sheets with
parchment paper. • Combine the flour, baking
powder, cinnamon, ginger, and pumpkin pie spice in
a medium bowl. • Beat the butter, sugar, and vanilla
using an electric mixer on medium-high speed until
pale and creamy. • Add the egg, beating to
combine. • With mixer on low speed, gradually beat
in the mixed dry ingredients. • Lightly flour a work
surface and knead the dough until smooth. • Roll
the dough out on a lightly floured work surface to
1/8-inch (3-mm) thick. • Cut out 36 rounds using a
2 1/2-inch (6-cm) plain cookie cutter. • Place on the
prepared cookie sheets, spacing 1 inch (2.5 cm)
apart. • Bake for 15 minutes, or until golden brown.
• Let cool on the cookie sheets for a few minutes.
Transfer to a rack and let cool completely. •
Frosting: Place the confectioners' sugar in a small
bowl, add the food coloring, then gradually stir in
enough water to obtain a spreadable frosting. •
Spread half the cookies with raspberry preserves
and sandwich together. • Frost the tops of the
cookie sandwiches using a small spatula or knife
and, if liked, sprinkle with jelly crystals.

Spiced Cookies

2 cups (300 g) all-purpose (plain) flour
1 teaspoon baking powder
1 teaspoon ground cinnamon
1 teaspoon ground ginger
1 teaspoon pumpkin pie spice (all-spice)
1/2 cup (125 g) butter, softened
1/4 cup (50 g) firmly packed light brown sugar
1/4 teaspoon vanilla extract (essence)
1 large egg
1/3 cup (110 g) raspberry preserves (jam)

Frosting

1 cup (150 g) confectioners' (icing) sugar
Few drops red food coloring
2 tablespoons boiling water
Red jelly crystals, to decorate (optional)

Makes: 18 filled cookies
Preparation: 25 minutes
Cooking: 15 minutes
Level: 1

AFGHAN COOKIES

Cookies: Preheat the oven to 350°F (180°C/gas 4).
• Line two large cookie sheets with parchment
paper. • Beat the butter and sugar using an electric
mixer on medium-high speed until pale and creamy.
• With mixer on low speed, gradually add the flour
and cocoa, beating until combined. • Stir in the
cornflakes and coconut by hand using a wooden or
large kitchen spoon. • Put spoonfuls of mixture onto
the prepared cookie sheets, spacing 1 inch (2.5 cm)
apart). • Bake for 15 minutes, or until set. • Let cool
on the cookie sheets for a few minutes. Transfer to
a rack and let cool completely. • Frosting: Combine
the confectioners' sugar and cocoa in a small bowl.
Add the vanilla and gradually pour in enough water
to obtain a spreadable frosting. • Frost the tops of
the cooled cookies and top with chopped walnuts.

Cookies

3/4 **cup (180 g) butter,
softened**

1/2 **cup (100 g) sugar**

1 1/3 **cups (175 g) all-purpose
(plain) flour**

1/4 **cup (30 g)
unsweetened cocoa
powder**

1/2 **cup (50 g) cornflakes**

1/3 **cup (40 g) shredded
(desiccated) coconut**

1/4 **cup (30 g) walnuts,
coarsely chopped**

Chocolate Frosting

1 **cup (150 g)
confectioners' (icing)
sugar**

2 **tablespoons
unsweetened cocoa
powder**

1/8 **teaspoon vanilla extract
(essence)**

1 **tablespoon boiling
water**

Makes: about 25 cookies
Preparation: 15 minutes
Cooking: 15 minutes
Level: 1

RASPBERRY DELIGHTS

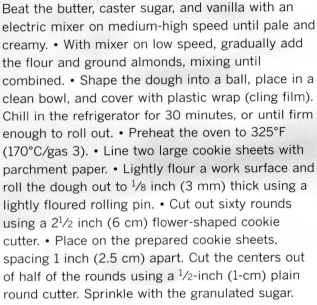

Beat the butter, caster sugar, and vanilla with an electric mixer on medium-high speed until pale and creamy. • With mixer on low speed, gradually add the flour and ground almonds, mixing until combined. • Shape the dough into a ball, place in a clean bowl, and cover with plastic wrap (cling film). Chill in the refrigerator for 30 minutes, or until firm enough to roll out. • Preheat the oven to 325°F (170°C/gas 3). • Line two large cookie sheets with parchment paper. • Lightly flour a work surface and roll the dough out to $1/8$ inch (3 mm) thick using a lightly floured rolling pin. • Cut out sixty rounds using a $2^1/2$ inch (6 cm) flower-shaped cookie cutter. • Place on the prepared cookie sheets, spacing 1 inch (2.5 cm) apart. Cut the centers out of half of the rounds using a $1/2$-inch (1-cm) plain round cutter. Sprinkle with the granulated sugar.
• Bake for 10–15 minutes, or until golden brown.
• Let cool on the baking sheet for a few minutes. Transfer to a rack and let cool completely. • Spoon a small dollop of raspberry preserves onto the cookies without holes. Sandwich together with the cookies with holes.

1   cup (250 g) butter, softened

½   cup (100 g) superfine (caster) sugar,

1   teaspoon vanilla extract (essence)

1½ cups (225 g) all-purpose (plain) flour

¾   cup (125 g) finely ground almonds

2   tablespoons granulated sugar

¾   cup (250 g) raspberry jam, warmed slightly

Makes: 30 filled cookies
Preparation: 30 minutes
  + 30 minutes to chill
Cooking: 10–15 minutes
Level: 1

APRICOT AND COCONUT MACAROONS

Whisk the egg whites, sugar, and vanilla together in a heatproof bowl over a saucepan of barely simmering water until the sugar has dissolved. • Remove from the heat and stir in the flour. • Fold in the coconut and dried apricots with a large kitchen spoon. • Cover the bowl with plastic wrap (cling film) and refrigerate for 30 minutes, or until the mixture is firm. • Preheat the oven to 325°F (170°C/gas 3). • Line two large cookie sheets with parchment paper. • Spoon 24 small mounds of mixture onto the prepared cookie sheets, spacing 1 inch (2.5 cm) apart. • Bake for 15–20 minutes, or until golden. • Let cool on the baking sheet for a few minutes. Transfer to a rack and let cool completely.

4   large egg whites

1   cup (200 g) sugar

1   teaspoon vanilla extract (essence)

½   cup (75 g) all-purpose (plain) flour

1¾ cups (215 g) shredded (desiccated) coconut

¾   cup (135 g) dried apricots, finely chopped

Makes: 24 cookies
Preparation: 20 minutes
  + 30 minutes to chill
Cooking: 15–20 minutes
Level: 1

FLORENTINES

Preheat the oven to 350°F (180°C/gas 4). • Line two large cookie sheets with parchment paper. • Melt the butter and brown sugar in a small saucepan over medium heat. • Combine the almonds, cherries, ginger, and orange peel in a medium bowl. • Pour in the melted butter mixture and add the flour, stirring to combine. • Place tablespoons of the mixture on the prepared cookie sheets, spacing 3 inches (7 cm) apart as they will double in size during baking. Flatten each one using the back of a fork and shape into rounds. • Bake for 10 minutes, or until golden. • Let cool on the cookie sheets for 5 minutes. Transfer to a rack and let cool completely. • When completely cooled, melt the chocolate in a heatproof bowl over a saucepan of barely simmering water. • Spread the smooth undersides of each Florentine with chocolate using a small spatula or knife and place back onto the rack, chocolate side up to set.

¼ **cup (60 g) butter**

¼ **cup (50 g) firmly packed light brown sugar**

¼ **cup (40 g) slivered almonds**

2 **tablespoons candied (glacé) cherries, coarsely chopped**

2 **tablespoons candied (glacé) ginger, coarsely chopped**

2 **tablespoons candied (glacé) orange peel, finely chopped**

⅓ **cup (50 g) all-purpose (plain) flour**

4 **oz (125 g) dark chocolate, coarsely chopped**

Makes: about 12 cookies
Preparation: 20 minutes
Cooking: 10 minutes
Level: 2

FILLED CATS' TONGUES

Cats' Tongue Cookies: Preheat the oven to 350°F (180°C/gas 4). • Line two cookie sheets with parchment paper. • Combine the flour and salt in a medium bowl. • Beat the butter and both sugars in a large bowl with an electric mixer at high speed until creamy. • Add the egg whites and lemon zest, beating until pale and thick. • With mixer on low speed, beat in the dry ingredients. • Fit a pastry bag with a 2-inch (5-cm) plain tip. Fill the pastry bag, twist the opening tightly closed, and squeeze out 2-inch (5-cm) lengths, spacing $1^1/2$ inches (4-cm) apart on the prepared cookie sheets. • Bake, one sheet at a time, for 5–7 minutes, or until faintly tinged with brown on top and slightly darker at the edges. • Working quickly, use a spatula to lift each cookie from the sheet and transfer to racks to cool. • Melt the chocolate in a double boiler over barely simmering water. Dip both ends of the cookies in the melted chocolate and let stand for 30 minutes to set. • Chocolate-Nougat Filling: Chop the nougat in a food processor until finely ground. • Transfer to a small bowl and mix in the chocolate hazelnut spread and confectioners' sugar to form a stiff cream. • Stick the cookies together in pairs with the filling.

Cats' Tongue Cookies

- $2/3$ cup (100 g) all-purpose (plain) flour
- $1/8$ teaspoon salt
- $1/3$ cup (90 g) butter, softened
- $1/3$ cup (75 g) granulated sugar
- 1 tablespoon vanilla sugar
- 2 large egg whites
- 1 teaspoon finely grated lemon zest
- 4 oz (125 g) dark chocolate, coarsely chopped

Chocolate–Nougat Filling

- 2 oz (60 g) nougat, broken into large pieces
- 3 tablespoons chocolate hazelnut spread (Nutella)
- 1 tablespoon confectioners' (icing) sugar

Makes: 16 filled cookies
Preparation: 40 minutes
 + 30 minutes to set
Cooking: 12–15 minutes
Level: 3

CHOCOLATE BISCOTTI

Preheat the oven to 325°F (170°C/gas 3). • Spread the hazelnuts out on a large baking sheet. Toast for 7 minutes, or until lightly golden. Transfer to a large cotton kitchen towel. Fold the towel over the nuts and rub them to remove the skins. Pick out the nuts and chop coarsely. • Increase the oven temperature to 350°F (180°C/gas 4). • Butter a cookie sheet. • Combine the flour, cocoa, baking soda, and salt into a medium bowl. • Beat the eggs, sugar, and vanilla in a large bowl with an electric mixer at high speed until pale and thick. • Mix in the dry ingredients, coffee granules, chocolate chips, and hazelnuts to form a stiff dough. • Divide the dough in half. Form into two 12-inch (30-cm) logs and place 2 inches apart on the prepared cookie sheet, flattening them slightly. • Bake for 25–30 minutes, or until firm to the touch. • Transfer to a cutting board to cool for 15 minutes. • Reduce the oven temperature to 325°F (170°C/gas 3). • Cut the cookie logs on the diagonal into 1-inch (2.5-cm) slices. • Arrange the slices cut-side down on two cookie sheets and bake for 10–15 minutes, or until golden and toasted. • Transfer to racks to cool.

¾ cup (100 g) shelled hazelnuts

1⅓ cups (200 g) all-purpose (plain) flour

½ cup (75 g) unsweetened cocoa powder

1½ teaspoons baking soda (bicarbonate of soda)

¼ teaspoon salt

3 large eggs

1 cup (200 g) sugar

½ teaspoon vanilla extract (essence)

2 teaspoons freeze-dried coffee granules

⅓ cup (60 g) dark chocolate chips

Makes: 24 cookies
Preparation: 40 minutes
Cooking: 35–40 minutes
Level: 2

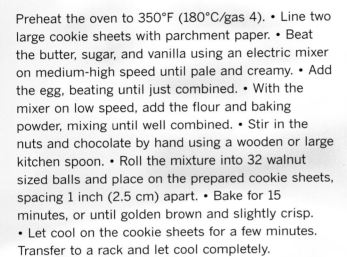

CHOCOLATE AND BRAZIL NUT COOKIES

Preheat the oven to 350°F (180°C/gas 4). • Line two large cookie sheets with parchment paper. • Beat the butter, sugar, and vanilla using an electric mixer on medium-high speed until pale and creamy. • Add the egg, beating until just combined. • With the mixer on low speed, add the flour and baking powder, mixing until well combined. • Stir in the nuts and chocolate by hand using a wooden or large kitchen spoon. • Roll the mixture into 32 walnut sized balls and place on the prepared cookie sheets, spacing 1 inch (2.5 cm) apart. • Bake for 15 minutes, or until golden brown and slightly crisp. • Let cool on the cookie sheets for a few minutes. Transfer to a rack and let cool completely.

½ cup (125 g) butter, softened

½ cup (100 g) firmly packed light brown sugar

½ teaspoon vanilla extract (essence)

1 large egg, lightly beaten

1⅓ cups (200 g) all-purpose (plain) flour

½ teaspoon baking powder

⅔ cup (100 g) Brazil nuts, coarsely chopped

4 oz (125 g) dark chocolate, coarsely chopped

Makes: 32 cookies
Preparation: 15 minutes
Cooking: 15 minutes
Level: 1

SHORTBREAD STARS

Preheat the oven to 350°F (180°C/gas 4). • Line three large cookie sheets with parchment paper. • Beat the butter, sugar, and vanilla using an electric mixer on medium-high speed until pale and creamy. • With mixer on low speed, gradually the flour and cornstarch, mixing until well combined. • Place the dough in a medium bowl, cover with plastic wrap (cling film) and refrigerate for 30 minutes, or until firm enough to roll out. • Lightly flour a work surface and roll the dough out to $1/2$-inch (1-cm) thick using a lightly floured rolling pin. • Cut out 35–40 shapes using a star- or other-shaped cookie cutter. • Place on the prepared cookie sheets, spacing 1 inch (2.5 cm) apart. Prick the stars with a fork and sprinkle with the granulated sugar. • Bake for 15 minutes or until light golden brown. • Let cool on the cookie sheets for a few minutes. Transfer to a rack and let cool completely.

1   cup (250 g) butter, softened

½   cup (100 g) superfine (caster) sugar

½   teaspoon vanilla extract (essence)

2   cups (300 g) all-purpose (plain) flour

1   cup (150 g) cornstarch (cornflour)

2   tablespoons granulated sugar

Makes: 35–40 cookies
Preparation: 30 minutes
Cooking: 15 minutes
Level: 1

CITRUS PINWHEELS

Combine the flour, baking powder, and salt in a medium bowl. • Beat the butter and sugar in a large bowl with an electric mixer at high speed until creamy. • Add the vanilla and egg yolk, beating until just blended. • Mix in the dry ingredients to form a smooth dough. • Dust two sheets of parchment paper with confectioners' sugar. • Divide the dough in four and place each on a piece of paper. • Roll out one dough portion to a 12 x 6-inch (30 x 15-cm) rectangle. • Knead the lemon extract and yellow food coloring into the second dough portion until well blended. • Roll out the dough to the same-sized rectangle as the plain dough. • Invert the lemon dough and place on top of the plain dough, peeling off the paper. • Roll the dough up tightly from the long side and refrigerate for at least 30 minutes. • Repeat with the remaining two dough portions, substituting the orange extract and red food coloring for the lemon extract and yellow food coloring. • Preheat the oven to 350°F (180°C/gas 4). • Set out two cookie sheets. • Slice the dough 1/4-inch (5-mm) thick and place 1 inch (2.5-cm) apart on the cookie sheets. • Bake for 12–15 minutes, or until lightly browned, rotating the sheets halfway through for even baking. • Let cool on the baking sheet for a few minutes. Transfer to a rack and let cool completely.

1⅓ cups (200 g) all-purpose (plain) flour

1 teaspoon baking powder

⅛ teaspoon salt

½ cup (125 g) butter, softened

½ cup (100 g) sugar

1 teaspoon vanilla extract (essence)

1 large egg yolk

¼ teaspoon lemon extract (essence)

3 drops yellow food coloring

½ teaspoon orange extract (essence)

3 drops red food coloring

Makes: 30–32 cookies
Preparation: 1 hour
  + 30 minutes to chill
Cooking: 12–15 minutes
Level: 2

WHITE MERINGUE MICE

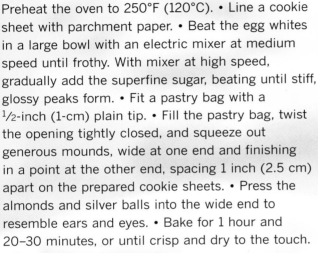

Preheat the oven to 250°F (120°C). • Line a cookie sheet with parchment paper. • Beat the egg whites in a large bowl with an electric mixer at medium speed until frothy. With mixer at high speed, gradually add the superfine sugar, beating until stiff, glossy peaks form. • Fit a pastry bag with a 1/2-inch (1-cm) plain tip. • Fill the pastry bag, twist the opening tightly closed, and squeeze out generous mounds, wide at one end and finishing in a point at the other end, spacing 1 inch (2.5 cm) apart on the prepared cookie sheets. • Press the almonds and silver balls into the wide end to resemble ears and eyes. • Bake for 1 hour and 20–30 minutes, or until crisp and dry to the touch. • Transfer to racks to cool.

2   large egg whites
2/3 cup superfine (caster) sugar
24 almond halves, to decorate
24 silver balls, to decorate

Makes: 12 cookies
Preparation: 30 minutes
Cooking: 80–90 minutes
Level: 2

■ ■ ■ *These cookies are ideal for children's birthday parties.*

BAVARIAN APPLE CONES

Apple Filling: Cook the apples with the orange or lemon juice in a medium saucepan over low heat for about 15 minutes, or until softened. • Transfer to a food processor and process until smooth. Transfer to a small bowl and refrigerate for 1 hour. • With mixer at high speed, beat the cream and vanilla sugar until stiff. • Fold into the apple mixture.
• Cones: Preheat the oven to 375°F (190°C/gas 5).
• Line a cookie sheet with parchment paper. Draw four 4-inch (10-cm) squares on the paper. • Combine the flour, cinnamon, and salt in a medium bowl. • Beat the eggs and sugar in a large bowl with an electric mixer at high speed until pale and thick.
• Fold in the mixed dry ingredients and lemon zest.
• Drop 1 tablespoon of the mixture onto each square on the prepared cookie sheet. Use a thin metal spatula to fill the 4-inch (10-cm) squares. • Bake for 5–7 minutes, or until lightly browned. • Peel each square away from the parchment paper and use a thin metal spatula to lift the cookies. • Twist the squares into cones, smooth-side inward, working quickly. • Cool the cookies completely on racks. • Repeat to make twelve cones. • Fill the cones with the apple filling.

Apple Filling

2   apples, cored, and coarsely chopped

1   tablespoon freshly squeezed orange or lemon juice

1   cup (250 ml) heavy (double) cream

½   cup (100 g) vanilla sugar

Cones

⅔   cup (100 g) all-purpose (plain) flour

½   teaspoon ground cinnamon

⅛   teaspoon salt

3   large eggs

½   cup (100 g) sugar

1   teaspoon finely grated lemon zest

Makes: 30 cookies
Preparation: 55 minutes
    + 1 hour to chill
Cooking: 15 minutes
Level: 3

COOKIE CONES
WITH HAZELNUT CREAM

Cones: Preheat the oven to 400°F (200°C/gas 6).
• Butter four cookie sheets. • Butter two rolling
pins. • Combine the flour and salt in a medium
bowl. • Beat the butter and confectioners' sugar in
a bowl with an electric mixer at high speed until
creamy. • Mix in the dry ingredients and vanilla.
• Stir in the egg whites until well blended. • Fit a
pastry bag with a 1/2-inch (1-cm) plain tip. Fill the
pastry bag, twist the opening tightly closed, and
squeeze out small ovals, spacing them 3 inches
(7 cm) apart on the prepared cookie sheets. • Do
not pipe more than 5 cookies on one sheet. • Bake,
one sheet at a time, for 5–8 minutes, or until just
golden at the edges. • Working quickly, use a
spatula to lift each cookie from the sheet and drape
it over a rolling pin. Remove from the rolling pin
and overlap the edges to form a cone. Let cool
completely. • Butter the cookie sheets again and
continue to bake in batches until all the batter has
been used. • Hazelnut Cream: Heat the chocolate
hazelnut cream in a double boiler over barely
simmering water until liquid. • Transfer to a large
bowl and let cool. • Beat the cream in a large bowl
with an electric mixer at high speed until thick. •
Use a large rubber spatula to fold the cream into
the chocolate mixture until well blended. • Fit a
pastry bag with a 1/4-inch (5-mm) star tip. Fill the
pastry bag and pipe the cream into the cones.

Cones

- 2/3 **cup (100 g) all-purpose (plain) flour**
- 1/8 **teaspoon salt**
- 1/3 **cup (90 g) butter, softened**
- 2/3 **cup (100 g) confectioners' (icing) sugar**
- 1/2 **teaspoon vanilla extract (essence)**
- 4 **large egg whites, lightly beaten**

Hazelnut Cream

- 2/3 **cup (150 g) chocolate hazelnut cream (Nutella)**
- 1 **cup (250 ml) heavy (double) cream**

Makes: 36 cookies
Preparation: 40 minutes
Cooking: 20–30 minutes
Level: 3

ORANGE CRISPS

Beat the butter, sugar, and vanilla using an electric mixer on medium-high speed until pale and creamy. • Add the orange zest and egg, beating until just combined. • With mixer on low speed, add the flour and cinnamon, beating until well combined. • Divide the dough in half and roll two 2-inch (5-cm) round and 2½-inch (6-cm) long logs. Wrap in plastic wrap (cling film) and chill in the freezer for 30 minutes, or until firm enough to cut without flattening. • Preheat the oven to 375°F (190°C/gas 5). • Line two large cookie sheets with parchment paper. • Remove the cookie dough from the freezer and cut each one into thirteen rounds using a sharp knife. • Place the rounds on the prepared cookie sheets, spacing 1 inch (2.5 cm) apart. • Bake for 10 minutes, or until light golden. • Let cool on the baking sheet for a few minutes. Transfer to a rack and let cool completely.

½ cup (125 g) butter, softened

½ cup (100 g) superfine (caster) sugar

3 teaspoons vanilla extract (essence)

1 tablespoon finely grated orange zest

1 large egg

¾ cup (125 g) all-purpose (plain) flour

1 teaspoon ground cinnamon

Makes: 26 cookies
Preparation: 15 minutes
  + 30 minutes to chill
Cooking: 15 minutes
Level: 1

CHOC-MINT COOKIES

Chocolate Cookies: Preheat the oven to 350°F (180°C/gas 4). • Line two large cookie sheets with parchment paper. • Melt the chocolate and butter together in a small heatproof bowl over a saucepan of barely simmering water, stirring occasionally until smooth. • Whisk the egg and sugar together in a large bowl and pour in the melted chocolate, mixing until incorporated. • Stir in the flour, baking powder, and peppermint filled chocolate squares using a wooden or large kitchen spoon until well combined. • Cover the bowl with plastic wrap (cling film) and refrigerate for 30 minutes, or until firm enough to handle. • Roll the mixture into 25 walnut-sized balls and place on the prepared sheets, spacing 2 inches (5 cm) apart. • Bake for 8–10 minutes, or until firm slightly wrinkled. • Let cool on the baking sheet for a few minutes. Transfer to a rack and let cool completely. • Peppermint Frosting: Place the confectioners' sugar in a small bowl, add the food coloring, peppermint extract, and enough boiling water to obtain a spreadable frosting. Taste and adjust the flavor if necessary. • Place small dollops of frosting in the center of each cookie and spread using a small spatula or knife. • Drizzle melted chocolate over the top.

Chocolate Cookies

4 oz (125 g) dark chocolate, coarsely chopped

½ cup (125 g) butter

1 large egg

1 cup (200 g) firmly packed light brown sugar

1¼ cups (180 g) all-purpose (plain) flour

1 teaspoon baking powder

⅓ cup (60 g) peppermint filled chocolate squares, coarsely chopped

Peppermint Frosting

1 cup (150 g) confectioners' (icing) sugar

Few drops green food coloring

Few drops peppermint extract (essence)

2 tablespoons boiling water

3 oz (90 g) dark chocolate, melted

Makes: 25 cookies
Preparation: 30 minutes + 30 minutes to chill
Cooking: 8–10 minutes
Level: 2

CHEWY DATE AND GINGER SQUARES

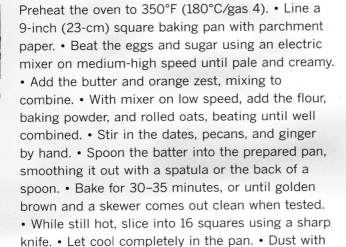

Preheat the oven to 350°F (180°C/gas 4). • Line a 9-inch (23-cm) square baking pan with parchment paper. • Beat the eggs and sugar using an electric mixer on medium-high speed until pale and creamy. • Add the butter and orange zest, mixing to combine. • With mixer on low speed, add the flour, baking powder, and rolled oats, beating until well combined. • Stir in the dates, pecans, and ginger by hand. • Spoon the batter into the prepared pan, smoothing it out with a spatula or the back of a spoon. • Bake for 30–35 minutes, or until golden brown and a skewer comes out clean when tested. • While still hot, slice into 16 squares using a sharp knife. • Let cool completely in the pan. • Dust with confectioners' sugar just before serving.

2   large eggs

1   cup (200 g) firmly packed light brown sugar

⅓   cup (90 g) butter, melted

1   tablespoon finely grated orange zest

1½   cups (225 g) all-purpose (plain) flour

1   teaspoon baking powder

½   cup (120 g) rolled oats

¾   cup (135 g) pitted dates, coarsely chopped

¾   cup (120 g) pecans, coarsely chopped

¾   cup (135 g) candied (glacé) ginger, coarsely chopped

Confectioners' (icing) sugar, to dust

Makes: 16 squares
Preparation: 20 minutes
Cooking: 30–35 minutes
Level: 1

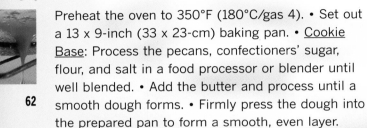

PECAN PIE BARS

Preheat the oven to 350°F (180°C/gas 4). • Set out a 13 x 9-inch (33 x 23-cm) baking pan. • <u>Cookie Base</u>: Process the pecans, confectioners' sugar, flour, and salt in a food processor or blender until well blended. • Add the butter and process until a smooth dough forms. • Firmly press the dough into the prepared pan to form a smooth, even layer. • Bake for 15–20 minutes, or until lightly golden. • <u>Pecan Pie Topping</u>: Melt the chocolate and butter in a double boiler over barely simmering water. • Transfer to a large bowl and mix in the brown sugar, corn syrup, vanilla, and rum until well blended. • Stir in the nuts. • Spread the filling over the baked cookie base. • Bake for 20–25 minutes, or until the filling is bubbling. • Cool completely before cutting into bars.

Cookie Base

¼ cup (30 g) finely chopped pecans

⅔ cup (100 g) confectioners' (icing) sugar

2 cups (300 g) all-purpose (plain) flour

⅛ teaspoon salt

1 cup (250 g) butter

Pecan Pie Topping

3 oz (100 g) dark chocolate, chopped

½ cup (125 g) butter

¾ cup (150 g) firmly packed dark brown sugar

¾ cup (180 ml) dark corn syrup (molasses)

½ teaspoon vanilla extract (essence)

1 tablespoon dark rum

3 cups (350 g) coarsely chopped pecans

Makes: 24–28 bars
Preparation: 40 minutes
Cooking: 35-45 minutes
Level: 1

TOFFEE AND WALNUT SQUARES

Preheat the oven to 350°F (180°C/gas 4). • Butter
an 11 x 7-inch (28 x 18-cm) baking pan. • Combine
the flour, baking powder, and salt in a medium bowl.
• Melt the butter with the brown sugar and corn
syrup in a medium saucepan over low heat until the
sugar has dissolved. • Remove from the heat and
add the vanilla and eggs, beating until just blended.
• Mix in the dry ingredients and walnuts. • Pour the
mixture into the prepared pan. • Bake for 25–30
minutes, or until dry on top and almost firm to the
touch. Do not overbake. • Cool completely in the
pan. • Caramel Frosting: Beat the confectioners'
sugar, butter, corn syrup, and vanilla extract in a
medium bowl until well blended. • Spread the
frosting over the cooled base in the pan. • Cut
into squares.

1¼ cups (180 g) all-purpose (plain) flour
1 teaspoon baking powder
⅛ teaspoon salt
1 cup (250 g) butter, cut up
1 cup (200 g) firmly packed light brown sugar
¼ cup (60 g) light corn (golden) syrup
½ teaspoon vanilla extract (essence)
4 large eggs
½ cup coarsely chopped walnuts

Caramel Frosting
2 cups (300 g) confectioners' (icing) sugar
3 tablespoons butter, melted
1 tablespoon light corn (golden) syrup
1 teaspoon vanilla extract (essence)

Makes: about 20 squares
Preparation: 25 minutes
Cooking: 25–30 minutes
Level: 1

CHOCOLATE CARAMEL SQUARES

Cookie Base: Preheat the oven to 325°F (170°C/ gas 3. • Line a 9-inch (23-cm) square pan with aluminum foil. • Combine the flour, baking powder, and salt in a large bowl. • Beat the butter and sugar in a large bowl with an electric mixer at high speed until pale and creamy. • With mixer on low speed, beat in the dry ingredients. • Spread the mixture evenly in the prepared pan. • Bake for 10–15 minutes, or until golden brown. Let cool in the pan on a rack. • Caramel Topping: Melt the butter with the sugar, corn syrup, and condensed milk in a medium saucepan over low heat, stirring constantly. Bring to a boil then simmer gently for 5 minutes. Remove from the heat and let cool slightly. • Spread the caramel topping evenly over the cookie base. • Melt the chocolate in a double boiler over barely simmering water. Pour the chocolate over the caramel topping and let stand for 1 hour or until set. • Cut into bars.

Cookie Base

1   cup (150 g) all-purpose (plain) flour

1   teaspoon baking powder

⅛   teaspoon salt

½   cup (125 g) butter, softened

¼   cup (50 g) sugar

Caramel Topping

½   cup (125 g) butter, cut up

½   cup (100 g) sugar

2   tablespoons light corn (golden) syrup

1   can (14 oz/400 g) sweetened condensed milk

8   oz (250 g) dark chocolate, coarsely chopped

Makes: 16–20 bars
Preparation: 20 minutes
    + 1–2 hour to cool
    and set
Cooking: 10–15 minutes
Level: 2

MARBLED CREAM CHEESE SQUARES

Cream Cheese Mixture: Preheat the oven to 350°F (180°C/gas 4). • Butter a 9-inch (23-cm) baking pan. • Beat the cream cheese and sugar in a large bowl with an electric mixer at high speed until creamy. • Beat in the orange zest and juice and cornstarch. Add the egg, beating until just blended. • Chocolate Mixture: Melt the chocolate and butter in a double boiler over barely simmering water. Set aside to cool. • Stir in the sugar and vanilla. • Add the beaten egg mixture, followed by the flour. • Pour the chocolate mixture into the prepared pan. • Drop tablespoons of the cream cheese mixture over the chocolate base. • Use a thin metal spatula to swirl the mixtures together to create a marbled effect. • Bake for 25–30 minutes, or until slightly risen around the edges and set in the center. • Cool completely in the pan before cutting into squares.

Cream Cheese Mixture

1 cup (250 g) cream cheese, softened
¼ cup (50 g) sugar
2 tablespoons finely grated orange zest
3 tablespoons freshly squeezed orange juice
1 teaspoon cornstarch (cornflour)
1 large egg

Chocolate Mixture

8 oz (250 g) dark chocolate, chopped
¼ cup (60 g) cold butter
¾ cup (150 g) sugar
2 teaspoons vanilla extract (essence)
2 large eggs, lightly beaten with 2 tablespoons cold water
½ cup (75 g) all-purpose (plain) flour

Makes: 16–20 squares
Preparation: 35 minutes
Cooking: 25–30 minutes
Level: 2

NANAIMO BARS

Cookie Base: Preheat the oven to 350°F (180°C/gas 4). • Butter a 13 x 9-inch (33 x 23-cm) baking pan. • Beat the egg and sugar in a large bowl with an electric mixer at high speed until pale and thick. • Use a wooden spoon to stir in the butter, vanilla, cocoa, graham cracker crumbs, coconut, and pecans. • Firmly press the mixture into the prepared pan to form a smooth, even layer. • Bake for 10–15 minutes, or until firm to the touch. • Let cool completely. • Creamy Filling: Beat the butter, cream, confectioners' sugar, and vanilla in a large bowl with an electric mixer at high speed until well blended. • Spread the mixture over the cookie base and freeze for 10 minutes. • Frosting: Melt the chocolate and butter in a double boiler over barely simmering water. • Spread over the creamy filling. • Refrigerate for at least 1 hour, or until set. • Cut into bars.

Cookie Base

1	large egg
¼	cup (50 g) sugar
½	cup (125 g) butter, softened
1	teaspoon vanilla extract
3	tablespoons unsweetened cocoa powder
2	cups (300 g) graham cracker (digestive biscuit) crumbs
1	cup (150 g) shredded (desiccated) coconut
½	cup (60 g) finely chopped pecans

Creamy Filling

¼	cup (60 g) butter, softened
3	tablespoons heavy (double) cream
2	cups (300 g) confectioners' (icing) sugar
½	teaspoon vanilla extract

Frosting

5	oz (150 g) dark chocolate, chopped
2	tablespoons butter

Makes: 30–36 bars
Preparation: 40 minutes + 1 hour to chill
Cooking: 10–15 minutes
Level: 2

■ ■ ■ *These delicious bar cookies take their name from the Canadian city of Nanaimo in British Columbia.*

ENERGY BARS

Preheat the oven to 375°F (190°C/gas 5). • Butter an 11 x 7-inch (28 x 18-cm) baking pan. • Melt the butter with the honey and raw sugar in a large saucepan over low heat, stirring constantly. • Bring to a boil and simmer until the sugar has dissolved completely. • Remove from the heat and stir in the oats, walnuts, raisins, pumpkin seeds, sunflower seeds, sesame seeds, coconut, cinnamon, and salt. • Spoon the mixture evenly into the prepared pan. • Bake for 30–35 minutes, or until just golden. • Cool completely before cutting into bars.

⅓ cup (90 g) butter, softened

⅓ cup (90 g) honey

½ cup (100 g) raw sugar (Demerara or Barbados)

1½ cups (225 g) old-fashioned rolled oats

½ cup (60 g) coarsely chopped walnuts

½ cup (60 g) raisins

2 tablespoons pumpkin seeds

2 tablespoons sunflower seeds

2 tablespoons sesame seeds

2 tablespoons shredded (desiccated) coconut

¾ teaspoon ground cinnamon

⅛ teaspoon salt

Makes: 16–20 bars
Preparation: 15 minutes
Cooking: 30–35 minutes
Level: 1

LEMON CHEESECAKE SQUARES

Cookie Base: Preheat the oven to 375°F (190°C/gas 5). • Butter a 9-inch (23-cm) square baking pan. • Mix the graham cracker crumbs and butter in a large bowl until well blended. • Firmly press the mixture into the prepared pan to form a smooth, even layer. • Topping: Beat the cream cheese and sugar in a large bowl with an electric mixer at low speed until smooth. • Beat in the lemon curd, cornstarch, and egg. • Spoon the topping over the cookie base. • Bake for 25–30 minutes, or until firm to the touch. • Cool completely before cutting into bars.

Cookie Base

1¼ cups (160 g) graham cracker (digestive biscuit) crumbs

⅓ cup (90 g) butter, melted

Topping

8 oz (250 g) cream cheese, softened

½ cup (100 g) sugar

5 tablespoons lemon curd

3 tablespoons cornstarch

1 large egg, lightly beaten

Makes: 16–20 bars
Preparation: 20 minutes
Cooking: 25–30 minutes
Level: 1

CLASSIC BROWNIES

Preheat the oven to 350°F (180°C/gas 4). • Butter a deep 8-inch (20-cm) square baking pan. • Combine the flour, baking powder, and salt in a large bowl. • Melt the butter and chocolate in a double boiler over barely simmering water. • Remove from the heat and stir in the sugar. • Set aside to cool slightly. • Add the eggs, beating until just blended. • Mix in the dry ingredients, vanilla, and walnuts until well blended. • Pour the mixture into the prepared pan. • Bake for 35–40 minutes, or until dry on top and almost firm to the touch. Do not overbake. • Cool completely in the pan before cutting into bars.

$^2/_3$ cup (100 g) all-purpose (plain) flour

½ teaspoon baking powder

¼ teaspoon salt

$^1/_3$ cup (90 g) butter

4 oz (125 g) dark chocolate, coarsely chopped

1 cup (200 g) sugar

2 large eggs, lightly beaten

½ teaspoon vanilla extract (essence)

$^1/_3$ cup (40 g) coarsely chopped walnuts

Makes: 16 brownies
Preparation: 25 minutes
Cooking: 35–40 minutes
Level: 1

WALNUT BLONDIES

Preheat the oven to 350°F (180°C/gas 4). • Butter a deep 8-inch (20-cm) square baking pan. • Combine the flour, baking powder, and salt in a medium bowl. • Beat the butter and brown sugar in a large bowl with an electric mixer at high speed until creamy. • Add the eggs, corn syrup, and vanilla, beating until just blended. • With mixer on low speed, beat in the dry ingredients and walnuts. • Pour the batter into the prepared pan, smoothing the top. • Bake for 25–30 minutes, or until dry on top and almost firm to the touch. Do not overbake. • Cool completely in the pan before cutting into bars.

$1\frac{1}{3}$ cups (200 g) all-purpose (plain) flour

$\frac{1}{2}$ teaspoon baking powder

$\frac{1}{8}$ teaspoon salt

$\frac{2}{3}$ cup (180 g) butter, softened

$\frac{3}{4}$ cup (150 g) firmly packed light brown sugar

2 large eggs

2 tablespoons light corn (golden) syrup

$1\frac{1}{2}$ teaspoons vanilla extract (essence)

1 cup (120 g) coarsely chopped walnuts

Makes: 16 bars
Preparation: 20 minutes
Cooking: 25–30 minutes
Level: 1

RICH CHOCOLATE BROWNIES

Preheat the oven to 325°F (170°C/gas 3). • Butter and flour a 9-inch (23-cm) baking pan. • Combine the flour, baking powder, and salt in a large bowl. • Melt the chocolate and butter in a double boiler over barely simmering water. Remove from the heat and let cool. • Beat the eggs, brown sugar, and vanilla in a large bowl with an electric mixer at high speed until pale and thick. • Use a large rubber spatula to fold in the chocolate mixture, followed by the dry ingredients. • Pour the batter into the prepared pan. • Bake for 35–40 minutes, or until dry on top and almost firm to the touch. Do not overbake. • Cool completely in the pan before cutting into squares.

1   cup (150 g) all-purpose (plain) flour

½   teaspoon baking powder

⅛   teaspoon salt

6   oz (180 g) dark chocolate, coarsely chopped

1½ cups (375 g) butter

5   large eggs

2   cups (400 g) firmly packed light brown sugar

1   teaspoon vanilla extract (essence)

Makes: 16–20 brownies
Preparation: 30 minutes
Cooking: 30–40 minutes
Level: 1

LEMON MERINGUE BARS

Cookie Base: Preheat the oven to 350°F (180°C/gas 4). • Butter an 11 x 7-inch (28 x 18-cm) baking pan. • Combine the flour, cornstarch, and salt in a medium bowl. • Beat the butter and sugar in a medium bowl with an electric mixer at high speed until creamy. • With mixer on low sped, gradually mix in the dry ingredients to form a stiff dough. • Firmly press the mixture into the prepared pan to form a smooth, even layer. • Bake for 12–15 minutes, or until just golden. • Lemon Meringue Topping: Mix the condensed milk, egg yolks, and lemon zest and juice in a large bowl until well blended. • Pour the mixture over the baked cookie base. • Bake for 8–10 minutes, or until set. • Lower the oven temperature to 325°F (170°C/gas 3). • Beat the egg whites in a large bowl with an electric mixer at medium speed until soft peaks form. • With mixer at high speed, gradually add the sugar, beating until stiff, glossy peaks form. • Use a thin metal spatula to spread the meringue over and sprinkle with the almonds. • Bake for 20–25 minutes more, or until the meringue is dry. • Cool completely in the pan. • Cut into bars.

Cookie Base

1   cup (150 g) all-purpose (plain) flour

⅓   cup (50 g) cornstarch

⅛   teaspoon salt

½   cup (125 g) butter, softened

2   tablespoons sugar

Lemon Meringue Topping

1   can (14 oz/400 g) sweetened condensed milk

2   large eggs, separated

2   teaspoons finely grated lemon zest

½   cup (125 ml) freshly squeezed lemon juice

¼   cup (50 g) sugar

½   cup (75 g) flaked almonds

Makes: 20-24 bars
Preparation: 1 hour
Cooking: 40–50 minutes
Level: 2

LINZER SQUARES

Beat the almonds, egg, sugar, flour, butter, cinnamon, lemon zest, and cloves in a large bowl with an electric mixer at medium speed until well blended. • Press the dough into a disk, wrap in plastic wrap (cling film) and refrigerate for 30 minutes. • Preheat the oven to 350°F (180°C/gas 4). • Butter an 11 x 7-inch (28 x 18-cm) baking pan. • Firmly press half the dough into the prepared pan to form a smooth, even layer. • Warm the raspberry preserves in a small saucepan over low heat until liquid. • Spread the jam over the dough. • Knead the remaining dough on a lightly floured surface and divide in half. • Cut one half of the dough into six portions. Roll each portion into an 11-inch (28-cm) rope. • Place the ropes lengthways on top of the preserves. • Cut the remaining dough into eight portions. Roll each portion into a 7-inch (18-cm) rope. • Place the ropes crosswise on top of the preserves to create a lattice pattern. • Bake for 35–40 minutes, or until the dough is lightly browned. • Cool completely in the pan before cutting into squares.

1   cup (125 g) finely ground almonds

1   large egg, lightly beaten

1¼ cups (250 g) sugar

1⅔ cups (250 g) all-purpose (plain) flour

¾ cup (180 g) butter, softened

1   teaspoon ground cinnamon

1   teaspoon finely grated lemon zest

⅛ teaspoon ground cloves

¾ cup (200 g) raspberry preserves (jam)

Makes: 20–24 squares
Preparation: 15 minutes
Cooking: 35–40 minutes
Level: 1

■ ■ ■ *These squares take their name from the famous Austrian dessert, Linzertorte, which combines a raspberry filling with spiced pastry layers.*

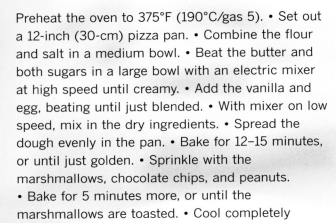

MARSHMALLOW PIZZA

Preheat the oven to 375°F (190°C/gas 5). • Set out a 12-inch (30-cm) pizza pan. • Combine the flour and salt in a medium bowl. • Beat the butter and both sugars in a large bowl with an electric mixer at high speed until creamy. • Add the vanilla and egg, beating until just blended. • With mixer on low speed, mix in the dry ingredients. • Spread the dough evenly in the pan. • Bake for 12–15 minutes, or until just golden. • Sprinkle with the marshmallows, chocolate chips, and peanuts. • Bake for 5 minutes more, or until the marshmallows are toasted. • Cool completely in the pan. • Cut into wedges.

1¾ cups (280 g) all-purpose (plain) flour

¼ teaspoon salt

1 cup (250 g) butter, softened

½ cup (100 g) sugar

½ cup (100 g) firmly packed light brown sugar

½ teaspoon vanilla extract (essence)

1 large egg

1¼ cups (120 g) coarsely chopped pink and white marshmallows

1 cup (180 g) dark chocolate chips

½ cup (60 g) roasted peanuts

Makes: about 20 wedge-shaped cookies
Preparation: 20 minutes
Cooking: 17–20 minutes
Level: 1

CHOCOLATE CHIP PIZZA

Preheat the oven to 375°F (190°C/gas 5). • Set out a 14-inch (35-cm) pizza pan. • Combine the flour, baking soda, and salt in a medium bowl. • Beat the butter and both sugars in a large bowl with an electric mixer at high speed until creamy. • Add the vanilla and eggs, beating until just blended. • Mix in the dry ingredients and chocolate chips. • Spread the mixture in the pan. • Bake for 20–25 minutes, or until lightly browned. • Cool completely in the pan. • Cut into wedges.

2¼ cups (330 g) all-purpose (plain) flour

1 teaspoon baking soda (bicarbonate of soda)

½ teaspoon salt

1 cup (250 g) butter, softened

¾ cup (150 g) sugar

¾ cup (150 g) firmly packed light brown sugar

½ teaspoon vanilla extract (essence)

2 large eggs

1 cup (180 g) dark chocolate chips

Makes: 20 wedge-shaped cookies
Preparation: 15 minutes
Cooking: 20–25 minutes
Level: 1

PANFORTE

Preheat the oven to 350°F (180°C/gas 4). • Line a baking sheet with rice paper. • Mix the candied peels, nuts, flour, and spices in a large bowl. • Heat the brown sugar, honey, and water in a medium saucepan over medium heat, stirring constantly, until the sugar has dissolved. • Wash down the sides of the pan with a pastry brush dipped in cold water to prevent sugar crystals from forming. Cook, without stirring, until small bubbles form on the surface and the syrup registers 238°F (112°C) on a candy thermometer, or reaches the soft-ball stage. • Remove from the heat and stir into the nut mixture. The mixture should be very firm; add a little more boiling water if it is too firm. • Pour onto the prepared sheet. Shape into a round about 1/2-inch (1-cm) thick. • Spice Powder: Mix the cardamom and cinnamon. Sprinkle the spice powder over the panforte. • Bake for 25–35 minutes, or until golden brown. • Cool the panforte completely on the baking sheet. • Remove the excess rice paper from the edges before serving. Dust with confectioners' sugar.

■ ■ ■ *Panforte comes from Siena, a town in central Italy, and dates from the Middle Ages. The rice paper used for lining the pan is edible. It can be found in cake decorating stores or Asian markets.*

1   cup (180 g) candied (glacé) orange peel, cut into small diamonds

2   tablespoons candied (glacé) lemon peel, cut into small diamonds

1²/₃ cups (200 g) unblanched, toasted almonds, coarsely chopped

²/₃ cup (90 g) walnuts, coarsely chopped

1   cup (150 g) all-purpose (plain) flour

1/2 teaspoon each ground coriander, mace, cloves, and nutmeg

1   cup (200 g) firmly packed brown sugar

1/2 cup (125 g) honey

1/4 cup (60 ml) boiling water + extra, as needed

Spice Powder

3   tablespoons ground cardamom

1   tablespoon ground cinnamon

1/3 cup (50 g) confectioners' (icing) sugar, to dust

Serves: 12
Preparation: 25 minutes
Cooking: 25–35 minutes
Level: 2

GLAZED CHOCOLATE PANFORTE

Panforte: Soak the raisins in a small bowl of warm water for 20 minutes. Drain well. • Preheat the oven to 325°F (170°C/gas 3). • Butter and flour a 10-inch (25-cm) round cake pan. • Mix together the walnuts, almonds, hazelnuts, pine nuts, candied peel, raisins, cocoa, chocolate, cinnamon, nutmeg, coriander, and pepper in a large bowl. Stir in the honey, flour, fennel seeds, and enough warm water to make a stiff dough. • Spoon the batter into the prepared pan. • Bake for 25–30 minutes, or until light golden brown. • Cool the cake in the pan for 30 minutes. Turn out onto a rack to cool completely. • Glaze: Melt the chocolate in a double boiler over barely simmering water. Set aside to cool for 10 minutes. Spread over the cake. Let set for at least 1 hour before serving.

2 tablespoons raisins

½ cup (60 g) walnuts, chopped

¼ cup (30 g) almonds, chopped

¼ cup (30 g) hazelnuts, chopped

¼ cup (30 g) pine nuts

⅔ cup (150 g) mixed candied (glacé) orange and lemon peel, cut into small cubes

⅓ cup (50 g) unsweet-ened cocoa powder

4 oz (125 g) dark chocolate, chopped

½ teaspoon each ground cinnamon, nutmeg, coriander, black pepper

¼ cup (60 g) honey, warmed

2⅓ cups (350 g) all-purpose (plain) flour

¼ teaspoon fennel seeds

½ cup (125 ml) warm water + extra, as needed

Glaze

12 oz (350 g) dark chocolate, chopped

Serves: 12
Preparation: 30 minutes
    + 1 hour to set
Cooking: 25–30 minutes
Level: 2

SMALL
CAKES

RASPBERRY AND WHITE CHOCOLATE MUFFINS

Preheat the oven to 350°F (180°C/gas 4). • Line a 12-cup muffin pan with paper baking cups. • Combine the flour, sugar, baking powder, cinnamon, and salt in a large bowl. • Beat the milk, sour cream, butter, and eggs in a large bowl until just blended. • Stir the milk mixture into the dry ingredients, followed by the chocolate and raspberries. • Spoon the batter into the cups, filling each three-quarters full. • Bake for 25–30 minutes, or until golden brown and firm to the touch. • Serve warm or at room temperature.

2 cups (300 g) all-purpose (plain) flour

³/₄ cup (150 g) superfine (caster) sugar

2 teaspoons baking powder

1 teaspoon ground cinnamon

⅛ teaspoon salt

½ cup (125 ml) milk

½ cup (125 ml) sour cream

¼ cup (60 g) butter, melted

1 large egg, lightly beaten

5 oz (150 g) white chocolate, coarsely chopped

½ cup (150 g) fresh or frozen raspberries

Makes: 12 muffins
Preparation: 15 minutes
Cooking: 25–30 minutes
Level: 1

BLUEBERRY AND COCONUT MUFFINS

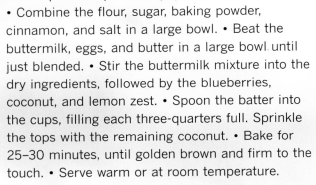

Preheat the oven to 350°F (180°C/gas 4). • Line a 12-cup muffin pan with paper baking cups. • Combine the flour, sugar, baking powder, cinnamon, and salt in a large bowl. • Beat the buttermilk, eggs, and butter in a large bowl until just blended. • Stir the buttermilk mixture into the dry ingredients, followed by the blueberries, coconut, and lemon zest. • Spoon the batter into the cups, filling each three-quarters full. Sprinkle the tops with the remaining coconut. • Bake for 25–30 minutes, until golden brown and firm to the touch. • Serve warm or at room temperature.

2 cups (300 g) all-purpose (plain) flour

¾ cup (150 g) superfine (caster) sugar

1½ teaspoons baking powder

1 teaspoon ground cinnamon

⅛ teaspoon salt

1 cup (250 ml) buttermilk

1 large egg

¼ cup (60 g) butter, melted

½ cup (150 g) fresh or frozen blueberries

¼ cup (30 g) shredded (desiccated) coconut

1 teaspoon finely grated lemon zest

Makes: 12 muffins
Preparation: 15 minutes
Cooking: 25–30 minutes
Level: 1

FIG AND ORANGE MUFFINS

Preheat the oven to 350°F (180°C/gas 4). • Line a 12-cup muffin pan with paper baking cups. • Mix the milk and lemon juice in a large bowl and set aside for 5 minutes. • Bring the orange juice to a boil in a small saucepan. Remove from the heat, add the figs, and let cool slightly. • Combine the flour, sugar, baking powder, and salt in a large bowl. • Add the eggs and butter to the milk and beat until just blended. Stir the milk mixture into the dry ingredients, followed by the figs, orange juice and zest, and almonds. • Spoon the batter into the cups, filling each one three-quarters full. • Bake for 25–30 minutes, until golden brown and firm to the touch. • Serve warm or at room temperature.

1 cup (250 ml) milk

½ tablespoon freshly squeezed lemon juice

3 tablespoons (45 ml) freshly squeezed orange juice

½ cup (90 g) dried figs, coarsely chopped

2 cups (300 g) all-purpose flour

¾ cup (150 g) superfine (caster) sugar

2 teaspoons baking powder

⅛ teaspoon salt

1 large egg

¼ cup (60 g) butter, melted

¼ cup (30 g) finely chopped almonds

½ tablespoon finely grated orange zest

Makes: 12 muffins
Preparation: 20 minutes
Cooking: 25–30 minutes
Level: 1

PLUM CRUMBLE MUFFINS

Muffins: Preheat the oven to 350°F (180°C/gas 4).
• Line a 12-cup muffin pan with paper baking cups.
• Combine the flour, sugar, baking powder, and salt
in a large bowl. • Beat the milk, yogurt, butter, eggs,
and vanilla in a large bowl until just blended. • Stir
the milk mixture into the dry ingredients, followed
by the plums. • Spoon the batter into the cups,
filling each three-quarters full. • Crumble Topping:
Mix the oats, flour, coconut, brown sugar, cinnamon,
and honey in a small bowl. • Use a pastry blender
to cut in the butter until the mixture resembles fine
crumbs. • Sprinkle the topping evenly over the
cups. • Bake for 25–30 minutes, or until golden
brown and firm to the touch. • Serve warm or at
room temperature.

Muffins

2   cups (300 g)
    all-purpose (plain) flour

3/4 cup (150 g) superfine
    (caster) sugar

2   teaspoons baking
    powder

1/8 teaspoon salt

1/2 cup (125 ml) milk

1/2 cup (125 ml) plain
    yogurt

1/4 cup (60 g) butter, melted

1   large egg

1/2 teaspoon vanilla extract

4   plums, halved, pitted,
    and finely chopped

Crumble Topping

1/4 cup (30 g) old-fashioned
    rolled oats

1/4 cup (30 g) all-purpose
    (plain) flour

1/4 cup (30 g) shredded
    (desiccated) coconut

1/4 cup (50 g) brown sugar

1/2 teaspoon ground
    cinnamon

1   tablespoon clear honey

1/4 cup (60 g) butter

Makes: 12 muffins
Preparation: 20 minutes
Cooking: 25–30 minutes
Level: 1

APPLE MUFFINS

Preheat the oven to 350°F (180°C/gas 4). • Butter a 12-cup muffin pan. • Combine the flour, baking powder, cinnamon, nutmeg, coriander, cloves, and salt in a large bowl. Stir in the brown sugar. • Beat the milk, eggs, and butter in a medium bowl until just blended. • Stir the milk mixture into the dry ingredients, followed by the apples and raisins. • Spoon the batter into the prepared muffin pans, filling each three-quarters full. Sprinkle with the brown sugar. • Bake for 25–30 minutes, until golden brown and firm to the touch. • Let cool in the pans for 5 minutes. • Turn the muffins out onto racks. Serve warm or at room temperature.

2 cups (300 g) all-purpose (plain) flour

2 teaspoons baking powder

1 teaspoon ground cinnamon

¼ teaspoon ground nutmeg

¼ teaspoon ground coriander

⅛ teaspoon ground cloves

⅛ teaspoon salt

¾ cup (150 g) firmly packed light brown sugar

1 cup (250 ml) milk

1 large egg

¼ cup (60 g) butter, melted

2 small sweet cooking apples, peeled, cored, and finely chopped

¼ cup (45 g) raisins

2 tablespoons dark brown sugar

Makes: 12 muffins
Preparation: 15 minutes
Cooking: 25–30 minutes
Level: 1

PEAR AND PECAN MINI MUFFINS

Preheat the oven to 350°F (180°C/gas 4). • Line a 24-cup mini muffin pan with paper baking cups. • Combine the flour, sugar, almonds, cinnamon, and salt in a large bowl. • Beat the milk, eggs, and butter in a medium bowl until just blended. • Stir the milk mixture into the dry ingredients, followed by the pears and pecans. • Spoon the batter into the prepared muffin pans, filling each three-quarters full. • Bake for 25–30 minutes, or until golden brown and firm to the touch. • Transfer the muffins onto racks and let cool completely. • Maple Frosting: Beat the butter and maple syrup in a medium bowl until creamy. Mix in the confectioners' sugar until well blended. • Fit a pastry bag with a ¹⁄₄-inch (5-mm) tip. Fill the pastry bag with the frosting and pipe over the muffins. Top with a pecan half.

1³⁄₄ cups (275 g) self-rising flour

³⁄₄ cup (150 g) superfine (caster) sugar

¹⁄₄ cup (30 g) finely ground almonds

1 teaspoon ground cinnamon

¹⁄₈ teaspoon salt

1 cup (250 ml) milk

1 large egg

¹⁄₄ cup (60 g) butter, melted

2 small ripe pears, peeled, cored, and finely chopped

¹⁄₃ cup (35 g) coarsely chopped pecans

Maple Frosting

2 tablespoons butter, softened

2 tablespoons pure maple syrup

1¹⁄₂ cups (225 g) confectioners' (icing) sugar

Pecan halves, to decorate

Makes: 24 mini muffins
Preparation: 25 minutes
Cooking: 25–30 minutes
Level: 2

PEACH AND PASSION FRUIT MUFFINS

Preheat the oven to 350°F (180°C/gas 4). • Line a 12-cup muffin pan with paper baking cups. • Combine the flour, sugar, coconut, baking powder, and salt in a large bowl. • Beat the milk, eggs, and butter in a medium bowl until just blended. • Stir the milk mixture into the dry ingredients, followed by the peaches and passion fruit pulp. • Spoon the batter into the prepared muffin pans, filling each one three-quarters full. • Bake for 25–30 minutes, or until golden brown and firm to the touch. Dust with the confectioners' sugar. • Serve warm or at room temperature.

2 cups (300 g) all-purpose (plain) flour

3/4 cup (150 g) sugar

1/4 cup (30 g) shredded (desiccated) coconut

2 teaspoons baking powder

1/8 teaspoon salt

3/4 cup (180 ml) milk

1 large eggs

1/4 cup (60 g) butter, melted

2 fresh or canned peaches, halved, pitted, and finely chopped

1/4 cup (60 ml) fresh or canned passion fruit pulp

Confectioners' (icing) sugar, to dust

Makes: 12 muffins
Preparation: 15 minutes
Cooking: 25–30 minutes
Level: 1

BLACKBERRY AND VANILLA MUFFINS

Preheat the oven to 350°F (180°C/gas 4). • Line a 12-cup muffin pan with paper baking cups. • Combine the flour, sugar, baking powder, and salt in a large bowl. Stir in the sugar. • Beat the milk, sour cream, eggs, butter, and vanilla in a large bowl until just blended. • Stir the milk mixture into the dry ingredients, followed by the blackberries. • Spoon the batter into the prepared cups, filling each one three-quarters full. • Bake for 25–30 minutes, or until golden brown and firm to the touch. • Serve warm or at room temperature.

2 cups (300 g) all-purpose (plain) flour

³/₄ cup (150 g) sugar

2 teaspoons baking powder

¹/₈ teaspoon salt

¹/₂ cup (125 ml) milk

¹/₂ cup (125 ml) sour cream

2 large egg

¹/₄ cup (60 g) butter, melted

1 teaspoon vanilla extract (essence)

¹/₂ cup (120 g) fresh or frozen blackberries

Makes: 12 muffins
Preparation: 15 minutes
Cooking: 25–30 minutes
Level: 1

BANANA BRAN MUFFINS

Preheat the oven to 350°F (180°C/gas 4). • Butter a 12-cup muffin pan. • Combine the bran, flour, dark brown sugar, raisins, and salt in a large bowl. • Melt the corn syrup and butter in a small saucepan over low heat. • Mix the milk and baking soda in a small bowl. • Mix the corn syrup mixture, milk mixture, and eggs into the dry ingredients until just blended. Stir in the mashed bananas. • Spoon the batter into the prepared muffin pans, filling each one three-quarters full. Place a slice of banana on top of each muffin and sprinkle with the light brown sugar. • Bake for 25–30 minutes, until golden brown and firm to the touch. • Let cool in the pans for 5 minutes. • Turn the muffins out onto racks. Serve warm or at room temperature.

112

$1\frac{1}{2}$ cups (150 g) bran

1 cup (150 g) self-rising flour

$\frac{1}{4}$ cup (50 g) firmly packed dark brown sugar

$\frac{1}{4}$ cup (45 g) raisins

$\frac{1}{4}$ teaspoon salt

1 tablespoon light corn (golden) syrup

1 tablespoon butter

1 cup (250 ml) milk

1 teaspoon baking soda (bicarbonate of soda)

1 large egg

2 firm-ripe bananas, $1\frac{1}{2}$ peeled and mashed, $\frac{1}{2}$ peeled and thinly sliced

2 tablespoons light brown sugar

Makes: 12 muffins
Preparation: 15 minutes
Cooking: 25–30 minutes
Level: 1

DATE AND LEMON MUFFINS

Preheat the oven to 350°F (180°C/gas 4). • Butter a 12-cup muffin pan. • Bring the lemon juice to a boil in a small saucepan. Remove from the heat, add the dates, and let cool slightly. • Combine the flour, baking powder, and salt in a large bowl. Stir in the brown sugar and lemon zest. • Beat the milk, eggs, and butter in a medium bowl until just blended. • Stir the milk mixture into the dry ingredients, followed by the figs and lemon juice. • Spoon the batter into the prepared muffin pans, filling each one three-quarters full. • Bake for 25–30 minutes, until golden brown and firm to the touch. • Let cool in the pans for 5 minutes. • Turn the muffins out onto racks. Serve warm or at room temperature.

3 tablespoons freshly squeezed lemon juice

¾ cup (125 g) dates, pitted and finely chopped

2 cups (300 g) all-purpose (plain) flour

2 teaspoons baking powder

⅛ teaspoon salt

¾ cup (150 g) firmly packed light brown sugar

1 tablespoon finely grated lemon zest

1 cup (250 ml) milk

1 large egg

¼ cup (60 g) butter, melted

Makes: 12 muffins
Preparation: 15 minutes
Cooking: 25–30 minutes
Level: 1

PINK LAMINGTON CUPCAKES

116

Cupcakes: Preheat the oven to 325°F (170°C/gas 3). • Butter a 12-cup muffin pan. • Combine the flour and salt in a small bowl. • Beat the butter, sugar, and vanilla in a large bowl with an electric mixer at medium-high speed until pale and creamy. • Add the milk and eggs, beating until just blended. • Use a large rubber spatula to fold in the dry ingredients. • Spoon the batter into the prepared cups, filling each one three-quarters full. • Bake for 25–30 minutes, or until golden brown and firm to the touch. Let cool in the pans for 5 minutes. Turn the cupcakes out onto racks and let cool completely. • Raspberry Glaze: Mix the jell-o crystals and water in a medium bowl until the crystals have dissolved. Add the ice and let it melt. • Refrigerate for 10 minutes, stirring occasionally to prevent any lumps from forming, until the jelly has set slightly. • Dip the cupcakes in the raspberry jelly, turning them over so they are completely coated. Then dip them in the coconut, making sure that they are evenly coated. Place on racks to set for 15 minutes. If the jell-o begins to set too much as you are preparing the cupcakes, add a little hot water. • Cut each cupcake in half, fill with whipped cream, and sandwich them together.

Cupcakes

1½ cups (225 g) self-raising flour

⅛ teaspoon salt

½ cup (125 g) butter, softened

¾ cup (150 g) superfine (caster) sugar

1 teaspoon vanilla extract (essence)

½ cup (125 ml) milk

2 large eggs

Raspberry Glaze

1 3-oz (85-g) packet raspberry jell-o (jelly) crystals

1 cup (250 ml) boiling water

½ cup (125 g) ice

1½ cups (185 g) shredded (desiccated) coconut

½ cup (125 ml) whipped cream

Makes: 12 cupcakes
Preparation: 30 minutes
   + 10 minutes to chill
Cooking: 25–30 minutes
Level: 2

PASSION FRUIT CUPCAKES

Cupcakes: Preheat the oven to 325°F (170°C/gas 3).
• Line a 12-cup muffin pan with paper baking cups.
• Combine the flour, and salt in a large bowl. • Beat the butter and sugar in a large bowl with an electric mixer on high speed until pale and creamy. • Add the eggs one at a time, beating until just combined after each addition. • With mixer on low speed, add the mixed dry ingredients, sour cream, lemon zest, and passion fruit pulp. • Spoon the batter into the prepared cups, filling each one three-quarters full. • Bake for 25–30 minutes, or until golden brown and firm to the touch. • Let cool completely.
• Passion fruit Frosting: Beat the cream cheese, butter, and lemon zest in a small bowl until creamy. • Stir in the passion fruit pulp and confectioners' sugar until well blended. • Spread the frosting on top of the cupcakes.

Cupcakes

1 cup (150 g) self-rising flour

⅛ teaspoon salt

½ cup (125 g) butter, softened

¾ cup (150 g) superfine (caster) sugar

3 large eggs

½ cup (125 ml) sour cream

1 teaspoon finely grated lemon zest

¼ cup (60 ml) fresh or canned passion fruit pulp

Passion fruit Frosting

⅓ cup (90 ml) cream cheese, softened

2 tablespoons butter, softened

1 teaspoon finely grated lemon zest

3 tablespoons fresh or canned passion fruit pulp

1½ cups (225 g) confectioners' (icing) sugar

Makes: 12 cupcakes
Preparation: 25 minutes
Cooking: 25–30 minutes
Level: 1

BLUEBERRY DELIGHT CUPCAKES

Preheat the oven to 325°F (170°C/gas 3). • Line a 12-cup muffin pan with paper baking cups. • Combine the flour, sugar, baking powder, cinnamon, and salt in a large bowl. • • Beat the butter, sugar, and vanilla in a large bowl with an electric mixer on high speed until pale and creamy. • Add the eggs one at a time, beating until just combined after each addition. • With mixer on low speed, add the mixed dry ingredients and milk. Stir the blueberries in by hand. • Spoon the batter into the prepared cups, filling each one three-quarters full. • Bake for 25–30 minutes, or until golden brown and firm to the touch. • Let cool completely. • Lemon Butter Frosting: Beat the butter, lemon zest, and vanilla in a small bowl until creamy. Stir in the confectioners' sugar until well blended. • Spread the frosting on top of the cupcakes. Decorate with the remaining blueberries.

1½ cups (225 g) all-purpose (plain) flour

1 teaspoon baking powder

1 teaspoon ground cinnamon

⅛ teaspoon salt

½ cup (125 g) butter, softened

¾ cup (150 g) superfine (caster) sugar

½ teaspoon vanilla extract (essence)

½ cup (125 ml) milk

2 large eggs

½ cup (125 g) fresh or frozen blueberries, + extra, to decorate

Lemon Butter Frosting

½ cup (125 g) butter, softened

1 teaspoon finely grated lemon zest

½ teaspoon vanilla extract (essence)

1½ cups (225 g) confectioners' (icing) sugar

Makes: 12 cupcakes
Preparation: 25 minutes
Cooking: 25–30 minutes
Level: 1

FIG, VANILLA, AND HONEY CUPCAKES

Cupcakes: Preheat the oven to 325°F (170°C/gas 3).
• Line a 12-cup muffin pan with paper baking cups.
• Combine the flour and salt in a large bowl. Stir in the sugar. • Beat the butter, honey, eggs, vanilla, and orange zest in a large bowl with an electric mixer on medium-high speed until just blended.
• Stir the honey mixture into the dry ingredients, followed by the figs and walnuts. • Spoon the batter into the prepared cups, filling each three-quarters full. • Bake for 25–30 minutes, until golden brown and firm to the touch. • Let cool completely. •
Honey Frosting: Beat the butter, 1 teaspoon honey, and vanilla seeds in a small bowl. Stir in the confectioners' sugar until well blended. • Spread the frosting on top of the cupcakes. Decorate each cupcake with two fig quarters and drizzle with the remaining honey.

Cupcakes

1 cup (150 g) self-rising flour

1/8 teaspoon salt

1/2 cup (100 g) superfine (caster) sugar

1/4 cup (125 g) butter, softened

1/4 cup (60 ml) clear honey

2 large eggs

1 teaspoon vanilla extract (essence)

1/2 teaspoon finely grated orange zest

1/2 cup (90 g) finely chopped dried figs

1/4 cup (30 g) finely chopped walnuts

Honey Frosting

1/3 cup (90 g) butter, softened

2 teaspoons clear honey

1/2 teaspoon vanilla extract

1 cup (150 g) confectioners' (icing) sugar

6 fresh figs, cut into quarters

Makes: 12 cupcakes
Preparation: 25 minutes
Cooking: 25–30 minutes
Level: 1

APPLE AND PECAN CUPCAKES

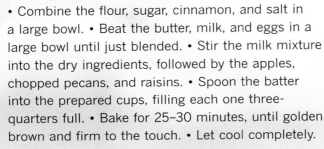

124

Preheat the oven to 325°F (170°C/gas 3). • Line a 12-cup muffin pan with paper baking cups. • Combine the flour, sugar, cinnamon, and salt in a large bowl. • Beat the butter, milk, and eggs in a large bowl until just blended. • Stir the milk mixture into the dry ingredients, followed by the apples, chopped pecans, and raisins. • Spoon the batter into the prepared cups, filling each one three-quarters full. • Bake for 25–30 minutes, until golden brown and firm to the touch. • Let cool completely.

1 cup (150 g) self-rising flour

½ cup (100 g) superfine (caster) sugar

1 teaspoon ground cinnamon

⅛ teaspoon salt

¼ cup (60 g) butter, softened

¼ cup (60 ml) milk

2 large eggs, lightly beaten

½ cup (90 g) apples, peeled, cored, and finely chopped

⅓ cup (50 g) pecans, finely chopped

¼ cup (45 g) raisins

Makes: 12 cupcakes
Preparation: 25 minutes
Cooking: 25–30 minutes
Level: 2

CHOCOLATE COCONUT CUPCAKES

Cupcakes: Preheat the oven to 325°F (170°C/gas 3). • Line a 12-cup muffin pan with paper baking cups. • Melt the chocolate with the cream in a double boiler over barely simmering water. • Set aside and let cool slightly. • Combine the flour, coconut, cocoa, and salt in a medium bowl. • Beat the butter and sugar in a medium bowl with an electric mixer on high speed. Add the eggs one at a time, beating until just combined after each addition. • With mixer on low speed, gradually beat in the mixed dry ingredients and melted chocolate mixture. • Spoon the batter into the prepared cups, filling each one three-quarters full. • Bake for 25–30 minutes, or until golden brown and firm to the touch. • Let cool completely. • Chocolate Ganache: Melt the chocolate with the cream in a double boiler over barely simmering water. • Remove from the heat and stir in the shredded coconut. • Refrigerate for 20 minutes until thickened. • Spread the frosting on the cupcakes and top with the coconut shavings.

Cupcakes

3 oz (90 g) dark chocolate, chopped

²/₃ cup (150 ml) light (single) cream

²/₃ cup (100 g) self-raising flour

½ cup (60 g) shredded (desiccated) coconut

2 tablespoons unsweetened cocoa powder

⅛ teaspoon salt

⅓ cup (90 g) butter, softened

1 cup (200 g) superfine (caster) sugar

2 large eggs

Chocolate Ganache

2 oz (60 g) bittersweet (dark) chocolate, coarsely chopped

½ cup (125 ml) light (single) cream

2 tablespoons shredded (desiccated) coconut

Coconut shavings, to decorate

Makes: 12 cupcakes
Preparation: 25 minutes
+ 20 minutes to chill
Cooking: 25–30 minutes
Level: 1

PARTY CUPCAKES

Preheat the oven to 325°F (170°C/gas 3). • Line a 12-cup muffin pan with paper baking cups. • Combine the flour, baking powder, and salt in a medium bowl. • Beat the butter, sugar, and vanilla in a large bowl with an electric mixer on high speed until pale and creamy. • Add the eggs one at a time, beating until just blended after each addition. • With mixer on low speed, gradually add the mixed dry ingredients and milk. • Spoon the batter into the prepared cups, filling each one three-quarters full. • Bake for 25–30 minutes, until golden brown and firm to the touch. • Let cool completely. • <u>Pink Frosting</u>: Beat the butter and vanilla in a small bowl until creamy. Stir in the confectioners' sugar until well blended. • Gradually mix in the food coloring until the frosting becomes a light pink color. • Fit a pastry bag with a $1/4$-inch (5-mm) star tip. Fill the pastry bag with the frosting and pipe over the cupcakes.

$1\frac{1}{2}$ cups (225 g) all-purpose (plain) flour

$1\frac{1}{2}$ teaspoons baking powder

$\frac{1}{8}$ teaspoon salt

$\frac{1}{2}$ cup (125 g) butter, softened

$3/4$ cup (150 g) superfine (caster) sugar

1 teaspoon vanilla extract (essence)

2 large eggs

$\frac{1}{2}$ cup (125 ml) milk

Pink Frosting

$\frac{1}{2}$ cup (125 g) butter, softened

1 teaspoon vanilla extract (essence)

$1\frac{1}{2}$ cups (225 g) confectioners' (icing) sugar

$\frac{1}{8}$ teaspoon red food coloring

Makes: 12 cupcakes
Preparation: 25 minutes
Cooking: 25–30 minutes
Level: 2

LADYBUG CUPCAKES

Cupcakes: Preheat the oven to 325°F (170°C/gas 3).
• Line a 12-cup muffin pan with paper baking cups.
• Combine the flour and salt in a large bowl. Stir in
the sugar. • Beat the butter, sugar, and vanilla in a
large bowl with an electric mixer on high speed
until pale and creamy. • Add the eggs one at a time,
beating until just blended after each addition. •
With mixer on low speed, gradually add the mixed
dry ingredients and milk. • Spoon the batter into
the prepared cups, filling each three-quarters full. •
Bake for 25–30 minutes, until golden brown and
firm to the touch. • Let cool completely. • Red
Frosting: Beat the butter and vanilla in a small bowl
until creamy. Stir in the confectioners' sugar until
well blended. • Gradually mix in the food coloring
until the frosting becomes a deep red color.
• Spread the frosting on top of the cupcakes.
• Place a licorice strip in the center of each
cupcake. Arrange two licorice rounds on either side
of the licorice strip and top with chocolate buttons
to resemble a ladybug.

Cupcakes

1½ **cups (225 g) self-raising
flour**

⅛ **teaspoon salt**

½ **cup (125 g) butter,
softened**

¾ **cup (150 g) superfine
(caster) sugar**

1 **teaspoon vanilla extract
(essence)**

2 **large eggs**

½ **cup (125 ml) milk**

Red Frosting

½ **cup (125 g) butter,
softened**

1 **teaspoon vanilla extract
(essence)**

1½ **cups (225 g)
confectioners' (icing)
sugar**

⅛ **teaspoon red food
coloring**

6 **thin licorice strips,
cut in short lengths**

48 **small licorice rounds**

48 **chocolate buttons**

Makes: 12 cupcakes
Preparation: 30 minutes
Cooking: 25–30 minutes
Level: 2

POSIE CUPCAKES

Cupcakes: Preheat the oven to 325°F (170°C/gas 3).
• Line a 12-cup muffin pan with paper baking cups.
• Combine the flour, almonds, and salt in a large
bowl. • Beat the butter, sugar, orange and lemon
zests, and vanilla in a large bowl with an electric
mixer on high speed until pale and creamy. • Add
the eggs one at a time, beating until just blended
after each addition. • With mixer on low speed,
gradually add the mixed dry ingredients, yogurt,
and milk. • Spoon the batter into the prepared cups,
filling each one three-quarters full. • Bake for 25–30
minutes, until golden brown and firm to the touch.
• Let cool completely. • Citrus Frosting: Beat the
butter and confectioners' sugar in a small bowl until
well blended. Stir in the lemon and orange juice
until thick. • Spread the frosting on top of the
cupcakes. • Decorate with the sugar flowers.

Cupcakes

1 cup (150 g) self-rising flour

½ cup (50 g) finely ground almonds

⅛ teaspoon salt

½ cup (125 g) butter, softened

¾ cup (150 g) superfine (caster) sugar

1 teaspoon finely grated orange zest

1 teaspoon finely grated lemon zest

½ teaspoon vanilla extract (essence)

2 large eggs

¼ cup (60 ml) plain yogurt

¼ cup (60 ml) milk

Citrus Frosting

¼ cup (60 g) butter, softened

1½ cups (225 g) confectioners' (icing) sugar

½ tablespoon lemon juice

½ tablespoon orange juice

Sugar flowers, to decorate

Makes: 12 cupcakes
Preparation: 25 minutes
Cooking: 25–30 minutes
Level: 1

STRAWBERRY CREAM CUPCAKES

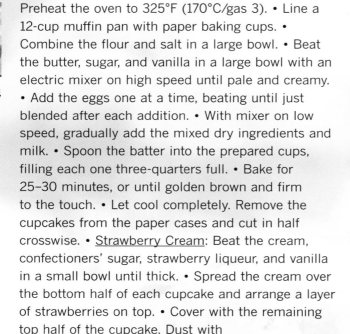

134

Preheat the oven to 325°F (170°C/gas 3). • Line a 12-cup muffin pan with paper baking cups. • Combine the flour and salt in a large bowl. • Beat the butter, sugar, and vanilla in a large bowl with an electric mixer on high speed until pale and creamy. • Add the eggs one at a time, beating until just blended after each addition. • With mixer on low speed, gradually add the mixed dry ingredients and milk. • Spoon the batter into the prepared cups, filling each one three-quarters full. • Bake for 25–30 minutes, or until golden brown and firm to the touch. • Let cool completely. Remove the cupcakes from the paper cases and cut in half crosswise. • Strawberry Cream: Beat the cream, confectioners' sugar, strawberry liqueur, and vanilla in a small bowl until thick. • Spread the cream over the bottom half of each cupcake and arrange a layer of strawberries on top. • Cover with the remaining top half of the cupcake. Dust with confectioners' sugar.

1½ cups (225 g) self-rising flour

⅛ teaspoon salt

½ cup (125 g) butter, softened

¾ cup (150 g) superfine (caster) sugar

½ teaspoon vanilla extract (essence)

2 large eggs

½ cup (125 ml) milk

1 tablespoon strawberry liqueur

Strawberry Cream

½ cup (125 ml) heavy (double) cream

1 tablespoon confectioners' (icing) sugar, + extra, to dust

½ tablespoon strawberry liqueur

½ teaspoon vanilla extract (essence)

36 strawberries, thinly sliced

Makes: 12 cupcakes
Preparation: 25 minutes
Cooking: 25–30 minutes
Level: 1

CHERRY CUPCAKES

Cupcakes: Preheat the oven to 325°F (170°C/gas 3).
• Line a 12-cup muffin pan with paper baking cups.
• Combine the flour and salt in a large bowl. •
• Beat the butter, sugar, and vanilla in a large bowl
with an electric mixer on high speed until pale and
creamy. • Add the eggs one at a time, beating until
just blended after each addition. • With mixer on
low speed, gradually add the mixed dry ingredients
and milk. • Spoon the batter into the prepared cups,
filling each one three-quarters full. • Bake for 25–30
minutes, until golden brown and firm to the touch.
• Let cool completely. • Vanilla Frosting: Mix the
confectioners' sugar, milk, and vanilla in a small
bowl until thick. • Spread the frosting on the
cupcakes. Place a cherry on top of each cupcake.

Cupcakes

1½ cups (225 g) self-rising flour

⅛ teaspoon salt

½ cup (125 g) butter, softened

¾ cup (150 g) superfine (caster) sugar

1 teaspoon vanilla extract (essence)

2 large eggs

½ cup (125 ml) milk

12 candied (glacé) cherries

Vanilla Frosting

1½ cups (225 g) confectioners' (icing) sugar

¼ cup (60 ml) milk

½ teaspoon vanilla extract (essence)

Makes: 12 cupcakes
Preparation: 25 minutes
Cooking: 25–30 minutes
Level: 1

RUM AND RAISIN CUPCAKES

Cupcakes: Dissolve the coffee in the rum in a small bowl. Add the raisins and set aside to plump for 15 minutes. • Preheat the oven to 325°F (170°C/gas 3). • Line a 12-cup muffin pan with paper baking cups. • Combine the flour and salt in a large bowl. • Beat the butter and brown sugar in a large bowl with an electric mixer on high speed until creamy. • Add the eggs one at a time, beating until just blended after each addition. • With mixer on low speed, gradually add the mixed dry ingredients and milk. • Spoon the batter into the prepared cups, filling each one three-quarters full. • Bake for 25–30 minutes, or until golden brown and firm to the touch. • Let cool completely. • Rum Butter Frosting: Beat the butter and rum in a small bowl. Stir in the confectioners' sugar until well blended. • Spread the frosting on the cupcakes. • Decorate with the remaining raisins.

Cupcakes

½ teaspoon freeze-dried coffee granules

5 tablespoons dark rum

¾ cup (135 g) raisins

1½ cups (225 g) self-rising flour

⅛ teaspoon salt

½ cup (125 g) butter, softened

¾ cup (150 g) firmly packed light brown sugar

2 large eggs

½ cup (125 ml) milk

Rum Butter Frosting

½ cup (125 g) butter, softened

1½ tablespoons dark rum

1½ cups (225 g) confectioners' (icing) sugar

Makes: 12 cupcakes
Preparation: 25 minutes + 15 minutes to plump raisins
Cooking: 25–30 minutes
Level: 1

MOCHA CUPCAKES

Cupcakes: Preheat the oven to 325°F (170°C/gas 3).
• Line a 12-cup muffin pan with paper baking cups.
• Melt the chocolate with the cream, coffee liqueur, and coffee granules in a double boiler over barely simmering water. • Set aside and let cool slightly.
• Combine the flour, almonds, cocoa, and salt in a large bowl. • Beat the butter and sugar in a large bowl with an electric mixer on high speed until pale and creamy. • Add the eggs one at a time, beating until just blended after each addition. • With mixer on low speed, gradually add the mixed dry ingredients and melted chocolate mixture. • Spoon the batter into the prepared cups, filling each one three-quarters full. • Bake for 25–30 minutes, or until golden brown and firm to the touch. • Let cool completely. • Mocha Ganache: Melt the chocolate with the cream, coffee liqueur and coffee granules in a double boiler over barely simmering water.
• Remove from the heat and let cool slightly.
• Refrigerate for 20 minutes until thickened.
• Spread the frosting on the cupcakes.

Cupcakes

3½ oz (100 g) dark chocolate, chopped

⅔ cup (150 ml) light (single) cream

3 tablespoons coffee liqueur

1 tablespoon freeze-dried coffee granules

⅔ cup (100 g) self-rising flour

½ cup (50 g) finely ground almonds

2 tablespoons unsweetened cocoa powder

⅛ teaspoon salt

⅓ cup (90 g) butter, softened

1 cup (200 g) superfine (caster) sugar

2 large eggs

Mocha Ganache

3½ oz (100 g) dark chocolate, chopped

½ cup (125 ml) light cream

1 tablespoon coffee liqueur

1 teaspoon coffee granules

Makes: 12 cupcakes
Preparation: 25 minutes
 + 20 minutes to chill
Cooking: 25–30 minutes
Level: 1

WHITE CHOCOLATE CUPCAKES

Preheat the oven to 325°F (170°C/gas 3). • Line a 12-cup muffin pan with paper baking cups. • Melt the chocolate with the cream in a double boiler over barely simmering water. • Set aside and let cool slightly. • Combine the flour and salt in a large bowl. • Beat the butter, sugar, and vanilla in a large bowl with an electric mixer on high speed until creamy. • Add the eggs one at a time, beating until just blended after each addition. • With mixer on low speed, gradually add the mixed dry ingredients and melted chocolate mixture. • Spoon the batter into the prepared cups, filling each one three-quarters full. • Bake for 25–30 minutes, or until golden brown and firm to the touch. • Let cool completely. • White Chocolate Frosting: Melt the chocolate with the cream in a double boiler over barely simmering water. • Remove from the heat and mix in the confectioners' sugar until well blended. • Refrigerate for 20 minutes until thickened. • Spread the frosting on the cupcakes.

3½ oz (100 g) white chocolate, coarsely chopped

⅔ cup (150 ml) light (single) cream

1 cup (150 g) self-rising flour

⅛ teaspoon salt

⅓ cup (90 g) butter, softened

1 cup (200 g) superfine (caster) sugar

1 teaspoon vanilla extract (essence)

2 large eggs

White Chocolate Frosting

3½ oz (100 g) white chocolate, coarsely chopped

½ cup (125 ml) light (single) cream

½ cup (75 g) confectioners' (icing) sugar

Makes: 12 cupcakes
Preparation: 15 minutes
  + 20 minutes to chill
Cooking: 25–30 minutes
Level: 1

PEANUT CUPCAKES

Cupcakes: Preheat the oven to 325°F (170°C/gas 3).
• Line a 12-cup muffin pan with paper baking cups.
• Melt the chocolate with the cream in a double
boiler over barely simmering water. • Set aside and
let cool slightly. • Combine the flour, peanuts, and
salt in a large bowl. • Beat the butter, brown sugar,
and vanilla in a large bowl with an electric mixer on
high speed until creamy. • Add the eggs one at a
time, beating until just blended after each addition.
• With mixer on low speed, gradually add the mixed
dry ingredients and melted chocolate mixture. •
Spoon the batter into the prepared cups, filling each
one three-quarters full. • Bake for 25–30 minutes,
or until golden brown and firm to the touch. • Let
cool completely. • Caramel Frosting: Beat the butter,
brown sugar, and molasses in a small bowl until
creamy. Stir in the confectioners' sugar until well
blended. • Spread the frosting on top of the
cupcakes and top with the peanut brittle.

Cupcakes

3½ oz (100 g) white
   chocolate, chopped

⅔ cup (150 ml) light
   (single) cream

1 cup (150 g) self-rising
   flour

½ cup (50 g) finely ground
   peanuts

⅛ teaspoon salt

⅓ cup (90 g) butter,
   softened

1 cup (200 g) firmly
   packed light brown
   sugar

½ teaspoon vanilla extract
   (essence)

2 large eggs

Caramel Frosting

½ cup (125 g) butter,
   softened

2 tablespoons dark
   brown sugar

½ tablespoon molasses
   (treacle)

1½ cups (225 g) confec-
   tioners' (icing) sugar

3 oz (90 g) store-bought
   peanut brittle

Makes: 12 cupcakes
Preparation: 25 minutes
Cooking: 25–30 minutes
Level: 1

ROSE WATER AND PISTACHIO CUPCAKES

Cupcakes: Preheat the oven to 325°F (170°C/gas 3). • Line a 12-cup muffin pan with paper baking cups. • Combine the flour, ground pistachios, and salt in a large bowl. • Beat the butter and sugar in a large bowl with an electric mixer on high speed until pale and creamy. • Add the eggs one at a time, beating until just blended after each addition. • With mixer on low speed, gradually add the rose water, mixed dry ingredients, and milk. • Spoon the batter into the prepared cups, filling each one three-quarters full. • Bake for 25–30 minutes, or until golden brown and firm to the touch. • Let cool completely. • Rose Frosting: Beat the butter and confectioners' sugar in a small bowl until well blended. Stir in the rose water until thick. • Gradually mix in the food coloring until the frosting becomes a light pink color. • Fit a pastry bag with a 1/4-inch (5-mm) star tip. Fill the pastry bag with the frosting and pipe over the cupcakes.

Cupcakes

1   cup (150 g) self-rising flour

1/2 cup (50 g) finely ground pistachios

1/8 teaspoon salt

1/2 cup (125 g) butter, softened

3/4 cup (150 g) superfine (caster) sugar

2   large eggs

2   tablespoons rose water

1/2 cup (125 ml) milk

Rose Frosting

1/2 cup (125 g) butter, softened

1 1/2 cups (225 g) confectioners' (icing) sugar

1/2 tablespoon rose water

1/8 teaspoon red food coloring

Makes: 12 cupcakes
Preparation: 25 minutes
Cooking: 25–30 minutes
Level: 1

COCONUT, LIME, AND MANGO FRIANDS

148

Preheat the oven to 400°F (200°C/gas 4). • Butter a
12-cup friand pan or muffin pan. • Melt the butter in
a small saucepan over low heat. Cook for 1 minute
until golden, making sure that you do not burn the
butter. • Remove from the heat and let cool
completely. • Combine the flour and salt in a large
bowl. Stir in the confectioners' sugar, coconut, and
lime zest. • Beat the egg whites in a large bowl until
frothy. • Use a large rubber spatula to fold the dry
ingredients and melted butter into the beaten
whites until well blended. • Spoon the batter into
the prepared pans, filling each three-quarters full.
• Arrange the mango slices on top of the friands.
• Bake for 15–18 minutes, until golden brown and
firm to the touch. • Let cool in the pan for
5 minutes. • Turn the friands out onto racks
and let cool completely.

3/4 cup (180 g) butter, cut up
1/2 cup (75 g) self-rising flour
1/8 teaspoon salt
1 1/2 cups (225 g) confectioners' (icing) sugar
1 cup (125 g) shredded (desiccated) coconut
1 tablespoon finely grated lime zest
6 large egg whites
1 mango, thinly sliced

Makes: 12 friands
Preparation: 15 minutes
Cooking: 15–18 minutes
Level: 1

PECAN AND BANANA FRIANDS

Preheat the oven to 400°F (200°C/gas 4). • Butter a 12-cup friand pan or muffin pan. • Melt the butter in a small saucepan over low heat. Cook for 1 minute until golden, making sure that you do not burn the butter. • Remove from the heat and let cool completely. • Combine the flour and salt in a large bowl. Stir in the confectioners' sugar, pecans, and vanilla. • Beat the egg whites in a large bowl until frothy. • Use a large rubber spatula to fold the dry ingredients and melted butter into the beaten whites until well blended. • Spoon the batter into the prepared pans, filling each three-quarters full. • Arrange the banana slices on top of the friands. • Bake for 15–18 minutes, until golden brown and firm to the touch. • Let cool in the pan for 5 minutes. • Turn the friands out onto racks and let cool completely.

3/4 cup (180 g) butter, cut up

1/2 cup (75 g) self-rising flour

1/8 teaspoon salt

1 1/2 cups (225 g) confectioners' (icing) sugar

1 cup (100 g) finely ground pecans

2 teaspoons vanilla extract (essence)

6 large egg whites

2 medium bananas, peeled and thinly sliced

Makes: 12 friands
Preparation: 15 minutes
Cooking: 15–20 minutes
Level: 1

WHITE CHOCOLATE AND PASSION FRUIT FRIANDS

Preheat the oven to 400°F (200°C/gas 4). • Butter a 12-cup friand pan or muffin pan. • Melt the chocolate and butter in a double boiler over barely simmering water. • Remove from the heat and let cool completely. • Combine the flour and salt in a large bowl. Stir in the confectioners' sugar, almonds, and orange zest. • Beat the egg whites in a large bowl until frothy. • Use a large rubber spatula to fold the dry ingredients, melted chocolate mixture, and half of the passion fruit pulp into the beaten whites until well blended. • Spoon the batter into the prepared pans, filling each one just over half full. • Arrange the remaining passion fruit pulp on top of the friands. • Bake for 15–18 minutes, until golden brown and firm to the touch. • Let cool in the pan for 5 minutes. • Turn the friands out onto racks and let cool completely.

3½ oz (100 g) white chocolate, coarsely chopped

⅓ cup (90 g) butter, cut up

½ cup (75 g) self-rising flour

⅛ teaspoon salt

1½ cups (225 g) confectioners' (icing) sugar

1 cup (100 g) finely ground almonds

1 teaspoon finely grated orange zest

6 large egg whites

⅓ cup (90 ml) fresh or canned passion fruit pulp, strained

Makes: 12 friands
Preparation: 15 minutes
Cooking: 15–18 minutes
Level: 1

CHOCOLATE, GINGER, AND ORANGE FRIANDS

154

Preheat the oven to 400°F (200°C/gas 4). • Butter a 12-cup friand pan or muffin pan. • Melt the chocolate and butter in a double boiler over barely simmering water. • Remove from the heat and let cool completely. • Combine the flour and salt in a large bowl. Stir in the confectioners' sugar, almonds, candied ginger, and orange zest. • Beat the egg whites in a large bowl until frothy. • Use a large rubber spatula to fold the dry ingredients and melted chocolate mixture into the beaten whites until well blended. • Spoon the batter into the prepared pans, filling each one just over half full. • Bake for 15–18 minutes, until golden brown and firm to the touch. • Let cool in the pan for 5 minutes. • Turn the friands out onto racks and let cool completely. Dust with the cocoa.

- 3½ oz (100 g) dark chocolate, coarsely chopped
- ⅓ cup (90 g) butter
- ½ cup (75 g) self-rising flour
- ⅛ teaspoon salt
- 1½ cups (225 g) confectioners' (icing) sugar
- 1 cup (100 g) finely ground almonds
- 2 tablespoons finely sliced candied ginger
- 1 tablespoon finely grated orange zest
- 6 large egg whites

  Unsweetened cocoa powder, to dust

Makes: 12 friands
Preparation: 15 minutes
Cooking: 15–18 minutes
Level: 1

SPICED PLUM AND HAZELNUT FRIANDS

156

Preheat the oven to 400°F (200°C/gas 4). • Butter a 12-cup friand pan or muffin pan. • Melt the butter in a small saucepan over low heat. Cook for 1 minute until golden, making sure it does not burn. • Remove from the heat and let cool completely. • Combine the flour, cinnamon, nutmeg, coriander, cloves, and salt in a large bowl. Stir in the confectioners' sugar and hazelnuts. • Beat the egg whites in a large bowl until frothy. • Use a large rubber spatula to fold the dry ingredients and melted butter into the beaten whites until well blended. • Spoon the batter into the prepared pans, filling each one just over half full. • Arrange the plum slices on top of the friands. Bake for 15–18 minutes, until golden brown and firm to the touch. • Let cool in the pan for 5 minutes. • Turn the friands out onto racks and let cool completely.

¾ cup (180 g) butter, melted

½ cup (75 g) self-rising flour

1 teaspoon ground cinnamon

½ teaspoon ground nutmeg

¼ teaspoon ground coriander

¼ teaspoon ground cloves

⅛ teaspoon salt

1½ cups (225 g) confectioners' (icing) sugar

1 cup (100 g) finely ground hazelnuts

6 large egg whites

5 plums, halved, pitted, and thinly sliced

Makes: 12 friands
Preparation: 15 minutes
Cooking: 15–18 minutes
Level: 1

GINGER MADELEINES

Preheat the oven to 375°F (190°C/gas 5). • Butter and flour a 12-cup madeleine pan. • Combine the flour, pumpkin pie spice, and salt in a medium bowl. • Beat the eggs and sugar in a large bowl with an electric mixer on medium-high speed until tripled in volume and very thick, about 5 minutes. • Use a large rubber spatula to fold in the dry ingredients, melted butter, and ginger until just blended. • Spoon tablespoons of the batter into the prepared pan. • Bake for 11–13 minutes, until golden brown and firm to the touch. • Turn the madeleines out onto racks. Dust with the confectioners' sugar. Serve warm or at room temperature.

¾ cup (125 g) self-rising flour

½ teaspoon pumpkin pie spice (all-spice)

⅛ teaspoon salt

2 large eggs

1 cup (200 g) superfine (caster) sugar

⅓ cup (90 g) butter, melted

1 tablespoon finely chopped candied (glacé) ginger

Confectioners' (icing) sugar, to dust

Makes: 12 madeleines
Preparation: 15 minutes
Cooking: 11–13 minutes
Level: 1

ORANGE MADELEINES

Preheat the oven to 375°F (190°C/gas 5). • Butter and flour a 12-cup madeleine pan. • Combine the flour and salt in a medium bowl. • Beat the eggs and sugar in a large bowl with an electric mixer on medium-high speed until tripled in volume and very thick, about 5 minutes. • Use a large rubber spatula to fold in the dry ingredients, melted butter, and orange zest until just blended. • Spoon tablespoons of the batter into the prepared pan. • Bake for 11–13 minutes, until golden brown and firm to the touch. • Turn the madeleines out onto racks. Dust with the confectioners' sugar. Serve warm or at room temperature.

¾ cup (125 g) self-rising flour

⅛ teaspoon salt

2 large eggs

1 cup (200 g) superfine (caster) sugar

⅓ cup (90 g) butter, melted

1 tablespoon finely grated orange zest

Confectioners' (icing) sugar, to dust

Makes: 12 madeleines
Preparation: 15 minutes
Cooking: 11–13 minutes
Level: 1

SPICED MADELEINES

Preheat the oven to 375°F (190°C/gas 5). • Butter and flour a 12-cup madeleine pan. • Combine the flour, cinnamon, nutmeg, coriander, cloves, and salt in a medium bowl. • Beat the eggs and sugar in a large bowl with an electric mixer on medium-high speed until tripled in volume and very thick, about 5 minutes. • Use a large rubber spatula to fold in the dry ingredients and melted butter until just blended. • Spoon tablespoons of the batter into the prepared pan. • Bake for 11–13 minutes, until golden brown and firm to the touch. • Turn the madeleines out onto racks. Dust with the confectioners' sugar. Serve warm or at room temperature.

$3/4$ **cup (125 g) self-rising flour**

$1/2$ **teaspoon ground cinnamon**

$1/4$ **teaspoon ground nutmeg**

$1/4$ **teaspoon ground coriander**

$1/8$ **teaspoon ground cloves**

$1/8$ **teaspoon salt**

2 **large eggs**

1 **cup (200 g) superfine (caster) sugar**

$1/3$ **cup (90 g) butter, melted**

Confectioners' (icing) sugar, to dust

Makes: 12 madeleines
Preparation: 15 minutes
Cooking: 11–13 minutes
Level: 1

CHOCOLATE MADELEINES

Preheat the oven to 375°F (190°C/gas 5). • Butter and flour a 12-cup madeleine pan. • Combine the flour, cocoa, cinnamon, and salt in a medium bowl. • Beat the eggs and sugar in a large bowl with an electric mixer on medium-high speed until tripled in volume and very thick, about 5 minutes. • Use a large rubber spatula to fold in the dry ingredients and melted butter until just blended. • Spoon tablespoons of the batter into the prepared pan. • Bake for 11–13 minutes, until golden brown and firm to the touch. • Turn the madeleines out onto racks. Serve warm or at room temperature.

3/4 cup (125 g) self-rising flour

2 tablespoons unsweetened cocoa powder

1/2 teaspoon ground cinnamon

1/8 teaspoon salt

2 large eggs

1 cup (200 g) superfine (caster) sugar

1/3 cup (90 g) butter, melted

Makes: 12 madeleines
Preparation: 15 minutes
Cooking: 11–13 minutes
Level: 1

LEMON AND LIME MADELEINES

Preheat the oven to 375°F (190°C/gas 5). • Butter and flour a 12-cup madeleine pan. • Combine the flour and salt in a medium bowl. • Beat the eggs and sugar in a large bowl with an electric mixer on medium-high speed until tripled in volume and very thick, about 5 minutes. • Use a large rubber spatula to fold in the dry ingredients, melted butter, and lemon and lime zests until just blended. • Spoon tablespoons of the batter into the prepared pan. • Bake for 11–13 minutes, until golden brown and firm to the touch. • Turn the madeleines out onto racks. Dust with the confectioners' sugar. Serve warm or at room temperature.

¾ cup (125 g) self-rising flour

⅛ teaspoon salt

2 large eggs

1 cup (200 g) superfine (caster) sugar

⅓ cup (90 g) butter, melted

1½ teaspoons finely grated lemon zest

1½ teaspoons finely grated lime zest

Confectioners' (icing) sugar, to dust

Makes: 12 madeleines
Preparation: 15 minutes
Cooking: 11–13 minutes
Level: 1

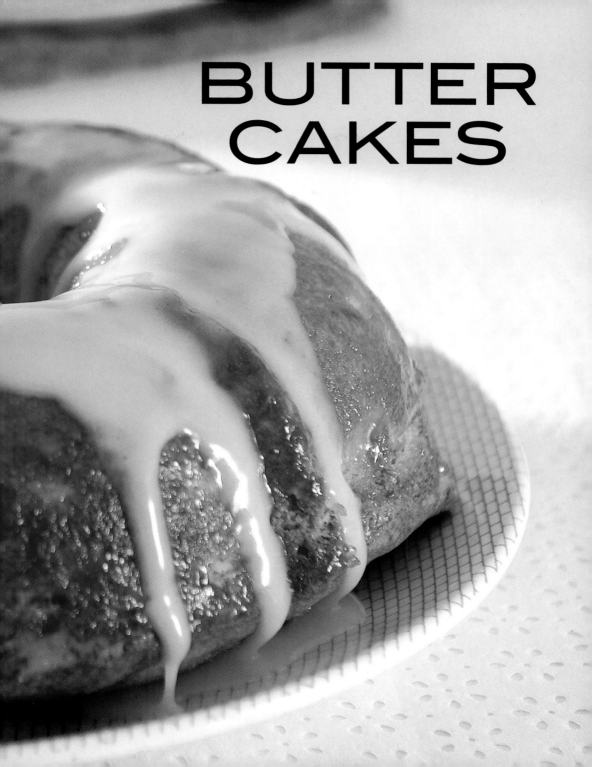

BUTTER CAKES

BASIC POUND CAKE

Preheat the oven to 350°F (180°C/gas 4). • Butter and flour a 10-inch (25-cm) tube pan. • Combine the flour, baking powder, baking soda, and salt in a large bowl. • Beat the butter, sugar, and vanilla and almond extracts in a large bowl with an electric mixer at medium speed until creamy. • Add the eggs, one at a time, beating until just blended after each addition. • With mixer at low speed, gradually beat in the dry ingredients, alternating with the milk. • Spoon the batter into the prepared pan. • Bake for 50–60 minutes, or until a toothpick inserted into the center comes out clean. • Run a knife around the edges of the pan to loosen the cake. Cool the cake in the pan for 15 minutes. Turn the cake out onto a rack and let cool completely.

3 cups (450 g) all-purpose (plain) flour

1 teaspoon baking powder

½ teaspoon baking soda (bicarbonate of soda)

½ teaspoon salt

1 cup (250 g) butter, softened

2 cups (400 g) sugar

2 teaspoons vanilla extract (essence)

1 teaspoon almond extract

5 large eggs

1 cup (250 ml) milk

Serves: 10–12
Preparation: 15 minutes
Cooking: 50–60 minutes
Level: 1

■■■ *Vary the flavor of this cake by changing the extracts used. Orange and coconut are a good combination, as are butterscotch and vanilla. For a different flavor, add finely grated citrus zests or a teaspoon each of ginger, nutmeg, cinnamon, and/or pumpkin pie spice (all-spice). Serve with whipped cream and chopped fresh fruit, if liked.*

HONEY AND SPICE POUND CAKE

Cake: Preheat the oven to 325°F (160°C/gas 3).
• Butter and flour a 10-inch (25-cm) Bundt pan.
• Mix the flour, baking powder, baking soda, and salt in a medium bowl. • Beat the butter, sugar, honey, and vanilla in a large bowl with an electric mixer at medium speed until pale and creamy.
• Add the eggs, one at a time, beating until just blended after each addition. • With mixer at low speed, gradually beat in the dry ingredients, alternating with the sour cream. • Spoon half the batter into the prepared pan. • Filling: Mix the sugar, cinnamon, and ginger in a small bowl. Sprinkle over the batter in the pan. Spoon the remaining batter over the top. • Bake for 70–80 minutes, or until golden brown and a toothpick inserted into the center comes out clean. • Run a knife around the edges of the pan to loosen the cake. Cool the cake in the pan for 15 minutes. Turn out onto a rack and let cool completely. • Dust with the confectioners' sugar.

Cake

2 cups (300 g) all-purpose (plain) flour

1 teaspoon baking powder

½ teaspoon baking soda (bicarbonate of soda)

½ teaspoon salt

1 cup (250 g) butter, softened

1 cup (200 g) sugar

⅓ cup (90 ml) honey

2 teaspoons vanilla extract (essence)

3 large eggs

¾ cup (180 ml) sour cream

⅓ cup (50 g) confectioners' (icing) sugar, to dust

Filling

1 cup (200 g) sugar

2 teaspoons ground cinnamon

1 teaspoon ground ginger

Serves: 10–12
Preparation: 25 minutes
Cooking: 70–80 minutes
Level: 1

ALMOND POUND CAKE

Preheat the oven to 350°F (180°C/gas 4). • Butter and flour a 10-inch (25-cm) Bundt pan. • Mix the flour, ground almonds, baking powder, and salt in a large bowl. • Beat the butter, sugar, almond extract, and vanilla in a large bowl with an electric mixer at medium speed until pale and creamy. • Add the eggs, one at a time, beating until just blended after each addition. • With mixer at low speed, gradually beat in the dry ingredients, alternating with the milk. • Spoon the batter into the prepared pan. • Sprinkle with the almonds. • Bake for 75–85 minutes, or until a toothpick inserted into the center comes out clean. • Run a knife around the edges of the pan to loosen the cake. Cool the cake in the pan for 15 minutes. Turn out onto a rack and let cool completely.

2 cups (300 g) all-purpose (plain) flour

1 cup (125 g) finely ground almonds

1 teaspoon baking powder

¼ teaspoon salt

1½ cups (375 g) butter, softened

3 cups (600 g) sugar

2 teaspoons almond extract (essence)

1 teaspoon vanilla extract (essence)

6 large eggs

1 cup (250 ml) milk

¾ cup (75 g) slivered almonds or almond pieces

Serves: 12–14
Preparation: 20 minutes
Cooking: 75–85 minutes
Level: 1

APPLE AND WALNUT POUND CAKE

Preheat the oven to 350°F (180°C/gas 4). • Butter and flour a 9-inch (23-cm) Bundt pan. • Mix the flour, cinnamon, ginger, baking powder, baking soda, and salt in a large bowl. • Beat the butter, sugar, eggs, and vanilla in a large bowl with an electric mixer at medium speed until creamy.
• With mixer at low speed, gradually beat in the dry ingredients. • By hand, stir in the apple and walnuts. • Spoon the batter into the prepared pan.
• Bake for 55–65 minutes, or until a toothpick inserted into the center comes out clean. • Run a knife around the edges of the pan to loosen the cake. Cool the cake in the pan for 15 minutes. Turn out onto a rack and let cool completely.

2 cups (300 g) all-purpose (plain) flour

1½ teaspoons ground cinnamon

1½ teaspoons ground ginger

¾ teaspoon baking powder

¼ teaspoon baking soda (bicarbonate of soda)

¼ teaspoon salt

1 cup (250 g) butter, softened

1⅓ cups (270 g) sugar

2 large eggs

2 teaspoons vanilla extract (essence)

2 cups (300 g) grated peeled apple

1 cup (100 g) walnuts, coarsely chopped

Serves: 10–12
Preparation: 20 minutes
Cooking: 55–65 minutes
Level: 1

DOUBLE CHOCOLATE POUND CAKE

Cake: Preheat the oven to 350°F (180°C/gas 4).
• Butter and flour a 10-inch (25-cm) Bundt pan. Sprinkle the pan with 2 tablespoons of the sugar.
• Melt the chocolate in a double boiler over barely simmering water. Set aside to cool. • Mix the flour, baking powder, baking soda, and salt in a large bowl. • Beat the butter, remaining sugar, and vanilla and almond extracts in a large bowl with an electric mixer at medium speed until creamy. • Add the eggs, one at a time, beating until just blended after each addition. • With mixer at low speed, gradually beat in the dry ingredients, alternating with the yogurt. • Spoon the batter into the prepared pan.
• Bake for 75–85 minutes, or until a toothpick inserted into the center comes out clean. • Run a knife around the edges of the pan to loosen the cake. Cool the cake in the pan for 15 minutes. Turn out onto the rack and let cool completely. • Glaze: Melt each type of chocolate separately in a double boiler over barely simmering water. • Drizzle alternate spoonfuls of the melted chocolate over the cake.

■■■If liked, serve this luscious big cake with fresh raspberries to contrast with the sweetness of the chocolate.

Cake

2 cups (400 g) sugar

8 oz (250 g) white chocolate, chopped

3 cups (450 g) all-purpose (plain) flour

1 teaspoon baking powder

½ teaspoon baking soda (bicarbonate of soda)

½ teaspoon salt

1 cup (250 g) butter, softened

2 teaspoons vanilla extract (essence)

1 teaspoon almond extract (essence)

5 large eggs

1 cup (250 ml) plain yogurt

Glaze

4 oz (125 g) white chocolate, melted

4 oz (125 g) dark chocolate

Serves: 16
Preparation: 25 minutes
Cooking: 75–85 minutes
Level: 1

CHOCOLATE POUND CAKE WITH PEPPERMINT FROSTING

Cake: Preheat the oven to 350°F (180°C/gas 4).
• Butter and flour a 10-inch tube pan. • Combine the flour, cocoa, baking powder, and salt in a large bowl. • Beat the butter, shortening, sugar, and vanilla in a large bowl with an electric mixer at medium speed until creamy. • Add the eggs, one at a time, beating until just blended after each addition. • With mixer at low speed, gradually beat in the dry ingredients, alternating with the milk.
• Spoon the batter into the prepared pan. • Bake for 1 hour and 35–45 minutes, or until a toothpick inserted into the center comes out clean. • Run a knife around the edges of the pan to loosen the cake. Cool the cake in the pan for 15 minutes. Turn out onto a rack and let cool completely. •
Peppermint Frosting: With mixer at medium speed, beat the confectioners' sugar and butter in a large bowl until creamy. Beat in the cocoa, milk, and peppermint extract until smooth. • Spread the top and sides of the cake with the frosting.

■■■*If you don't like the peppermint flavored frosting, omit the peppermint extract and go with the creamy, plain chocolate frosting.*

Cake

3⅓ cups (500 g) all-purpose (plain) flour

1 cup (150 g) unsweetened cocoa powder

1 teaspoon baking powder

½ teaspoon salt

1 cup (250 g) butter, softened

½ cup (125 g) vegetable shortening

3 cups (600 g) sugar

1 tablespoon vanilla extract (essence)

5 large eggs

1¼ cups (300 ml) milk

Peppermint Frosting

2 cups (300 g) confectioners' (icing) sugar

¼ cup (60 g) butter, softened

⅓ cup (50 g) unsweetened cocoa powder

1 tablespoon milk

½ teaspoon peppermint extract (essence)

Serves: 16–20
Preparation: 25 minutes
Cooking: 1 hour 35–45 minutes
Level: 1

CHOCOLATE CHIP POUND CAKE

Preheat the oven to 350°F (180°C/gas 4). • Butter and flour a 10-inch (25-cm) tube pan. • Mix the flour, baking powder, and salt in a large bowl. • Beat the butter, sugar, and vanilla in a large bowl with an electric mixer at medium speed until pale and creamy. • Add the eggs, one at a time, beating until just blended after each addition. • With mixer at low speed, gradually beat in the dry ingredients, alternating with the buttermilk. • By hand, stir in the chocolate chips. • Spoon the batter into the prepared pan. Bake for 75–85 minutes, or until a toothpick inserted into the center comes out clean. • Run a knife around the edges of the pan to loosen the cake. Cool the cake in the pan for 15 minutes. Turn out onto a rack and let cool completely.

2½ cups (375 g) all-purpose (plain) flour

1 teaspoon baking powder

½ teaspoon salt

1½ cups (375 g) butter, softened

2¼ cups (450 g) sugar

2 teaspoons vanilla extract (essence)

5 large eggs

¾ cup (180 ml) buttermilk

1 cup (180 g) dark chocolate chips

Serves: 14–16
Preparation: 25 minutes
Cooking: 75–85 minutes
Level: 1

PUMPKIN POUND CAKE

186

Preheat the oven to 375°F (160°C/gas 3). • Butter and flour a 10-inch (25-cm) tube pan. • Mix the flour, baking powder, baking soda, cinnamon, ginger, nutmeg, and salt in a large bowl. • Beat the sugar and oil in a large bowl with an electric mixer at medium speed until well blended. • Add the eggs, one at a time, beating until just blended after each addition. • With mixer at low speed, gradually beat in the pumpkin and mixed dry ingredients. • By hand, stir in the pecans. • Spoon the batter into the prepared pan. • Bake for 70–80 minutes, or until golden brown on top and a toothpick inserted into the center comes out clean. • Run a knife around the edges of the pan to loosen the cake. Cool the cake in the pan for 15 minutes. Turn out onto a rack and let cool completely. • Dust with the confectioners' sugar just before serving.

■■■ This is the perfect cake to bake at Thanksgiving time.

3 cups (450 g) all-purpose (plain) flour

2 teaspoons baking powder

1 teaspoon baking soda (bicarbonate of soda)

1 teaspoon ground cinnamon

1 teaspoon ground ginger

1 teaspoon ground nutmeg

½ teaspoon salt

2 cups (400 g) sugar

1¼ cups (300 ml) vegetable oil

4 large eggs

2 cups (400 g) plain canned pumpkin

½ cup (60 g) finely ground pecans

⅓ cup (50 g) confectioners' (icing) sugar, to dust

Serves: 12–14
Preparation: 25 minutes
Cooking: 70–80 minutes
Level: 1

187

APPLESAUCE POUND CAKE

Preheat the oven to 350°F (180°C/gas 4). • Butter and flour a 10-inch (25-cm) tube pan. • Mix the flour, baking soda, cinnamon, ginger, nutmeg, cloves, and salt in a large bowl. • Beat the butter and brown sugar in a large bowl with an electric mixer at medium speed until creamy. • Add the eggs, one at a time, beating until just combined after each addition. • With mixer at low speed, gradually beat in the dry ingredients, alternating with the applesauce. By hand, stir in the dates and walnuts. • Spoon the batter into the prepared pan. • Bake for 80–90 minutes, or until golden brown and a toothpick inserted into the center comes out clean. • Run a knife around the edges of the pan to loosen the cake. Cool the cake in the pan for 15 minutes. Turn out onto a rack and let cool completely.

$3\frac{1}{3}$ cups (500 g) all-purpose (plain) flour

2 teaspoons baking soda (bicarbonate of soda)

1 teaspoon ground cinnamon

1 teaspoon ground ginger

1 teaspoon ground nutmeg

½ teaspoon ground cloves

½ teaspoon salt

½ cup (125 g) butter, softened

2 cups (400 g) firmly packed brown sugar

2 large eggs e

3 cups (450 g) unsweetened applesauce

1 cup (120 g) chopped dates

1 cup (100 g) coarsely chopped walnuts

Serves: 12–14
Preparation: 20 minutes
Cooking: 80–90 minutes
Level: 1

POUND CAKE WITH RASPBERRY SAUCE

Cake: Preheat the oven to 325°F (160°C/gas 3).
• Butter and flour a 10-inch (25-cm) tube pan. •
Mix the flour, nutmeg, baking soda, and salt in a
large bowl. • Beat the butter, sugar, vanilla, and
almond extract in a large bowl with an electric
mixer at medium speed until pale and creamy.
• Add the eggs, one at a time, beating until just
blended after each addition. • With mixer at low
speed, gradually beat in the dry ingredients,
alternating with the milk. • Spoon the batter into
the prepared pan. • Bake for 80–90 minutes, or
until a toothpick inserted into the center comes out
clean. • Run a knife around the edges of the pan to
loosen the cake. Cool the cake in the pan for 15
minutes. Turn out onto a rack to cool completely.
• Raspberry Sauce: Place the mashed raspberries,
sugar, and liqueur in a medium bowl and stir until
the sugar has dissolved. • Refrigerate for at least
3 hours before serving. • Drizzle the sauce over
the cake, or pass the sauce on the side.

■■■ This is a lovely light pound cake. Serve plain for
breakfast or morning tea, or with the raspberry sauce
on special occasions.

Cake

3⅓ cups (500 g) all-
purpose (plain) flour

1 teaspoon ground
nutmeg

½ teaspoon baking soda
(bicarbonate of soda)

½ teaspoon salt

2 cups (500 g) butter,
softened

3 cups (600 g) sugar

2 teaspoons vanilla
extract (essence)

1 teaspoon almond
extract (essence)

6 large eggs

½ cup (125 ml) milk

Raspberry Sauce

3 cups (500 g) fresh
raspberries, lightly
mashed with a fork

¼ cup (50 g) sugar

1 tablespoon crème de
cassis or orange liqueur

Serves: 12–14
Preparation: 30 minutes
+ 3 hours to chill
Cooking: 80–90 minutes
Level: 1

CITRUS POUND CAKE

Cake: Preheat the oven to 325°F (160°C/gas 3).
• Butter and flour a 10-inch (25-cm) Bundt pan.
• Mix the flour, baking soda, and salt in a large bowl. • Beat the butter, cream cheese, sugar, and lemon and orange extracts in a large bowl with an electric mixer at medium speed until creamy. • Add the eggs, one at a time, beating until just blended after each addition. • With mixer at low speed, gradually beat in the dry ingredients. The batter will be quite thick. • Spoon the batter into the prepared pan. • Bake for 1 hour and 35–45 minutes, or until golden brown and a toothpick inserted into the center comes out clean. • Run a knife around the edges of the pan to loosen the cake. Cool the cake in the pan for 15 minutes. Turn out onto a rack and let cool completely. • Frosting: Beat the confectioners' sugar, butter, and lemon zest in a medium bowl. Beat in enough lemon or orange juice to make a spreadable frosting. • Spread the cake with the frosting. Top with the almonds.

Cake

2⅓ cups (350 g) all-purpose (plain) flour

½ teaspoon baking soda (bicarbonate of soda)

½ teaspoon salt

¾ cup (180 g) butter, softened

1 package (8 oz/250 g) cream cheese, softened

2¼ cups (450 g) sugar

1 teaspoon lemon extract (essence)

1 teaspoon orange extract (essence)

5 large eggs

Frosting

2 cups (300 g) confectioners' (icing) sugar

¼ cup (60 g) butter, melted

1 tablespoon finely grated lemon zest

2 tablespoons freshly squeezed lemon or orange juice

¼ cup (30 g) almond pieces, to top

Serves: 10–12
Preparation: 15 minutes
Cooking: 1 hour 35–45 minutes
Level: 1

PINEAPPLE POUND CAKE

Cake: Preheat the oven to 350°F (180°C/gas 4).
• Butter and flour a 10-inch (23-cm) Bundt pan.
• Mix the flour, baking powder, cinnamon, ginger, nutmeg, baking soda, and salt in a large bowl.
• Beat the butter, sugar, pineapple extract, and vanilla in a large bowl with an electric mixer at medium speed until creamy. • Add the eggs, one at a time, beating until just blended after each addition. • With mixer at low speed, gradually beat in the sweet potatoes and dry ingredients. • Spoon the batter into the prepared pan. • Bake for 70–80 minutes, or until a toothpick inserted into the center comes out clean. • Run a knife around the edges of the pan to loosen the cake. Cool the cake in the pan for 15 minutes. Turn out onto a rack and let cool completely. • Glaze: Beat the confectioners' sugar, butter, and pineapple extract in a medium bowl until smooth. Beat in enough of the water to make a soft glaze. Drizzle over the cake.

Cake

- 3 cups (450 g) all-purpose (plain) flour
- 2 teaspoons baking powder
- 1 teaspoon cinnamon
- 1 teaspoon ground ginger
- 1 teaspoon ground nutmeg
- ½ teaspoon baking soda (bicarbonate of soda)
- ½ teaspoon salt
- 1 cup (250 g) butter, softened
- 2 cups (400 g) sugar
- 2 teaspoons pineapple extract (essence)
- 1 teaspoon vanilla extract (essence)
- 4 large eggs
- 2 cups (400 g) cooked, mashed sweet potatoes

Glaze

- 2 cups (300 g) confectioners' (icing) sugar
- ¼ cup (60 g) butter, melted
- 2 teaspoons pineapple extract (essence)
- 2 tablespoons hot water

Serves: 14–16
Preparation: 25 minutes
Cooking: 70–80 minutes
Level: 1

LEMON POPPY SEED SYRUP CAKE

Cake: Preheat the oven to 350°F (180°C/gas 4).
• Butter and flour a 9-inch (23-cm) springform pan.
• Mix the flour, almonds, baking powder, and salt in a large bowl. • Place the poppy seeds and milk in a small bowl and set aside for 15 minutes. • Beat the butter, sugar, and lemon zest in a large bowl with an electric mixer at medium speed until creamy. • Add the eggs, one at a time, beating until just blended after each addition. • With mixer at low speed, gradually beat in the dry ingredients, alternating with the lemon juice and poppy seed mixture.
• Spoon the batter into the prepared pan. • Bake for 50–60 minutes, or until a toothpick inserted into the center comes out clean. • Cool the cake in the pan for 10 minutes. Turn out onto a rack. • Lemon Syrup: Heat the sugar, lemon juice, and water in a small saucepan over low heat. Bring to a boil and simmer for 2 minutes. • Place the cake on the rack over a jelly-roll pan. Poke holes in the cake with a skewer or fork. Spoon the hot syrup over the warm cake. Scoop up any syrup from the pan and drizzle over the cake until it is all absorbed.

Cake

2 cups (300 g) all-purpose (plain) flour

½ cup (50 g) finely ground almonds

2 teaspoons baking powder

¼ teaspoon salt

⅓ cup (50 g) poppy seeds

¼ cup (60 ml) milk

¾ cup (180 g) butter, softened

1 cup (200 g) firmly packed light brown sugar

1 tablespoon finely grated lemon zest

3 large eggs

½ cup (125 ml) freshly squeezed lemon juice

Lemon Syrup

1 cup (200 g) sugar

⅔ cup (150 ml) freshly squeezed lemon juice

⅓ cup (90 ml) water

Serves: 8–10
Preparation: 20 minutes
Cooking: 50–60 minutes
Level: 1

196

LEMON CROWN

Preheat the oven to 400°F (200°C/gas 6). • Butter and flour a 9-inch (23-cm) tube pan. • Mix the flour, baking powder, and salt in a medium bowl. • Beat the butter, sugar, and lemon zest in a large bowl with an electric mixer at medium speed until pale and creamy. • Add the eggs, one at a time, beating until just blended after each addition. • With mixer at low speed, gradually beat in the dry ingredients and 2 tablespoons of lemon juice. • Spoon the batter into the prepared pan. • Bake for 30–40 minutes, or until a toothpick inserted into the center comes out clean. • Cool the cake in the pan for 15 minutes. Turn out onto a rack and let cool completely. • Warm the apricot preserves in a small saucepan over low heat. Spread over the cake. • Beat the confectioners' sugar and enough of the remaining lemon juice to make a thin glaze. Drizzle over the cake.

1²⁄₃ cups (250 g) all-purpose (plain) flour

2 teaspoons baking powder

¼ teaspoon salt

¾ cup (180 g) butter, softened

1¼ cups (250 g) sugar

2 tablespoons finely grated lemon zest

3 large eggs

⅓ cup (90 ml) freshly squeezed lemon juice

½ cup (125 g) apricot preserves (jam)

1²⁄₃ cups (250 g) confectioners' (icing) sugar

Serves: 8–10
Preparation: 25 minutes
Cooking: 30–40 minutes
Level: 1

LEMON YOGURT CAKE

Cake: Preheat the oven to 325°F (160°C/gas 3).
• Butter a 9-inch (23-cm) round cake pan. Line with parchment paper. Butter the paper. • Mix the flour, baking powder, and salt in a medium bowl.
• Beat the butter, sugar, and lemon zest in a large bowl with an electric mixer at medium speed until pale and creamy. • Add the egg yolks, one at a time, beating until just blended after each addition.
• With mixer at low speed, gradually beat in the dry ingredients, alternating with the yogurt.
• With mixer at high speed, beat the egg whites in a medium bowl until stiff peaks form. Use a large rubber spatula to fold them into the batter. • Spoon the batter into the prepared pan. • Bake for 35–45 minutes, or until the cake shrinks from sides of the pan and a toothpick inserted into the center comes out clean. • Cool the cake in the pan for 5 minutes. Turn out onto a rack. Carefully remove the paper and let cool completely. • Lemon Frosting: Mix the confectioners' sugar and butter in a medium bowl. Beat in enough of the lemon juice to make a thick, spreadable frosting. Spread the top and sides of the cake with the frosting. Decorate with the candied lemon peel.

Cake

2 cups (300 g) all-purpose (plain) flour

2 teaspoons baking powder

¼ teaspoon salt

½ cup (125 g) butter, softened

1 cup (200 g) sugar

1 tablespoon finely grated lemon zest

3 large eggs, separated

1 cup (250 ml) lemon-flavored yogurt

Lemon Frosting

2 cups (300 g) confectioners' (icing) sugar

3 tablespoons butter, melted

2 tablespoons freshly squeezed lemon juice

2 tablespoons candied (glacé) lemon peel, coarsely chopped

Serves: 8–10
Preparation: 20 minutes
Cooking: 35–45 minutes
Level: 1

FROSTED LEMON BUTTER CAKE

<u>Cake</u>: Preheat the oven to 350°F (180°C/gas 4).
• Butter and flour a 9-inch (23-cm) ring pan or
savarin mold. • Mix the flour, baking powder, and
salt in a medium bowl. • Beat the butter, sugar,
lemon zest, lemon extract, and vanilla in a large
bowl with an electric mixer at medium speed until
pale and creamy. • Add the eggs, one at a time,
beating until just blended after each addition.
• With mixer at low speed, gradually beat in the dry
ingredients, alternating with the milk. • Spoon the
batter into the prepared pan. • Bake for 40–50
minutes, or until a toothpick inserted into the center
comes out clean. • Cool the cake in the pan for
10 minutes. Turn out onto a rack and let cool
completely. • <u>Lemon Frosting</u>: Mix the confectioners'
sugar, butter, and lemon extract in a medium bowl.
Beat in the lemon juice to make a spreadable
frosting. Spread over the top of the cake.

Cake

2 cups (300 g) all-
    purpose (plain) flour

2 teaspoons baking
    powder

¼ teaspoon salt

½ cup (125 g) butter,
    softened

1 cup (200 g) sugar

1 tablespoon finely grated
    lemon zest

1 teaspoon lemon extract
    (essence)

½ teaspoon vanilla extract
    (essence)

3 large eggs

2 tablespoons milk

Frosting

1½ cups (225 g)
    confectioners' (icing)
    sugar

2 tablespoons butter,
    melted

1 teaspoon lemon extract
    (essence)

1 tablespoon freshly
    squeezed lemon juice

Serves: 8–10
Preparation: 30 minutes
Cooking: 40–50 minutes
Level: 1

LIME AND HONEY SYRUP CAKE

Cake: Preheat the oven to 350°F (180°C/gas 4).
• Butter and flour a 9-inch (23-cm) Bundt pan.
• Stir the flour, coconut, almonds, baking powder, and salt in a large bowl. • Beat the butter, sugar, and lime zest in a large bowl with an electric mixer at medium speed until pale and creamy.
• Add the eggs, one at a time, beating until just blended after each addition. • With mixer at low speed, gradually beat in the dry ingredients, alternating with the yogurt and lime juice. • Spoon the batter into the prepared pan. • Bake for 45–55 minutes, or until a toothpick inserted into the center comes out clean. • Cool in the pan for 10 minutes. Turn out onto a rack. Place the cake on the rack in a jelly-roll pan. • Honey-Lime Syrup: Peel the limes and slice the zest into thin strips. Squeeze the juice from the limes and place it in a small saucepan with the zest, water, honey, and cardamom pods. Bring to a boil over low heat and simmer for 5 minutes. Scoop out the cardamom. Poke holes in the cake with a skewer. • Pour the syrup over the hot cake. Scoop up any syrup from the pan and drizzle over the cake until it is all absorbed.

■■■ *Serve this cake while it is still warm. It is delicious with softly whipped cream or vanilla ice cream.*

Cake

2½ cups (375 g) cake flour

¾ cup (120 g) shredded (desiccated) coconut

¼ cup (30 g) almonds, finely ground

2 teaspoons baking powder

¼ teaspoon salt

1 cup (250 g) butter, softened

1 cup (200 g) sugar

1 tablespoon finely grated lime zest

3 large eggs

¾ cup (180 ml) plain yogurt

2 tablespoons freshly squeezed lime juice

Honey-Lime Syrup

2 limes

½ cup (125 ml) cold water

¼ cup (60 g) honey

Cardamom pods, smashed with flat side of chef's knife

Serves: 8–10
Preparation: 30 minutes
Cooking: 45–55 minutes
Level: 1

ALMOND TORTE

Preheat the oven to 350°F (180°C/gas 4). • Butter a 9-inch (23-cm) round cake pan. Line with parchment paper. Butter the paper. • Mix the flour, baking powder, and salt in a large bowl. • Beat the butter, sugar, and almond paste in a large bowl with an electric mixer at medium speed until creamy. • Add the eggs, one at a time, beating until just blended after each addition. • With mixer at low speed, gradually beat in the dry ingredients and almond extract. • Spoon the batter into the prepared pan. • Bake for 45–55 minutes, or until a toothpick inserted into the center comes out clean. • Cool the cake in the pan for 15 minutes. Turn out onto a rack. Carefully remove the paper and let cool completely. • With mixer at high speed, beat the cream and confectioners' sugar in a medium bowl until stiff. Spoon the cream over the top of the cake.

1⅓ cups (200 g) all-purpose (plain) flour

1½ teaspoons baking powder

¼ teaspoon salt

½ cup (125 g) butter, softened

¾ cup (150 g) sugar

1 package (7 oz/200 g) almond paste, softened

4 large eggs

½ teaspoon almond extract (essence)

1 cup (250 ml) heavy (double) cream

2 tablespoons confectioners' (icing) sugar

Serves: 8–10
Preparation: 25 minutes
Cooking: 45–55 minutes
Level: 1

■■■ *Serve this cake with a raspberry coulis. To prepare the coulis, purée 1 pound (500 g) of fresh raspberries with ½ cup (100 g) of sugar and 2 tablespoons of kirsch or raspberry liqueur.*

RICH BUTTER CAKE WITH HAZELNUT FROSTING

208

Cake: Preheat the oven to 350°F (180°C/gas 4).
• Butter and flour a 10-inch (26-cm) springform pan. • Stir together the flour, cornstarch, baking powder, and salt in a large bowl. • Beat the butter, sugar, orange and lemon zests, and vanilla in a large bowl with an electric mixer at medium speed until creamy. • Add the eggs, one at a time, beating until just blended after each addition. • With mixer at low speed, gradually beat in the dry ingredients, alternating with the milk. • Spoon the batter into the prepared pan. • Bake for 50–60 minutes, or until a toothpick inserted into the center comes out clean. • Cool the cake in the pan on a rack for 15 minutes. Loosen and remove the pan sides. Invert the cake onto the rack. Remove the pan bottom and let cool completely. • Hazelnut Frosting: With mixer at medium speed, beat the cream cheese and sugar in a large bowl until smooth. • Beat in the hazelnut oil, rum, and vanilla. • With mixer at high speed, beat the cream in a medium bowl until thick. Use a large rubber spatula to fold it into the cream cheese mixture. • Split the cake horizontally. Place one layer on a serving plate and spread with one-third of the frosting. Top with the remaining layer. Spread the top and sides with one-third of the frosting. Spoon the remaining frosting into a pastry bag. Pipe a decorative pattern over the cake. Top with the hazelnuts.

Cake

2⅓ cups (350 g) all-purpose (plain) flour

1 cup (150 g) cornstarch (cornflour)

1 tablespoon baking powder

¼ teaspoon salt

1 cup (250 g) butter, softened

1 cup (200 g) sugar

1 tablespoon finely grated orange zest

1 tablespoon finely grated lemon zest

1 teaspoon vanilla extract

5 large eggs

½ cup (125 ml) milk

Hazelnut Frosting

1 package (8 oz/250 g) cream cheese, softened

½ cup (100 g) sugar

2 teaspoons hazelnut oil

1½ teaspoons rum

1 teaspoon vanilla extract

1 cup (250 ml) heavy (double) cream

Whole hazelnuts, to top

Serves: 10
Preparation: 40 minutes
Cooking: 50–60 minutes
Level: 2

BANANA CRUNCH CAKE

210

Preheat the oven to 350°F (180°C/gas 4). • Butter and flour a 9-inch (23-cm) tube pan. • Topping: Stir the flour, brown sugar, cinnamon, and nutmeg in a medium bowl. Use a pastry blender to cut in the butter until the mixture resembles fine crumbs. Stir in the almonds. • Cake: Stir together the flour, baking soda, baking powder, and salt in a large bowl. • Beat the butter, sugar, orange zest, and vanilla in a large bowl with an electric mixer at medium speed until pale and creamy. • Add the eggs, one at a time, beating until just blended after each addition. • With mixer at low speed, beat in the bananas and sour cream. Gradually beat in the dry ingredients and raisins. • Spoon the batter into the prepared pan. Sprinkle with the topping. • Bake for 25–30 minutes, or until the topping is golden brown and a toothpick inserted into the center comes out clean. • Cool the cake completely in the pan on a rack. Serve warm or at room temperature.

Topping

½ cup (75 g) all-purpose (plain) flour

½ cup (100 g) firmly packed brown sugar

1 teaspoon cinnamon

½ teaspoon ground nutmeg

¼ cup (60 g) cold butter

½ cup (60 g) almonds, coarsely chopped

Cake

2 cups (300 g) all-purpose (plain) flour

1 teaspoon baking soda (bicarbonate of soda)

½ teaspoon baking powder

¼ teaspoon salt

½ cup (125 g) butter, softened

¾ cup (150 g) sugar

1 tablespoon finely grated orange zest

1 teaspoon vanilla extract

2 large eggs

2 large, very ripe bananas, peeled and mashed

2 tablespoons sour cream

½ cup (90 g) raisins

Serves: 8–10
Preparation: 25–30 minutes
Cooking: 25–30 minutes
Level: 1

GLAZED LEMON LOAF

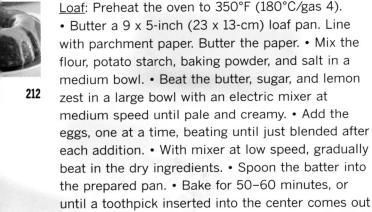

Loaf: Preheat the oven to 350°F (180°C/gas 4).
• Butter a 9 x 5-inch (23 x 13-cm) loaf pan. Line with parchment paper. Butter the paper. • Mix the flour, potato starch, baking powder, and salt in a medium bowl. • Beat the butter, sugar, and lemon zest in a large bowl with an electric mixer at medium speed until pale and creamy. • Add the eggs, one at a time, beating until just blended after each addition. • With mixer at low speed, gradually beat in the dry ingredients. • Spoon the batter into the prepared pan. • Bake for 50–60 minutes, or until a toothpick inserted into the center comes out clean. • Cool the cake in the pan for 15 minutes. Turn out onto a rack. Carefully remove the paper. • Lemon Glaze: Place the confectioners' sugar in a medium bowl. Beat in the lemon juice to obtain a pouring glaze. Drizzle the glaze over the cake.

1 cup (150 g) all-purpose (plain) flour

1 cup (150 g) potato starch

½ teaspoon baking powder

¼ teaspoon salt

1 cup (250 g) butter, softened

2 tablespoons finely grated lemon zest

1¼ cups (250 g) sugar

4 large eggs

Lemon Glaze

1½ cups (225 g) confectioners' (icing) sugar

3 tablespoons freshly squeezed lemon juice

Serves: 6–8
Preparation: 15 minutes
Cooking: 50–60 minutes
Level: 1

PECAN CRUNCH YOGURT CAKE

214

Preheat the oven to 350°F (180°C/gas 4). • Butter and flour a 9-inch (23-cm) square baking pan. Topping: Stir together the pecans, sugar, flour, butter, cinnamon, and vanilla in a medium bowl. • Cake: Mix the flour, baking powder, and salt in a medium bowl. • Beat the butter, sugar, and vanilla in a large bowl with an electric mixer at medium speed until pale and creamy. • Add the eggs, one at a time, beating until just blended after each addition. • With mixer at low speed, beat in the dry ingredients, alternating with the yogurt. • Spoon half the batter into the prepared pan. Sprinkle with half the topping. Spoon the remaining batter over the top and sprinkle with the remaining topping. • Bake for 55–65 minutes, or until springy to the touch and a toothpick inserted into the center comes out clean. • Cool the cake completely in the pan on a rack. Serve warm or at room temperature.

Topping

1 cup (150 g) pecans, coarsely chopped

½ cup (100 g) sugar

½ cup (75 g) all-purpose (plain) flour

¼ cup (60 g) butter, melted

2 teaspoons ground cinnamon

1 teaspoon vanilla extract (essence)

Cake

2 cups (300 g) all-purpose (plain) flour

2 teaspoons baking powder

¼ teaspoon salt

½ cup (125 g) butter, softened

1 cup (200 g) sugar

2 teaspoons vanilla extract (essence)

2 large eggs

1 cup (250 ml) plain yogurt

Serves: 8–10
Preparation: 25 minutes
Cooking: 55–65 minutes
Level: 1

■■■ *This is an excellent cake with a lovely flavor and texture and a pretty swirl of crunch throughout.*

216

CRUNCHY CHOCOLATE CHIP COFFEE CAKE

Preheat the oven to 350°F (180°C/gas 4). • Butter and flour a 13 x 9-inch (33 x 23-cm) baking pan. • Topping: Stir the sugar and flour in a medium bowl. Use a pastry blender to cut in the butter until the mixture resembles fine crumbs. Stir in the chocolate chips and walnuts. • Cake: Stir together the flour, baking powder, baking soda, and salt in a large bowl. • Beat the butter, cream cheese, sugar, and vanilla in a large bowl with an electric mixer at medium speed until creamy. • Add the eggs, one at a time, beating until just blended after each addition. • With mixer at low speed, gradually beat in the dry ingredients, alternating with the milk. • Spoon the batter into the prepared pan. Sprinkle with the topping. • Bake for 50–60 minutes, or until a toothpick inserted into the center comes out clean. • Cool the cake completely in the pan on a rack.

Topping

½ cup (100 g) firmly packed brown sugar

½ cup (75 g) all-purpose (plain) flour

¼ cup (60 g) cold butter, cut up

1 cup (180 g) dark chocolate chips

½ cup (60 g) walnuts, coarsely chopped

Cake

2½ cups (375 g) all-purpose (plain) flour

2 teaspoons baking powder

½ teaspoon baking soda (bicarbonate of soda)

¼ teaspoon salt

¾ cup (180 g) butter, softened

1 package (8 oz/250 g) cream cheese, softened

1½ cups (300 g) sugar

1 teaspoon vanilla extract (essence)

3 large eggs

¾ cup (180 ml) milk

Serves: 8–10
Preparation: 20 minutes
Cooking: 50–60 minutes
Level: 1

WALNUT CRUNCH CAKE

218

Preheat the oven to 350°F (180°C/gas 4). • Butter and flour a 9-inch (23-cm) Bundt pan. • Crunch: Stir the brown sugar and flour in a medium bowl. Use a pastry blender to cut in the butter until the mixture resembles fine crumbs. Stir in the walnuts. • Cake: Stir together the flour, baking powder, nutmeg, and salt in a medium bowl. • Beat the butter, brown sugar, and vanilla in a large bowl with an electric mixer at medium speed until creamy. • Add the eggs, one at a time, beating until just blended after each addition. • With mixer at low speed, gradually beat in the dry ingredients, alternating with the milk. • Spoon half the batter into the prepared pan. Sprinkle with half the crunch mixture. Spoon the remaining batter over the top and sprinkle with the remaining crunch mixture. • Bake for 50–60 minutes, or until the topping is golden brown. • Cool the cake in the pan on a rack for 15 minutes. Carefully turn out, turn topping-side up, and serve warm.

Crunch

- ¾ cup (150 g) firmly packed brown sugar
- ⅓ cup (50 g) all-purpose (plain) flour
- ¼ cup (60 g) cold butter, cut up
- ¾ cup (90 g) walnuts, coarsely chopped

Cake

- 2 cups (300 g) all-purpose (plain) flour
- 2 teaspoons baking powder
- 1 teaspoon nutmeg
- ¼ teaspoon salt
- ½ cup (125 g) butter, softened
- ¾ cup firmly (150 g) packed brown sugar
- 1 teaspoon vanilla extract (essence)
- 4 large eggs
- ¾ cup (180 ml) milk

Serves: 8–10
Preparation: 20 minutes
Cooking: 50–60 minutes
Level: 1

OLD-FASHIONED SOUR CREAM COFFEE CAKE

220

Preheat the oven to 325°F (160°C/gas 3). • Butter and flour a 13 x 9-inch (33 x 23-cm) baking pan. • Topping: Stir the flour, brown sugar, cinnamon, and nutmeg in a medium bowl. Use a pastry blender to cut in the butter until the mixture resembles fine crumbs. Stir in the nuts. • Cake: Mix the flour, baking powder, baking soda, cinnamon, and salt in a large bowl. • Beat the butter, brown sugar, molasses, and vanilla in a large bowl with an electric mixer at medium speed until creamy. • Add the eggs, one at a time, beating until just blended after each addition. • With mixer at low speed, gradually beat in the dry ingredients, alternating with the sour cream. • Spoon the batter into the prepared pan. Sprinkle with the topping. • Bake for 50–60 minutes, or until a toothpick inserted into the center comes out clean. • Cool the cake completely in the pan on a rack.

Topping

⅓ cup (50 g) all-purpose (plain) flour

¼ cup (50 g) firmly packed brown sugar

1 teaspoon cinnamon

½ teaspoon ground nutmeg

¼ cup (60 g) cold butter

½ cup (50 g) mixed nuts, chopped

Cake

2 cups (300 g) all-purpose (plain) flour

1 teaspoon baking powder

1 teaspoon baking soda (bicarbonate of soda)

1 teaspoon cinnamon

½ teaspoon salt

1 cup (250 g) butter, softened

1 cup (200 g) firmly packed brown sugar

2 tablespoons molasses

2 teaspoons vanilla extract (essence)

3 large eggs

1 cup (250 ml) sour cream

Serves: 8–10
Preparation: 15 minutes
Cooking: 50–60 minutes
Level: 1

GINGER BUTTER CAKE

Cake: Preheat the oven to 350°F (180°C/gas 4).
• Butter and flour two 8-inch (20-cm) round cake pans. Line with parchment paper. Butter the paper.
• Mix the flour, baking powder, ginger, and salt in a large bowl. • Beat the butter, sugar, and vanilla in a large bowl with an electric mixer at high speed until pale and creamy. • With mixer at medium speed, add the eggs, one at a time, beating until just blended after each addition. • With mixer at low speed, gradually beat in the dry ingredients. • Spoon half the batter into each of the prepared pans. • Bake for 25–35 minutes, or until a toothpick inserted into the center comes out clean. • Cool the cakes in the pans for 10 minutes. Turn out onto a rack. Carefully remove the paper and let cool completely. • Ginger Cream Filling: With mixer at high speed, beat the cream, confectioners' sugar, and ginger in a large bowl until stiff. • Place one cake on a serving plate and spread with the cream. Top with the remaining cake.

Cake

2 cups (300 g) all-purpose (plain) flour

2 teaspoons baking powder

2 teaspoons ground ginger

¼ teaspoon salt

¾ cup (180 g) butter, softened

¾ cup (150 g) firmly packed brown sugar

1 teaspoon vanilla extract (essence)

3 large eggs

Ginger Cream Filling

1 cup (250 ml) heavy (double) cream

2 tablespoons confectioners' (icing) sugar

1 teaspoon ground ginger

Serves: 8
Preparation: 25 minutes
Cooking: 25–35 minutes
Level: 1

MARBLE CAKE

Marble Cake: Preheat the oven to 350°F (180°C/gas 4). • Butter and flour a 9-inch (23-cm) tube pan. • Mix the flour, baking powder, and salt in a large bowl. • Beat the butter, sugar, and vanilla in a large bowl with an electric mixer at high speed until pale and creamy. • With mixer at medium speed, add the eggs, one at a time, beating until just combined. • With mixer at low speed, gradually beat in the dry ingredients, alternating with the milk. • Divide the batter evenly among three small bowls. Stir the cocoa into one, and red food coloring into another. Leave one bowl plain. • Drop alternate spoonfuls of the batters into the prepared pan, swirling them together with a knife to create a marbled effect. • Bake for 40–50 minutes, or until a toothpick inserted into the center comes out clean. • Cool the cake in the pan on a rack for 10 minutes. Turn out onto the rack and let cool completely. • Chocolate Frosting: Mix the confectioners' sugar and cocoa in a medium bowl. Add the butter and vanilla extract. Beat in almost all the water, adding more or less to obtain a thick frosting. • Spread the top and sides of the cake with the frosting.

Marble Cake

2¼ cups (330 g) all-purpose (plain) flour

2½ teaspoons baking powder

¼ teaspoon salt

1 cup (250 g) butter, softened

1 cup (200 g) sugar

1 teaspoon vanilla extract (essence)

3 large eggs

¾ cup (180 ml) milk

¼ cup (30 g) unsweetened cocoa powder

½ teaspoon red food coloring

Chocolate Frosting

2 cups (300 g) confectioners' (icing) sugar

⅓ cup (50 g) unsweetened cocoa powder

2 tablespoons butter

½ teaspoon vanilla extract (essence)

2 tablespoons boiling water

Serves: 8–10
Preparation: 30 minutes
Cooking: 40–50 minutes
Level: 1

CHOCOLATE-RASPBERRY MARBLE CAKE

Marble Cake: Preheat the oven to 350°F (180°C/ gas 4). • Butter an 11 x 7-inch (28 x 18-cm) baking pan. Line with parchment paper. Butter the paper. • Mix the flour, baking powder, and salt in a medium bowl. • Beat the butter and sugar in a large bowl with an electric mixer at medium speed until pale and creamy. • Add the eggs, one at a time, beating until just blended after each addition. • With mixer at low speed, gradually beat in the dry ingredients, alternating with the milk and vanilla. • Place half the batter in a separate bowl. Stir the cocoa into one bowl and the red food coloring into the other. • Drop alternate spoonfuls of the two batters into the prepared pan. • Bake for 30–40 minutes, or until a toothpick inserted into the center comes out clean. • Cool the cake in the pan for 15 minutes. Turn out onto a rack. Carefully remove the paper and let cool completely. • Cream Cheese Frosting: With mixer at medium speed, beat the cream cheese and confectioners' sugar in a large bowl until creamy. Add the cocoa and milk and beat until smooth and spreadable. Spread the top of the cake with the frosting. • Decorate with the raspberries.

Marble Cake

1²⁄₃ cups (250 g) all-purpose (plain) flour

1½ teaspoons baking powder

¼ teaspoon salt

²⁄₃ cup (150 g) butter, softened

¾ cup (150 g) sugar

2 large eggs

½ cup (125 ml) milk

1 teaspoon vanilla extract

¼ cup (30 g) unsweetened cocoa powder

½ teaspoon red food coloring

Cream Cheese Frosting

2 (3-oz) packages (180 g) cream cheese, softened

1½ cups (225 g) confectioners' (icing) sugar

¼ cup (30 g) unsweetened cocoa powder

1 tablespoon hot milk

Fresh raspberries, to top

Serves: 8–10
Preparation: 30 min
Cooking: 30–40 min
Level: 1

IRISH CREAM CAKE

Cake: Preheat the oven to 350°F (180°C/gas 4).
• Butter and flour a 10-inch (26-cm) tube pan.
• Mix the flour, sugar, baking powder, and salt in a large bowl. • Melt the chocolate with the oil, liqueur, water, and coffee granules in a double boiler over barely simmering water. • Transfer to a large bowl and beat in the egg yolks with a wooden spoon until well blended. • Add the dry ingredients and stir until smooth. • Beat the egg whites in a large bowl with an electric mixer at high speed until stiff peaks form. Use a large rubber spatula to fold them into the batter. • Spoon the batter into the prepared pan. • Bake for 30–40 minutes, or until firm to the touch and a slightly sugary crust has formed. • Cool the cake in the pan for 15 minutes. Turn out onto a rack to cool completely. • Coffee Frosting: Beat the coffee mixture and butter into the confectioners' sugar until the frosting is thick and spreadable. Spread over the top and sides of the cake.

Cake

2 cups (300 g) all-purpose (plain) flour

1½ cups (300 g) sugar

2 teaspoons baking powder

¼ teaspoon salt

4 oz (125 g) dark chocolate, coarsely chopped

½ cup (125 ml) vegetable oil

⅓ cup (90 ml) Irish cream liqueur

⅓ cup (90 ml) water

2 tablespoons freeze-dried coffee granules

7 large eggs, separated

Coffee Frosting

1 tablespoon freeze-dried coffee granules dissolved in 2 tablespoons Irish cream liqueur

3 tablespoons butter, melted

2 cups (300 g) confectioners' (icing) sugar

Serves: 8–10
Preparation: 20 min
Cooking: 30–40 min
Level: 2

BUTTER CAKE WITH SHERRY SAUCE

Butter Cake: Preheat the oven to 350°F (180°C/gas 4). • Butter and flour a 9-inch (23-cm) round cake pan. • Mix the flour, baking powder, and salt in a medium bowl. • Beat the butter, sugar, and vanilla in a large bowl with an electric mixer at medium speed until pale and creamy. • Add the eggs, one at a time, beating until just blended after each addition. • With mixer at low speed, gradually beat in the dry ingredients. • Spoon the batter into the prepared pan. • Bake for 25–30 minutes, or until golden and a toothpick inserted into the center comes out clean. • Cool the cake in the pan for 10 minutes. Turn out onto a rack and let cool completely. • Sherry Sauce: Bring the water and sugar to a boil in a small saucepan over medium heat. Cook over low heat, without stirring, until the mixture reaches 238°F (112°C), or the soft-ball stage. Remove from the heat and let cool for 15 minutes. • Stir in the sherry. • Place the cake on the rack over a jelly-roll pan. Poke holes in the cake with a skewer. Spoon the sherry sauce over the cake. Scoop up any sauce from the pan and drizzle on the cake until it is all absorbed.

Butter Cake

1½ cups (225 g) all-purpose (plain) flour

1½ teaspoons baking powder

¼ teaspoon salt

½ cup (125 g) butter, softened

¾ cup (150 g) sugar

1 teaspoon vanilla extract (essence)

4 large eggs

Sherry Sauce

1 cup (250 ml) water

1 cup (200 g) sugar

¼ cup (60 ml) medium dry sherry

Serves: 8–10
Preparation: 35 minutes
Cooking: 25–30 minutes
Level: 1

GINGERBREAD WITH LIME FROSTING

232

Loaf: Preheat the oven to 350°F (180°C/gas 4).
• Butter a 9 x 5-inch (23 x 13-cm) loaf pan. Line with parchment paper. Butter the paper. • Stir the butter and molasses in a small saucepan over low heat until the butter has melted. Keep warm. • Stir together the flour, sugar, baking powder, baking soda, ginger, cinnamon, cloves, mace, and salt in a large bowl. With an electric mixer at low speed, gradually beat in the milk and egg. • By hand, stir the hot butter mixture into the batter. • Spoon the batter into the prepared pan. • Bake for 45–55 minutes, or until a toothpick inserted into the center comes out clean. • Cool the loaf in the pan for 15 minutes. Turn out onto a rack. Carefully remove the paper and let cool completely. • Lime Frosting: With mixer at medium speed, beat the butter and lime zest in a medium bowl until creamy. • With mixer at low speed, gradually beat in the confectioners' sugar and enough of the lime juice to make a thick, spreadable frosting. • Spread the frosting over the top and sides of the loaf.

Loaf

½ cup (120 ml) molasses

¼ cup (60 g) butter

1 cup (150 g) all-purpose (plain) flour

¾ cup (150 g) sugar

1 teaspoon baking powder

½ teaspoon baking soda (bicarbonate of soda)

1 teaspoon ground ginger

1 teaspoon ground cinnamon

¼ teaspoon ground cloves

¼ teaspoon ground mace

¼ teaspoon salt

½ cup (125 ml) milk

1 large egg, lightly beaten

Lime Frosting

½ cup (125 g) butter, softened

1 tablespoon finely grated lime zest

2 cups (300 g) confectioners' (icing) sugar

2 tablespoons freshly squeezed lime juice

Serves: 6–8
Preparation: 30 minutes
Cooking: 45–55 minutes
Level: 1

CHOCOLATE POTATO CAKE

234

Cake: Preheat the oven to 350°F (180°C/gas 4).
• Butter and flour a 10-inch (23-cm) tube pan.
• Mix the flour, cocoa, baking powder, and salt in
a medium bowl. • Beat the butter and sugar in a
large bowl with an electric mixer at medium speed
until pale and until creamy. • Add the eggs, one at
a time, beating until just blended after each
addition. • With mixer at low speed, gradually beat
in the potato, followed by the dry ingredients, and
alternating with the milk. • Spoon the batter into
the prepared pan. • Bake for 30–40 minutes, or
until a toothpick inserted into the center comes out
clean. • Cool the cake in the pan for 30 minutes.
Turn out onto a rack to cool completely. Chocolate
Frosting: Mix the confectioners' sugar and cocoa in
a medium bowl. Add the butter and vanilla extract.
Beat in almost all the water, adding more or less to
obtain a thick frosting. • Spread the top and sides
of the cake with the frosting.

Cake

½ cup (75 g) unsweetened cocoa powder

2 cups (300 g) all-purpose (plain) flour

1½ teaspoons baking powder

¼ teaspoon salt

½ cup (125 g) butter, softened

¾ cup (150 g) sugar

3 large eggs

1 cup (200 g) cold unseasoned mashed potato

½ cup (125 ml) milk

Chocolate Frosting

2 cups (300 g) confectioners' (icing) sugar

⅓ cup (50 g) unsweetened cocoa powder

2 tablespoons butter

½ teaspoon vanilla extract (essence)

2 tablespoons boiling water

Serves: 10–12
Preparation: 20 minutes
Cooking: 30–40 minutes
Level: 1

CHOCOLATE PEANUT BUTTER CAKE

Cake: Preheat the oven to 325°F (160°C/gas 3).
• Butter a 9-inch (23-cm) square baking pan.
• Mix the flour, baking powder, and salt in a large bowl. • Melt the chocolate in a double boiler over barely simmering water. Set aside to cool. • Beat the butter, sugar, and vanilla in a large bowl with an electric mixer at medium speed until pale and creamy. • Add the egg yolks, one at a time, beating until just blended after each addition. • With mixer at low speed, gradually beat in the chocolate and peanut butter, followed by the dry ingredients, alternating with the milk. • With mixer at high speed, beat the egg whites in a large bowl until stiff peaks form. Use a large rubber spatula to fold them into the batter. • Spoon the batter into the prepared pan. • Bake for 1 hour and 15–25 minutes, or until a toothpick inserted into the center comes out clean. • Cool the cake in the pan for 10 minutes. Turn out onto a rack and let cool completely. • Peanut Butter Frosting: With mixer at medium speed, beat the confectioners' sugar, butter, and peanut butter in a large bowl until smooth. • Spread the top and sides of the cake with the frosting.

Cake

- 2 cups (300 g) all-purpose (plain) flour
- 2 teaspoons baking powder
- ¼ teaspoon salt
- 6 oz (180 g) dark chocolate, coarsely chopped
- ½ cup (125 g) butter, softened
- 1¾ cups (350 g) sugar
- 1 teaspoon vanilla extract (essence)
- 4 large eggs, separated
- ½ cup (125 g) smooth peanut butter
- 1 cup (250 ml) milk

Peanut Butter Frosting

- 2 cups (300 g) confectioners' (icing) sugar
- ½ cup (125 g) butter, melted
- ½ cup (125 g) smooth peanut butter

Serves: 12–14
Preparation: 20 minutes
Cooking: 1 hour 15–25 minutes
Level: 1

CHOCOLATE CHIP LOAF

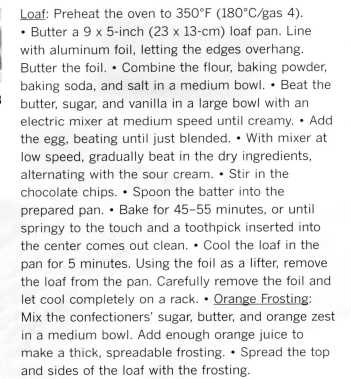

Loaf: Preheat the oven to 350°F (180°C/gas 4).
• Butter a 9 x 5-inch (23 x 13-cm) loaf pan. Line with aluminum foil, letting the edges overhang. Butter the foil. • Combine the flour, baking powder, baking soda, and salt in a medium bowl. • Beat the butter, sugar, and vanilla in a large bowl with an electric mixer at medium speed until creamy. • Add the egg, beating until just blended. • With mixer at low speed, gradually beat in the dry ingredients, alternating with the sour cream. • Stir in the chocolate chips. • Spoon the batter into the prepared pan. • Bake for 45–55 minutes, or until springy to the touch and a toothpick inserted into the center comes out clean. • Cool the loaf in the pan for 5 minutes. Using the foil as a lifter, remove the loaf from the pan. Carefully remove the foil and let cool completely on a rack. • Orange Frosting: Mix the confectioners' sugar, butter, and orange zest in a medium bowl. Add enough orange juice to make a thick, spreadable frosting. • Spread the top and sides of the loaf with the frosting.

Loaf

1½ cups (225 g) all-purpose (plain) flour

1 teaspoon baking powder

½ teaspoon baking soda (bicarbonate of soda)

¼ teaspoon salt

⅓ cup (90 g) butter, softened

¾ cup (150 g) sugar

1 teaspoon vanilla extract (essence)

1 large egg

1 cup (250 ml) sour cream

¾ cup (120 g) bittersweet or dark chocolate chips

Orange Frosting

2 cups (300 g) confectioners' (icing) sugar

3 tablespoons butter, melted

1 tablespoon finely grated orange zest

2 tablespoons freshly squeezed orange juice

■■■ *This is a delicious cake, even without the orange frosting. Children will enjoy it just as much as the grown-ups.*

Serves: 8–10
Preparation: 20 minutes
Cooking: 45–55 minutes
Level: 1

SACHERTORTE

Cake: Preheat the oven to 325°F (160°C/gas 3).
• Set out a 9-inch (23-cm) springform pan.
• Melt the chocolate in a double boiler over barely simmering water. Set aside to cool. • Beat the butter and sugar in a large bowl with an electric mixer at medium speed until creamy. • Add the egg yolks, one at a time, beating until just blended after each addition. • Use a large rubber spatula to fold in the chocolate and flour. • With mixer at high speed, beat the egg whites until stiff peaks form. Fold them into the batter. • Spoon the batter into the prepared pan. • Bake for 55–60 minutes, or until a toothpick inserted into the center comes out clean. • Cool the cake in the pan for 20 minutes. Loosen and remove the pan sides and let cool completely. • Split the cake horizontally. Place one layer on a serving plate. Spread with the preserves. Top with the remaining cake. • Frosting: Melt the butter and chocolate in a double boiler over barely simmering water. Stir in the coffee, confectioners' sugar and vanilla. Spread the top and sides of the cake with the frosting.

Cake

5 oz (150 g) dark chocolate, coarsely chopped

⅓ cup (90 g) butter, softened

½ cup (100 g) sugar

5 large eggs, separated

⅔ cup (100 g) all-purpose (plain) flour

⅓ cup (75 g) apricot preserves (jam)

Frosting

1 tablespoon butter

4 oz (125 g) dark chocolate, coarsely chopped

⅓ cup (90 ml) strong cold coffee

2 cups (300 g) confectioners' (icing) sugar

1 tablespoon vanilla extract (essence)

Serves: 8–10
Preparation: 25 minutes
Cooking: 55–60 minutes
Level: 2

QUICK-MIX CHOCOLATE APPLE CAKE

242

Cake: Preheat the oven to 350°F (180°C/gas 4).
• Butter a 13 x 9-inch (33 x 23-cm) baking pan. Line with parchment paper. Butter the paper. • Beat the apples, flour, butter, sugar, eggs, cocoa, water, baking powder, baking soda, and salt in a large bowl with an electric mixer at low speed until just blended. • Spoon the batter into the prepared pan. • Bake for 50–60 minutes, or until a toothpick inserted into the center comes out clean. • Cool the cake in the pan for 10 minutes. Turn out onto a rack. Carefully remove the paper and let cool completely. Chocolate Frosting: Mix the confectioners' sugar and cocoa in a medium bowl. Add the butter and vanilla extract. Beat in almost all the water, adding more or less to obtain a thick frosting. • Spread the top and sides of the cake with the frosting.

Cake

2   large tart apples (about 1 lb/500 g), coarsely grated

2   cups (300 g) all-purpose (plain) flour

1½ cups (375 g) butter, softened

1¼ cups (250 g) sugar

3   large eggs

⅓   cup (50 g) unsweetened cocoa powder

⅓   cup (90 ml) water

2   teaspoons baking powder

½   teaspoon baking soda (bicarbonate of soda)

¼   teaspoon salt

Chocolate Frosting

2   cups (300 g) confectioners' (icing) sugar

⅓   cup (50 g) unsweetened cocoa powder

2   tablespoons butter

½   teaspoon vanilla extract (essence)

2   tablespoons boiling water

Serves: 8–10
Preparation: 10 minutes
Cooking: 50–60 minutes
Level: 1

CHOCOLATE CARROT CAKE

244

Cake: Preheat the oven to 350°F (180°C/gas 4).
• Butter and flour a 13 x 9-inch (33 x 23-cm) baking pan. • Stir the flour, walnuts, raisins, coconut, cocoa, baking powder, cinnamon, baking soda, ginger, and salt in a large bowl. • Melt the chocolate in a double boiler over barely simmering water. Set aside to cool. • Beat the eggs, sugar, and oil in a large bowl with an electric mixer at medium speed until creamy. • With mixer at low speed, gradually beat in the dry ingredients, alternating with the chocolate and carrots. • Spoon the batter into the prepared pan. • Bake for 40–50 minutes, or until a toothpick inserted into the center comes out clean. • Cool the cake completely in the pan on a rack.
Milk Chocolate Frosting: Melt the chocolate in a double boiler over barely simmering water. Set aside to cool. • With mixer at medium speed, beat the cream cheese and confectioners' sugar in a large bowl. Beat in the melted chocolate. • Spread the top of the cake with the frosting.

Cake

1½ cups (225 g) all-purpose (plain) flour

½ cup (60 g) walnuts, chopped

½ cup (50 g) raisins

⅓ cup (50 g) shredded (desiccated) coconut

⅓ cup (50 g) unsweetened cocoa powder

1 teaspoon cinnamon

1 teaspoon baking powder

½ teaspoon baking soda

⅓ teaspoon ground ginger

¼ teaspoon salt

5 oz (150 g) milk chocolate

3 large eggs

¾ cup (150 g) firmly packed brown sugar

½ cup (125 ml) vegetable oil

2 cups (250 g) finely shredded carrots

Milk Chocolate Frosting

6 oz (180 g) milk chocolate, chopped

1 package (8 oz/250 g) cream cheese, softened

2 cups (300 g) confectioners' (icing) sugar

Serves: 10–12
Preparation: 30 minutes
Cooking: 40–50 minutes
Level: 1

CHOCOLATE CRUNCH APPLESAUCE CAKE

246

Preheat the oven to 350°F (180°C/gas 4). • Butter and flour an 8-inch (20-cm) square baking pan. • Mix the flour, cocoa, baking soda, and salt in a medium bowl. • Beat the butter, sugar, and vanilla in a large bowl with an electric mixer at medium speed until pale and creamy. • Add the eggs, one at a time, beating until just blended after each addition. • With mixer at low speed, gradually beat in the dry ingredients, alternating with the applesauce. • Spoon the batter into the prepared pan. Sprinkle with the chocolate chips and walnuts. • Bake for 30–35 minutes, or until a toothpick inserted into the center comes out clean. • Cool the cake completely in the pan on a rack.

1 cup (150 g) all-purpose (plain) flour

2 tablespoons unsweetened cocoa powder

¾ teaspoon baking soda (bicarbonate of soda)

¼ teaspoon salt

¼ cup (60 g) butter, softened

¾ cup (150 g) sugar

1 teaspoon vanilla extract (essence)

2 large eggs

1 cup (200 g) unsweetened applesauce

½ cup (90 g) dark chocolate chips

½ cup (60 g) walnuts, chopped

Serves: 6–8
Preparation: 20 minutes
Cooking: 35 minutes
Level: 1

FROSTED CHOCOLATE-BANANA CAKE

248

Cake: Preheat the oven to 350°F (180°C/gas 4).
• Butter a 9-inch (23-cm) square baking pan. Line with parchment paper. Butter the paper. • Mix the flour, cocoa, baking powder, baking soda, and salt in a large bowl. Stir in the sugar. • Beat in the eggs, water, banana, and vanilla. • Spoon the batter into the prepared pan. • Bake for 35–40 minutes, or until a toothpick inserted into the center comes out clean. • Cool the cake in the pan for 10 minutes. Turn out onto a rack. Carefully remove the paper and let cool completely. • Cream Cheese Frosting: Beat the cream cheese, butter, and vanilla in a large bowl with an electric mixer at medium speed until creamy. With mixer at low speed, beat in the confectioners' sugar and cocoa until smooth.
• Spread the cake with the frosting.

Cake

2 cups (300 g) all-purpose (plain) flour

½ cup (75 g) unsweetened cocoa powder

1½ teaspoons baking powder

½ teaspoon baking soda (bicarbonate of soda)

¼ teaspoon salt

1 cup (200 g) sugar

2 large eggs

¾ cup (180 ml) hot water

1 cup (250 g) mashed very ripe bananas (about 3 large bananas)

1½ teaspoons vanilla extract (essence)

Cream Cheese Frosting

3 oz (90 g) cream cheese, softened

¼ cup (60 g) butter, softened

1 teaspoon vanilla extract

2 cups (300 g) confectioners' (icing) sugar

¼ cup (30 g) unsweetened cocoa powder

Serves: 8–10
Preparation: 20 minutes
Cooking: 35–40 minutes
Level: 1

RICH CHOCOLATE SNACKING CAKE

Cake: Preheat the oven to 350°F (180°C/gas 4).
• Butter a 9-inch (23-cm) square pan. Line with parchment paper. Butter the paper. • Mix the flour, cocoa, baking powder, and salt in a large bowl.
• Beat the butter, sugar, and vanilla in a large bowl with an electric mixer at medium speed until pale and creamy. • Add the egg yolks, one at a time, beating until just blended after each addition.
• With mixer at low speed, beat in the dry ingredients and chocolate, alternating with the yogurt. • With mixer at high speed, beat the egg whites in a large bowl until stiff peaks form. Use a large rubber spatula to fold them into the batter.
• Spoon the batter into the prepared pan. • Bake for 40–50 minutes, or until a toothpick inserted into the center comes out clean. • Cool the cake in the pan for 15 minutes. Turn out of the pan, carefully remove the paper, and let cool completely.
Chocolate Frosting: Melt the chocolate and butter in a double boiler over barely simmering water. Remove from the heat and beat in the confectioners' sugar. • Spread the top of the cake with the frosting. Decorate with the walnut halves.

Cake

1 cup (150 g) all-purpose (plain) flour

½ cup (75 g) unsweetened cocoa powder

1½ teaspoons baking powder

¼ teaspoon salt

¾ cup (180 g) butter, softened

1½ cups (300 g) sugar

2 teaspoons vanilla extract (essence)

4 large eggs, separated

2 oz (60 g) dark chocolate, grated

1 cup (250 ml) plain yogurt

Chocolate Frosting

3 oz (90 g) dark chocolate, coarsely chopped

3 tablespoons butter, cut up

1 cup (150 g) confectioners' (icing) sugar

Walnut halves, to decorate

Serves: 8-10
Preparation: 35 minutes
Cooking 40–50 minutes
Level: 1

MUD CAKE WITH WHITE CHOCOLATE GANACHE AND WALNUTS

Cake: Preheat the oven to 325°F (160°C/gas 3).
• Butter a 9-inch (23-cm) round cake pan. Line
with parchment paper. • Place the sugar, milk,
butter, molasses, and chocolate in a saucepan over
low heat and stir, without boiling, until smooth. Set
aside to cool. • Mix the flour, baking powder, and
salt in a medium bowl. Gradually stir the dry
ingredients and eggs into the sugar mixture.
• Spoon the batter into the prepared pan. • Bake
for 60–70 minutes, or until a toothpick inserted
into the center comes out clean. • Cool the cake in
the pan for 15 minutes. Turn out onto a rack.
Carefully remove the paper and let cool completely.
• White Chocolate Ganache: Heat the cream almost
to a boil in a small saucepan over low heat. Place
the chocolate in a large bowl. Pour the cream over
the chocolate and stir until the chocolate is melted
and smooth. Refrigerate until thickened and
spreadable, about 30 minutes, stirring occasionally.
• Spread the top and sides of the cake with the
ganache. Decorate with the walnuts.

Cake

1   cup (200 g) firmly packed brown sugar

1   cup (250 ml) milk

¾   cup (180 g) butter, cut up

⅓   cup (90 g) molasses

5   oz (150 g) white chocolate, coarsely chopped

2   cups (300 g) all-purpose (plain) flour

2   teaspoons baking powder

¼   teaspoon salt

2   large eggs, lightly beaten

12 walnut halves

White Chocolate Ganache

½   cup (125 ml) heavy (double) cream

14 oz (400 g) white chocolate, coarsely chopped

Serves: 8–10
Preparation: 30 minutes
   + 30 minutes to chill
Cooking: 60–70 minutes
Level: 2

WHITE MUD CAKE

Cake: Preheat the oven to 325°F (160°C/gas 3).
• Butter a 9-inch (23-cm) round baking pan. Line
with parchment paper. Butter the paper. • Stir the
butter, sugar, chocolate, and milk in a large
saucepan over low heat until smooth. Do not boil.
Set aside to cool. • Mix the flour, baking powder,
and salt in a medium bowl. Gradually add the dry
ingredients, eggs, and vanilla to the saucepan,
stirring until smooth and well mixed. • Spoon the
batter into the prepared pan. • Bake for 50–60
minutes, or until a toothpick inserted into the center
comes out clean. • Cool the cake in the pan for 10
minutes. Turn out onto a rack. Carefully remove the
paper and let cool completely. • White Chocolate
Ganache: Heat the cream almost to a boil in a small
saucepan over low heat. Place the chocolate in a
large bowl. Pour the cream over the chocolate and
stir until melted and smooth. Refrigerate until
thickened and spreadable, about 30 minutes,
stirring occasionally. • Spread the top and sides
of the cake with the ganache.

Cake

1   cup (250 g) butter,
    cut up

2   cups (400 g) sugar

5   oz (150 g) white
    chocolate, coarsely
    chopped

1   cup (250 ml) milk

2   cups (300 g) all-
    purpose (plain) flour

2   teaspoons baking
    powder

¼   teaspoon salt

2   large eggs, lightly
    beaten

1   teaspoon vanilla extract
    (essence)

White Chocolate Ganache

½   cup (125 ml) heavy
    (double) cream

14 oz (400 g) white
    chocolate, coarsely
    chopped

Serves: 8–10
Preparation: 30 minutes
    + 30 minutes to cool
Cooking: 50–60 minutes
Level: 1

QUICK CHOCOLATE SWIRL

Cake: Preheat the oven to 350°F (180°C/gas 4).
• Butter a 9-inch (23-cm) square baking pan. Line
with parchment paper. Butter the paper. • Beat the
flour, sugar, cocoa, baking powder, salt, butter, eggs,
milk, water, vanilla, and vinegar in a large bowl with
an electric mixer at medium speed until creamy.
• Spoon the batter into the prepared pan. • Bake
for 50–60 minutes, or until the cake shrinks from
the pan sides and a toothpick inserted into the
center comes out clean. • Cool the cake in the
pan for 5 minutes. Turn out onto a rack. Carefully
remove the paper and let cool completely. •
Chocolate Frosting: Melt the chocolate and butter
in a double boiler over barely simmering water.
Set aside until cool enough to spread (make sure it
doesn't set). • Cream Cheese Frosting: With mixer
at medium speed, beat the cream cheese and
butter in a small bowl until creamy. Add the honey
and gradually beat in the confectioners' sugar.
• Spoon alternate dollops of each of the frostings
onto the top of the cake. Use a thin metal spatula
to spread the frosting. Use a fork to swirl the
frostings together to create a marbled effect.

Cake

2⅓ cups (350 g) all-
       purpose (plain) flour

1½ cups (300 g) sugar

⅔ cup (100 g) unsweet-
       ened cocoa powder

2½ teaspoons baking powder

¼ teaspoon salt

¾ cup (180 g) butter,
       softened

3 large eggs

1 cup (250 ml) milk

½ cup (125 ml) boiling
       water

1 teaspoon vanilla extract

1 teaspoon white vinegar

Chocolate Frosting

½ cup (125 g) butter

4 oz (125 g) dark
       chocolate, chopped

Cream Cheese Frosting

1 package (3 oz/90 g)
       cream cheese, softened

⅓ cup (90 g) butter,
       softened

1 tablespoon honey

1¼ cups (180 g) confec-
       tioners' (icing) sugar

Serves: 8–10
Preparation: 30 minutes
Cooking: 50–60 minutes
Level: 1

MOIST CHOCOLATE RING WITH CHOCOLATE SAUCE

Cake: Preheat the oven to 350°F (180°C/gas 4).
• Butter a 9-inch (23-cm) Bundt pan. Dust with cocoa. • Mix the flour, cocoa, baking powder, baking soda, and salt in a large bowl. Stir in both sugars.
• Beat the butter, buttermilk, milk, eggs, coffee mixture, and vanilla in a large bowl with an electric mixer at medium speed until well blended. With mixer at low speed, beat the butter mixture into the dry ingredients. • Spoon the batter into the prepared pan. • Bake for 40–50 minutes, or until a toothpick inserted into the center comes out clean.
• Cool the cake in the pan for 15 minutes. Turn out onto a rack and let cool completely. • Chocolate Sauce: Stir the chocolate and cream in a small saucepan over very low heat until the chocolate melts. Remove from the heat. Set aside to cool.
• Spoon the sauce over the cake and serve.

Cake

1¼ cups (180 g) all-purpose (plain) flour

⅓ cup (50 g) unsweetened cocoa powder

1 teaspoon baking powder

1 teaspoon baking soda (bicarbonate of soda)

¼ teaspoon salt

¾ cup (150 g) sugar

⅓ cup (75 g) firmly packed dark brown sugar

¼ cup (60 g) butter, melted

1 cup (250 ml) buttermilk

½ cup (125 ml) milk

2 large eggs

1 tablespoon freeze-dried coffee granules, dissolved in 1 tablespoon milk

1 teaspoon vanilla extract

Chocolate Sauce

1 cup (180 g) dark chocolate chips

½ cup (125 ml) heavy (double) cream

■■■ This cake has great flavor and texture. Serve it between meals with tea or coffee or add raspberries or sliced peaches and serve as a dessert.

Serves: 10–12
Preparation: 20 minutes
Cooking: 40–50 minutes
Level: 1

APPLE AND CREAM CHEESE CAKE

Cake: Preheat the oven to 350°F (180°C/gas 4).
• Butter and flour a 13 x 9-inch (33 x 23-cm) baking pan. • Mix the flour, baking powder, cinnamon, baking soda, and salt in a large bowl. • Beat the cream cheese, butter, sugar,, and almond extract in a large bowl with an electric mixer at medium speed until fluffy. • Add the eggs, one at a time, beating until just blended after each addition.
• With mixer at low speed, gradually beat in the dry ingredients, alternating with the milk. • Spoon the batter into the prepared pan. • Apple Topping: Place the apples in a medium bowl and toss with the lemon juice. • Mix the sugar, flour, and cinnamon in a small bowl. Add the sugar mixture to the apple slices and toss to coat well. • Arrange the apple slices over the batter. • Bake for 45–55 minutes, or until golden brown and a toothpick inserted into the center comes out clean. • Serve warm straight from the pan with a dollop of whipped cream.

Cake

2 cups (300 g) all-purpose (plain) flour

1½ teaspoons baking powder

1 teaspoon ground cinnamon

½ teaspoon baking soda (bicarbonate of soda)

¼ teaspoon salt

1 package (8 oz/250 g) cream cheese, softened

½ cup (125 g) butter, softened

1 cup (200 g) sugar

½ teaspoon almond extract (essence)

3 large eggs

¼ cup (60 ml) milk

Apple Topping

2 large tart apples, peeled, cored, and sliced

2 tablespoons freshly squeezed lemon juice

½ cup (100 g) sugar

2 tablespoons all-purpose (plain) flour

1 teaspoon cinnamon

   Whipped cream, to serve

Serves: 10–12
Preparation: 25 minutes
Cooking: 45–55 minutes
Level: 1

■■■*Apples were one of the earliest fruits to be cultivated and first mention of them in literature appears in Greek mythology. Many modern apple dishes have long histories. Apple pie, for example, is thought to date from medieval times. Today, apples are the most important fruit crop in Europe and North America. There are many varieties, loosely divided into cooking and eating apples, with many falling into both categories. Nutritionally, apples are a good source of soluble fiber, which helps to control blood sugar and reduce cholesterol. They also provide insoluble fiber, which helps move food quickly through the digestive system. Apples are low in calories and fat-free, making them an ideal snack food.*

UPSIDE-DOWN APPLE CAKE

264

Preheat the oven to 350°F (180°C/gas 4). • Butter a 9-inch (23-cm) round cake pan. • Sprinkle the pan with half the brown sugar. Slice one apple into thin rings and lay over the brown sugar. Sprinkle with the remaining brown sugar and drizzle with the lemon juice. • Mix the flour, baking powder, baking soda, cardamom, cinnamon, and salt in a medium bowl. • Beat the butter, sugar, and vanilla in a large bowl with an electric mixer at medium speed until pale and creamy. • Add the eggs, one at a time, beating until just blended after each addition. • With mixer at low speed, gradually beat in the dry ingredients, alternating with the milk. • Chop the remaining apple finely and stir into the batter. • Spoon the batter over the sliced apple. • Bake for 45–55 minutes, or until a toothpick inserted into the center comes out clean. • Cool the cake in the pan for 15 minutes. Turn out onto a rack. Serve warm or at room temperature.

⅓ cup (75 g) firmly packed brown sugar

2 large apples, peeled and cored

1 tablespoon freshly squeezed lemon juice

2 cups (300 g) all-purpose (plain) flour

1½ teaspoons baking powder

½ teaspoon baking soda (bicarbonate of soda)

1 teaspoon ground cardamom

1 teaspoon ground cinnamon

¼ teaspoon salt

¾ cup (180 g) butter, softened

¾ cup (150 g) sugar

1 teaspoon vanilla extract (essence)

2 large eggs

½ cup (125 ml) milk

Serves: 8–10
Preparation: 25 minutes
Cooking: 45–55 minutes
Level: 1

CINNAMON CRUMBLE APPLE CAKE

Cake: Preheat the oven to 350°F (180°C/gas 4).
• Butter a 9-inch (23-cm) square baking pan.
• Bring the apples, lemon juice, and brown sugar to a boil in a medium saucepan over medium heat. Cover, reduce the heat, and simmer for about 10 minutes, or until tender. Drain well and set aside to cool • Beat the butter and sugar in a large bowl with an electric mixer at medium speed until pale and creamy. • Add the eggs, one at a time, beating until just blended after each addition. • With mixer at low speed, gradually beat in the flour, baking powder, and salt, alternating with the milk. • Spoon two-thirds of the batter into the prepared pan. Spoon the apples over the top. Spread the remaining batter on top. • Cinnamon Crumble: Stir together the flour, brown sugar, and cinnamon in a large bowl. Use a pastry blender to cut in the butter until the mixture resembles coarse crumbs. Stir in the walnuts. • Sprinkle over the cake. • Bake for 40–50 minutes, or until a toothpick inserted into the center comes out clean. • Cool the cake completely in the pan on a rack.

Cake

3 medium tart apples, peeled, cored, and thinly sliced

¼ cup (60 ml) freshly squeezed lemon juice

2 tablespoons brown sugar

¾ cup (180 g) butter, softened

¾ cup (150 g) sugar

2 large eggs

2¼ cups (230 g) all-purpose (plain) flour

2 teaspoons baking powder

¼ teaspoon salt

¾ cup (180 ml) milk

Cinnamon Crumble

1 cup (150 g) all-purpose (plain) flour

½ cup (100 g) firmly packed brown sugar

1 tablespoon ground cinnamon

⅓ cup (90 g) cold butter

1 cup (120 g) walnuts, coarsely chopped

Serves: 8–10
Preparation: 30 minutes
Cooking: 40–50 minutes
Level: 1

GLAZED APPLE CRUMBLE CAKE

Cake: Preheat the oven to 350°F (180°C/gas 4). • Butter and flour a 9-inch (23-cm) square baking pan. • Mix the flour, baking powder, and salt in a medium bowl. • Beat the butter, sugar, and vanilla in a large bowl with an electric mixer at medium speed until pale and creamy. • Add the egg, beating until just blended. • With mixer at low speed, gradually beat in the dry ingredients, alternating with the buttermilk. • Spoon the batter into the prepared pan. Arrange the apples on top in overlapping layers. • Crumble: Mix the brown sugar, butter, cinnamon, and nutmeg in a small bowl until crumbly. Sprinkle over the apples. • Bake for 55–65 minutes, or until the apples are tender, the crumble is brown, and a toothpick inserted into the center comes out clean. • Cool the cake completely in the pan on a rack. • Glaze: Warm the apricot preserves and lemon juice in a saucepan over low heat. Brush the cake with the glaze just before serving.

■■■Use tart-tasting Granny Smith apples in this recipe for the best results.

Cake

2 cups (300 g) all-purpose (plain) flour

2 teaspoons baking powder

¼ teaspoon salt

½ cup (125 g) butter, softened

1 cup (200 g) sugar

1 teaspoon vanilla extract (essence)

1 large egg

1 cup (250 ml) buttermilk

2 tart apples, peeled, cored, and thinly sliced

Crumble

½ cup (100 g) firmly packed brown sugar

3 tablespoons butter, melted

1 teaspoon cinnamon

½ teaspoon nutmeg

Glaze

¾ cup (200 g) apricot preserves (jam)

1 tablespoon freshly squeezed lemon juice

Serves: 8–10
Preparation: 30 minutes
Cooking: 55–65 minutes
Level: 1

UPSIDE-DOWN CITRUS POLENTA CAKE

270

Preheat the oven to 350°F (180°C/gas 4). • Butter and flour a 9-inch (23-cm) springform pan. • Heat 1¼ cups (310 ml) of water and ¾ cup (150 g) of sugar in a large frying pan over medium heat until the sugar has dissolved. Bring to a boil and simmer for 5 minutes, or until the syrup begins to thicken. • Add the lemons and simmer for about 8 minutes, turning once, until the lemon peel is tender. • Using tongs, remove the lemon slices from the syrup and press them, overlapping, onto the bottom and sides of the prepared pan. • Return the syrup to medium heat and stir in the remaining water. Simmer until the syrup is pale gold. Carefully spoon the syrup over the lemon slices in the pan. • Stir together the flour, polenta, ground almonds, baking powder, and salt in a medium bowl. • Beat the butter, remaining sugar, lemon zest, and lemon extract in a large bowl with an electric mixer at medium speed until pale and creamy. • Add the eggs, one at a time, beating until just blended after each addition. • With mixer at low speed, gradually beat in the dry ingredients, alternating with the sour cream and lemon juice. • Spoon the batter into the prepared pan. • Bake for 50–60 minutes, or until a toothpick inserted into the center comes out clean. • Cool the cake in the pan for 15 minutes. Loosen and remove the pan sides. Invert onto a serving dish. Serve warm.

1½ cups (375 ml) water
1¾ cups (350 g) sugar
3 lemons, thinly sliced
1 cup (150 g) all-purpose (plain) flour
¾ cup (120 g) polenta (yellow cornmeal)
½ cup 875 g) finely ground almonds
1 teaspoon baking powder
¼ teaspoon salt
½ cup (125 g) butter, softened
1 tablespoon finely grated lemon zest
1 teaspoon lemon extract (essence)
3 large eggs
⅓ cup (90 ml) sour cream
¼ cup (60 ml) freshly squeezed lemon juice

Serves: 8–10
Preparation: 30 minutes
Cooking: 50–60 minutes
Level: 2

■■■*Polenta is the Italian word for cornmeal. It is usually golden yellow and medium or coarse-grained. Polenta is packed with energy-giving carbohydrates and is also a good source of phosphorus, thiamin, folate, and calcium.*

POLENTA CAKE WITH CANDIED PEEL

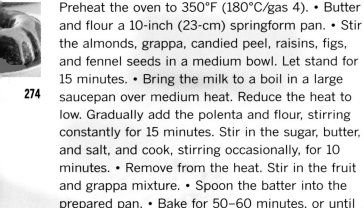

Preheat the oven to 350°F (180°C/gas 4). • Butter and flour a 10-inch (23-cm) springform pan. • Stir the almonds, grappa, candied peel, raisins, figs, and fennel seeds in a medium bowl. Let stand for 15 minutes. • Bring the milk to a boil in a large saucepan over medium heat. Reduce the heat to low. Gradually add the polenta and flour, stirring constantly for 15 minutes. Stir in the sugar, butter, and salt, and cook, stirring occasionally, for 10 minutes. • Remove from the heat. Stir in the fruit and grappa mixture. • Spoon the batter into the prepared pan. • Bake for 50–60 minutes, or until lightly browned. After 30 minutes, cover the top of the cake loosely with a piece of foil to prevent it from drying out. • Cool the cake completely in the pan on a rack. Loosen and remove the pan sides to serve.

⅓ cup (60 g) coarsely chopped blanched almonds

½ cup (50 g) chopped candied peel

¼ cup (60 ml) grappa

3 tablespoons golden raisins (sultanas)

2 tablespoons chopped dried figs

1 teaspoon fennel seeds

1 quart (1 liter) milk

2½ cups (375 g) polenta (yellow cornmeal)

⅓ cup (50 g) all-purpose (plain) flour

½ cup (100 g) sugar

⅔ cup (90 g) butter

¼ teaspoon salt

Serves: 10–12
Preparation: 20 minutes
Cooking: 75–85 minutes
Level: 2

PINEAPPLE UPSIDE-DOWN CAKE

Preheat the oven to 350°F (180°C/gas 4). • Melt ¼ cup (60 g) of the butter and pour into a 9-inch (23-cm) round cake pan. Sprinkle with the walnuts. Arrange the pineapple rings in the pan, cutting to fit, if necessary. • Beat the sugar, remaining butter, and eggs in a medium bowl with an electric mixer at medium speed until just blended. • Beat in the baking powder, vanilla, and salt. • With mixer at low speed, gradually beat in the flour, alternating with the milk. The batter should be smooth and quite sticky. • Spoon the batter over the pineapple. • Bake for 40–50 minutes, or until a toothpick inserted into the center comes out clean. • Cool the cake in the pan for 20 minutes. Invert onto a plate and serve warm.

½ cup (125 g) butter, softened

12 walnut halves, broken

9 rings drained canned pineapple

¾ cup (150 g) sugar

2 large eggs

1½ teaspoons baking powder

1 teaspoon vanilla extract (essence)

¼ teaspoon salt

1½ cups (225 g) all-purpose (plain) flour

½ cup (125 ml) milk

Serves: 8–10
Preparation: 20 minutes
Cooking: 40–50 minutes
Level: 1

■■■ *This cake is served warm and goes beautifully with lightly whipped cream or vanilla ice cream.*

ITALIAN POTATO CAKE

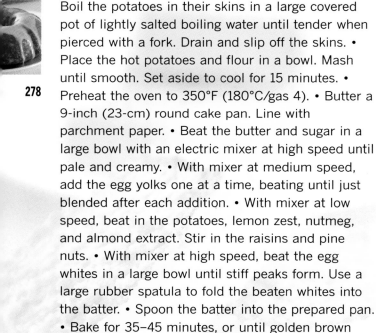

Boil the potatoes in their skins in a large covered pot of lightly salted boiling water until tender when pierced with a fork. Drain and slip off the skins. • Place the hot potatoes and flour in a bowl. Mash until smooth. Set aside to cool for 15 minutes. • Preheat the oven to 350°F (180°C/gas 4). • Butter a 9-inch (23-cm) round cake pan. Line with parchment paper. • Beat the butter and sugar in a large bowl with an electric mixer at high speed until pale and creamy. • With mixer at medium speed, add the egg yolks one at a time, beating until just blended after each addition. • With mixer at low speed, beat in the potatoes, lemon zest, nutmeg, and almond extract. Stir in the raisins and pine nuts. • With mixer at high speed, beat the egg whites in a large bowl until stiff peaks form. Use a large rubber spatula to fold the beaten whites into the batter. • Spoon the batter into the prepared pan. • Bake for 35–45 minutes, or until golden brown and a toothpick inserted into the center comes out clean. • Cool the cake in the pan for 15 minutes. Turn out onto a rack. Carefully remove the paper and let cool completely. • Dust with the confectioners' sugar just before serving.

1 lb (500 g) potatoes

¼ cup (30 g) all-purpose (plain) flour

½ cup (125 g) butter, softened

¾ cup (150 g) sugar

4 large eggs, separated

1 tablespoon finely grated lemon zest

1 teaspoon freshly grated nutmeg

½ teaspoon almond extract (essence)

¾ cup (135 g) raisins

⅓ cup (60 g) pine nuts

⅓ cup (50 g) confectioners' (icing) sugar, to dust

Serves: 8–10
Preparation: 45 minutes
Cooking: 35–45 minutes
Level: 1

ALMOND PUMPKIN CAKE

Boil the pumpkin until tender when pierced with a fork, about 15 minutes. Drain well. • Preheat the oven to 400°F (200°C/gas 6). • Butter and flour a 10-inch (26-cm) springform pan. • Dice the cooked pumpkin into small cubes. • Beat the egg yolks, $1/4$ cup (50 g) sugar, cinnamon, and salt with an electric mixer at high speed until frothy. Beat in the orange and lemon zest. • With mixer at low speed, gradually beat in the almonds, flour, orange peel, and pumpkin. • With mixer at high speed, beat the egg whites until frothy. Gradually beat in the remaining sugar until stiff peaks form. • Use a large rubber spatula to fold the beaten whites into the pumpkin mixture. • Spoon the batter into the prepared pan. • Bake for 25–30 minutes, or until a toothpick inserted into the center comes out clean. • Cool the cake in the pan for 10 minutes. Loosen and remove the pan sides. Invert the cake onto a rack to cool completely. • Spread with the marmalade. • Bring the citrus juices and sugar to a boil. Remove from the heat. Stir in the orange liqueur. • Prick the cake with a fork and drizzle with the syrup. • Serve with a dollop of cream to the side.

8   oz (250 g) pumpkin, peeled and sliced

6   large eggs, separated

1   cup (200 g) sugar

1   teaspoon cinnamon

$1/4$ teaspoon salt

2   tablespoons finely grated orange zest

2   tablespoons finely grated lemon zest

$1^2/_3$ cups (250 g) almonds, finely ground

$1/3$ cup (50 g) all-purpose (plain) flour

1   cup (200 g) candied (glacé) orange peel, finely chopped

$1/4$ cup (30 g) orange marmalade

$1/4$ cup (60 ml) freshly squeezed orange juice

2   tablespoons freshly squeezed lemon juice

$1/4$ cup (50 g) sugar

$3/4$ cup (180 ml) orange liqueur

$1/2$ cup (125 ml) heavy (double) cream, beaten

Serves: 10–12
Preparation: 30 minutes
Cooking: 40–45 minutes
Level: 2

BEST-EVER CARROT AND WALNUT CAKE

Cake: Preheat the oven to 350°F (180°C/gas 4).
• Butter and flour a deep 10-inch (26-cm) springform pan. • Stir together the flour, cinnamon, baking powder, baking soda, ginger, nutmeg, cloves, and salt in a large bowl. • Beat the butter, sugar, and vanilla in a large bowl with an electric mixer at medium speed until pale and creamy. • Add the eggs, one at a time, beating until just combined after each addition. • With mixer at low speed, gradually beat in the dry ingredients alternating with the milk. • Stir in the carrots, walnuts, and raisins. • Spoon the batter into the prepared pan.
• Bake for 45–55 minutes, or until a toothpick inserted into the center comes out clean. • Cool the cake in the pan for 10 minutes. Loosen and remove the pan sides. Invert the cake onto a rack. Loosen and remove the pan bottom and let cool completely.
• Cream Cheese Frosting: With mixer at medium speed, beat the cream cheese, butter, confectioners' sugar, and lemon zest and juice in a large bowl until creamy and smooth. • Spread the cake with the frosting. Decorate with the walnut halves.

Cake

- 2⅓ cups (350 g) all-purpose (plain) flour
- 2 teaspoons ground cinnamon
- 1 teaspoon baking powder
- 1 teaspoon baking soda (bicarbonate of soda)
- 1 teaspoon ground ginger
- ½ teaspoon ground nutmeg
- ¼ teaspoon ground cloves
- ¼ teaspoon salt
- 1½ cups (375 g) butter, softened
- 2 cups (400 g) sugar
- 2 teaspoons vanilla extract (essence)
- 4 large eggs
- ¾ cup (180 ml) milk
- 2 cups (250 g) finely grated carrots
- 1½ cups (200 g) fairly finely chopped chopped walnuts
- ⅓ cup (40 g) raisins

Cream Cheese Frosting

- **1 package (8 oz/250 g) cream cheese, softened**
- **⅓ cup (90 g) butter, softened**
- **2½ cups (375 g) confectioners' (icing) sugar**
- **1 tablespoon finely grated lemon zest**
- **2 teaspoons freshly squeezed lemon juice**
- **Walnut halves, to decorate**

Serves: 10–12
Preparation: 40 minutes
Cooking 45–55 minutes
Level: 1

■■■ *There are dozens of species of edible walnuts but the most common one is the Persian walnut (known in America as the English walnut). In France and northern Italy delicious walnut oils are made that can be used for cooking and to dress salads. Walnuts are an excellent source of omega-3 fatty acids and eating them regularly may help lower cholesterol.*

FROSTED SUNFLOWER CARROT CAKE

Cake: Preheat the oven to 350°F (180°C/gas 4).
• Butter and flour a 10-inch (26-cm) springform
pan. • Mix the flour, baking powder, ginger, nutmeg,
baking soda, and salt in a large bowl. • Beat the oil,
brown sugar, and eggs in a large bowl with an
electric mixer at high speed until creamy. • With
mixer at low speed, beat in the carrots, hazelnuts,
sunflower seeds, and mixed dry ingredients. •
Spoon the batter into the prepared pan. • Bake for
70–80 minutes, or until a toothpick inserted into
the center comes out clean. • Cool in the pan for
10 minutes. Loosen and remove the pan sides.
Invert the cake onto a rack. Loosen and remove the
pan bottom and let cool completely. • Orange
Frosting: Beat the cream cheese, butter, and
orange zest in a medium bowl until fluffy. Beat
in the confectioners' sugar. Spread the cake
with the frosting.

Cake

2½ cups (375 g) all-purpose (plain) flour

2½ teaspoons baking powder

1 teaspoon ground ginger

1 teaspoon ground nutmeg

½ teaspoon baking soda

½ teaspoon salt

1 cup (250 ml) vegetable oil

1¼ cups (250 g) firmly packed brown sugar

3 large eggs

2 cups (250 g) firmly packed coarsely grated carrots

1 cup (180 g) hazelnuts, coarsely chopped

2 tablespoons sunflower seeds

Orange Frosting

1 package (3 oz/90 g) cream cheese, softened

2 tablespoons butter, softened

1 tablespoon finely grated orange zest

2 cups (300 g) confectioners' (icing) sugar

Serves: 10–12
Preparation: 20 minutes
Cooking: 70–80 minutes
Level: 1

CRUMBLY ALMOND CAKE

Preheat the oven to 350°F (180°C/gas 4). • Butter and flour a 10-inch (26-cm) springform pan. • Mix the flour, almonds, sugar, and salt in a large bowl. • Use your fingers to rub the butter and eggs into the dry ingredients until the dough resembles large crumbs. It should be quite dry and crumbly. • Transfer the dough to the prepared pan, pressing it down firmly. • Bake for 35–45 minutes, or until a toothpick inserted into the center comes out clean. • Cool the cake in the pan for 10 minutes. Loosen the pan sides and let cool completely. • Cut or break into irregular diamond shapes to serve.

2 cups (300 g) all-purpose (plain) flour

2 cups (300 g) finely ground almonds

1 cup (200 g) sugar

¼ teaspoon salt

¾ cup (180 g) cold butter, cut up

4 large eggs, lightly beaten

Serves: 8–10
Preparation: 30 minutes
Cooking: 35–45 minutes
Level: 1

ALMOND-TOPPED CAKE

Cake: Preheat the oven to 350°F (180°C/gas 4).
• Butter and flour a 9-inch (23-cm) springform pan.
• Beat the butter, sugar, and vanilla in a large bowl
with an electric mixer at medium speed until pale
and creamy. • Add the eggs, one at a time, beating
until just blended after each addition. • With mixer
at low speed, gradually beat in the flour, baking
powder, and salt, alternating with the milk. • Spoon
the batter into the prepared pan. • Bake for 40
minutes. • Almond Topping: Stir the butter, sugar,
and almonds in a medium saucepan over low heat
until the butter has melted. • After the cake has
baked for 40 minutes, spread with the topping.
Brush with the milk. • Bake for 10–15 minutes more,
or until the topping is lightly browned. • Cool the
cake in the pan for 10 minutes. Loosen and remove
the pan sides. Place the cake on a rack and let
cool completely.

Cake

½ cup (125 g) butter,
  softened

1 cup (200 g) sugar

1 teaspoon vanilla extract
  (essence)

2 large eggs

2 cups (300 g) all-
  purpose (plain) flour

2 teaspoons baking
  powder

¼ teaspoon salt

¾ cup (180 ml) milk

Almond Topping

⅓ cup (90 g) butter, cut
  up

⅓ cup (75 g) sugar

¾ cup flaked almonds

3 tablespoons milk

Serves: 8–10
Preparation: 30 minutes
Cooking: 50–55 minutes
Level: 2

PISTACHIO CAKE

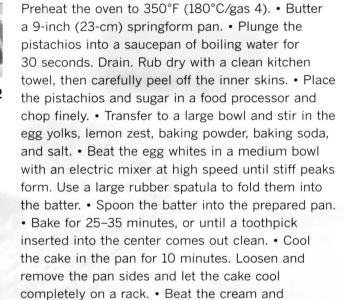

292

Preheat the oven to 350°F (180°C/gas 4). • Butter a 9-inch (23-cm) springform pan. • Plunge the pistachios into a saucepan of boiling water for 30 seconds. Drain. Rub dry with a clean kitchen towel, then carefully peel off the inner skins. • Place the pistachios and sugar in a food processor and chop finely. • Transfer to a large bowl and stir in the egg yolks, lemon zest, baking powder, baking soda, and salt. • Beat the egg whites in a medium bowl with an electric mixer at high speed until stiff peaks form. Use a large rubber spatula to fold them into the batter. • Spoon the batter into the prepared pan. • Bake for 25–35 minutes, or until a toothpick inserted into the center comes out clean. • Cool the cake in the pan for 10 minutes. Loosen and remove the pan sides and let the cake cool completely on a rack. • Beat the cream and confectioners' sugar in a medium bowl until thick. Place a dollop of cream on each slice.

1½ cups (225 g) pistachios
1 cup (200 g) sugar
3 large eggs, separated
2 tablespoons finely grated lemon zest
1 teaspoon baking powder
½ teaspoon baking soda (bicarbonate of soda)
¼ teaspoon salt
½ cup (125 ml) heavy (double) cream
1 tablespoon confectioners' (icing) sugar

Serves: 8
Preparation: 30 minutes
Cooking: 25–35 minutes
Level: 1

DUNDEE CAKE

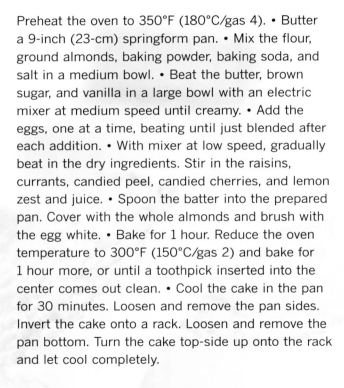

294

Preheat the oven to 350°F (180°C/gas 4). • Butter a 9-inch (23-cm) springform pan. • Mix the flour, ground almonds, baking powder, baking soda, and salt in a medium bowl. • Beat the butter, brown sugar, and vanilla in a large bowl with an electric mixer at medium speed until creamy. • Add the eggs, one at a time, beating until just blended after each addition. • With mixer at low speed, gradually beat in the dry ingredients. Stir in the raisins, currants, candied peel, candied cherries, and lemon zest and juice. • Spoon the batter into the prepared pan. Cover with the whole almonds and brush with the egg white. • Bake for 1 hour. Reduce the oven temperature to 300°F (150°C/gas 2) and bake for 1 hour more, or until a toothpick inserted into the center comes out clean. • Cool the cake in the pan for 30 minutes. Loosen and remove the pan sides. Invert the cake onto a rack. Loosen and remove the pan bottom. Turn the cake top-side up onto the rack and let cool completely.

1 cup (150 g) all-purpose (plain) flour

1/3 cup (50 g) finely ground almonds

1/2 teaspoon baking powder

1/2 teaspoon baking soda (bicarbonate of soda)

1/4 teaspoon salt

2/3 cup (150 g) butter, softened

3/4 cup (150 g) firmly packed brown sugar

1 teaspoon vanilla extract

2 large eggs, + 1 large egg white, lightly beaten

1 1/2 cups (270 g) raisins

1 1/2 cups (270 g) currants

1/2 cup (50 g) chopped mixed candied peel

1/4 cup (30 g) candied (glacé) cherries

1 tablespoon finely grated lemon zest

1 1/2 tablespoons freshly squeezed lemon juice

50 whole blanched almonds

Serves: 14–16
Preparation: 30 minutes
Cooking: 2 hours
Level: 1

LAYER CAKES

CHOCOHOLIC SUPREME

Cake: Preheat the oven to 350°F (180°C/gas 4).
• Butter and flour a 9-inch (23-cm) springform pan.
• Melt the chocolate in a double boiler over barely simmering water. Set aside to cool. • Mix the flour, almonds, baking powder, and salt in a medium bowl. • Beat the butter and sugar in a large bowl with an electric mixer at medium speed until pale and creamy. • Add the egg yolks, one at a time, beating until just blended after each addition. • With mixer at low speed, gradually beat in the cooled chocolate, followed by the dry ingredients and orange liqueur. • With mixer at high speed, beat the egg whites in a large bowl until stiff peaks form. Use a large rubber spatula to fold them into the chocolate mixture. • Spoon the batter into the prepared pan. • Bake for 40–50 minutes, or until springy to the touch and a toothpick inserted into the center comes out clean. • Cool the cake in the pan for 5 minutes. Turn out onto a rack and let cool completely. • Chocolate Frosting: Melt the chocolate and butter in a double boiler over barely simmering water. Set aside to cool enough to spread (make sure it doesn't set). • Warm the marmalade and liqueur in a small saucepan over low heat. • Split the cake in half horizontally. Place one layer on a serving plate. Spread with the marmalade and a quarter of the frosting. Top with the remaining layer and spread the top and sides with the remaining frosting.

Cake

8 oz (250 g) dark chocolate, coarsely chopped

⅔ cup (100 g) all-purpose (plain) flour

⅓ cup (30 g) almonds, finely ground

1 teaspoon baking powder

¼ teaspoon salt

½ cup (125 g) butter, softened

¾ cup (150 g) sugar

3 large eggs, separated

3 tablespoons orange liqueur

Chocolate Frosting

8 oz (250 g) dark chocolate, coarsely chopped

½ cup (125 g) butter

¼ cup (60 g) orange marmalade

2 tablespoons orange liqueur

Serves: 8–10
Preparation: 45 minutes
Cooking: 40–50 minutes
Level: 1

POPPY SEED LAYER CAKE

Cake: Bring the milk to a boil in a small saucepan over medium-low heat. Remove from the heat. Stir in the poppy seeds and set aside to cool. • Preheat the oven to 350°F (180°C/gas 4). • Butter and flour two 8-inch (20-cm) round cake pans. • Combine the flour, baking powder, and salt in a medium bowl. • Beat the butter, 1¼ cups (250 g) of sugar, and the vanilla in a large bowl with an electric mixer at medium-high speed until pale and creamy. • With mixer at low speed, gradually beat in the dry ingredients, alternating with the milk and poppy seed mixture. • With mixer at high speed, beat the egg whites in a large bowl until frothy. Gradually add the remaining sugar, beating until stiff, glossy peaks form. • Use a large rubber spatula to fold the beaten whites into the batter. • Spoon half the batter into each of the prepared pans. • Bake for 30–40 minutes, or until a toothpick inserted into the center comes out clean. • Cool the cakes in the pans for 10 minutes. Turn out onto racks and let cool completely. • Cream Cheese Frosting: With mixer at medium speed, beat the cream cheese, butter, confectioners' sugar, and vanilla until smooth. • Place one cake on a serving plate. Spread with one-third of the frosting. Top with the remaining cake and spread the top and sides with the remaining frosting.

Cake

1   cup (250 ml) milk

½   cup (75 g) poppy seeds

2   cups (300 g) all-purpose (plain) flour

2½ teaspoons baking powder

¼   teaspoon salt

¾   cup (180 g) butter, softened

1½ cups (300 g) sugar

2   teaspoons vanilla extract (essence)

3   large egg whites

Cream Cheese Frosting

1   package (8 oz/250 g) cream cheese, softened

¼   cup (60 g) butter, softened

2½ cups (375 g) confectioners' (icing) sugar

2   teaspoons vanilla extract (essence)

Serves: 8–10
Preparation: 35 minutes
Cooking 30–40 minutes
Level: 1

TRICOLORED CAKE

Cake: Preheat the oven to 350°F (180°C/gas 4).
• Butter three 8-inch (20-cm) round baking pans.
Line with parchment paper. Butter the paper. • Mix
the flour, baking powder, and salt in a large bowl.
• Beat the eggs and sugar in a large bowl with an
electric mixer at medium speed until pale and
thick. • Melt the butter with the milk in a medium
heavy-bottomed saucepan over medium heat. Stir
in the vanilla. • With mixer at low speed, gradually
beat in the dry ingredients, alternating with the milk
mixture. • Divide the batter evenly among three
small bowls. Stir the cocoa into one and the food
coloring into another. Leave one bowl plain. • Spoon
each type of batter into a separate prepared pan.
• Bake for 20–25 minutes, or until a toothpick
inserted into the center comes out clean. • Cool the
cakes in the pans for 5 minutes. Turn out onto
racks. Carefully remove the paper and let cool
completely. • Filling: With mixer at medium speed,
beat the cream in a large bowl until stiff. • Place the
plain layer of cake on a serving plate. Spread with
half the cream. Top with the pink cake and spread
with the remaining cream. Top with the chocolate
layer. • Vanilla Glaze: Beat the confectioners' sugar
and vanilla with enough water to make a spreadable
glaze. Drizzle over the cake.

Cake

2   cups (300 g) all-purpose
    (plain) flour

2   teaspoons baking
    powder

¼   teaspoon salt

4   large eggs

1   cup (200 g) sugar

2   tablespoons butter

1   cup (250 ml) milk,
    warmed

1   teaspoon vanilla extract
    (essence)

2   teaspoons red food
    coloring

3   tablespoons
    unsweetened cocoa
    powder

Filling

1½ cups (375 ml) heavy
    (double) cream

Vanilla Glaze

1½ cups (225 g)
    confectioners' (icing)
    sugar

½   teaspoon vanilla extract

2   tablespoons (30 ml)
    boiling water

Serves: 6–8
Preparation: 40 minutes
Cooking: 20–25 minutes
Level: 1

CHOCOLATE SOUR CREAM CAKE

Cake: Preheat the oven to 350°F (180°C/gas 4).
• Butter two 9-inch (23-cm) round cake pans. Line with parchment paper. Butter the paper. • Mix the flour, baking powder, and salt in a large bowl. • Melt the chocolate with the water in a double boiler over barely simmering water. Set aside to cool. • Beat the butter, brown sugar, and vanilla in a large bowl with an electric mixer at medium speed until creamy. • Add the eggs, one at a time, beating until just blended after each addition. • With mixer at low speed, gradually beat in the chocolate mixture, followed by the yogurt and dry ingredients. • Spoon half the batter into each of the prepared pans.
• Bake for 30–40 minutes, or until a toothpick inserted into the centers comes out clean. • Turn out onto racks and let cool completely. • Filling: With mixer at high speed, beat the cream, confectioners' sugar, and vanilla in a medium bowl until stiff. • Sour Cream Frosting: Melt the chocolate in a double boiler over barely simmering water. Remove from the heat. Stir in the sour cream and confectioners' sugar. Do not let the frosting cool completely or it will be too thick to spread. • Split each cake horizontally. Place one layer on a serving plate. Spread with one-third of the raspberry jam and one-third of the cream. Repeat with the remaining cake layers. Top with a plain cake layer.
• Spread the top and sides with the frosting.

Cake

2½ cups (375 g) all-purpose (plain) flour

2 teaspoons baking powder

¼ teaspoon salt

6 oz (180 g) dark chocolate, chopped

½ cup (125 ml) water

¾ cup (180 g) butter, softened

1¾ cups (350 g) firmly packed brown sugar

1 teaspoon vanilla extract

3 large eggs

½ cup (125 ml) plain yogurt

Filling

1½ cups (375 ml) heavy (double) cream

3 tablespoons confect- ioners' (icing) sugar

½ teaspoon vanilla extract

1 cup (300 g) raspberry jelly (jam)

Sour Cream Frosting

12 oz (350 g) dark chocolate, chopped

¾ cup (180 ml) sour cream

1½ cups (225 g) confect- ioners' (icing) sugar

Serves: 8–10
Preparation: 30 minutes
Cooking: 30–40 minutes
Level: 2

OLD-FASHIONED WHITE CHOCOLATE CAKE

Cake: Preheat the oven to 350°F (180°C/gas 4).
• Butter two 9-inch (23-cm) round cake pans. Line with parchment paper. Butter the paper. • Beat the egg yolks and sugar in a large bowl with an electric mixer at high speed until pale and thick. • With mixer at low speed, gradually beat in the butter. • Gradually beat in the pecans, almonds, flour, vanilla, and almond extract. • With mixer at high speed, beat the egg whites in a large bowl until stiff peaks form. Use a large rubber spatula to fold them into the batter. • Spoon half the batter into each of the prepared pans. • Bake for 45–50 minutes, or until a toothpick inserted into the centers comes out clean. • Cool the cakes in the pans for 10 minutes. Turn out onto racks and let cool completely. • Transfer the cakes to high-sided plates. Poke holes all over the cakes. Syrup: Bring the water and sugar to a boil in a medium saucepan over medium heat. Simmer for 20 minutes. Remove from the heat and stir in the kirsch. Spoon the hot syrup over the cakes. Set aside until the cakes have absorbed the syrup. • Place one cake layer on a serving plate. Spread with one-third of the ganache. Top with the remaining layer. Spread the top and sides with the remaining ganache. • Sprinkle with the grated white chocolate.

Cake

10 large eggs, separated

1½ cups (300 g) sugar

1¼ cups (300 g) butter, melted

2 cups (300 g) pecans, finely ground

2 cups (300 g) almonds, finely ground

⅓ cup (50 g) all-purpose (plain) flour

1 teaspoon vanilla extract (essence)

¼ teaspoon almond extract (essence)

Syrup

1¼ cups (300 ml) water

¾ cup (150 g) sugar

¼ cup (60 ml) kirsch

2 cups (500 g) White Chocolate Ganache (see page 252)

3 oz (90 g) white chocolate, coarsely grated, to decorate

Serves: 10–12
Preparation: 90 minutes
Cooking: 45–50 minutes
Level: 2

PEACH MELBA SANDWICH

Cake: Preheat the oven to 350°F (180°C/gas 4).
• Butter two 8-inch (20 cm) round cake pans and line with parchment paper. • Beat the butter, sugar, and vanilla in a large bowl with an electric mixer on medium-high speed, until pale and creamy. • Add the eggs one at a time, beating until just combined. • With mixer on low, gradually beat in the flour and milk until well incorporated • Divide the batter evenly between the prepared pans. • Bake for 25 minutes, or until golden brown and the cake springs back when lightly touched or a skewer comes out clean when tested. • Cool the cakes in the pans for 10 minutes then turn out onto a rack. Peel off the paper and let cool completely. • Vanilla Cream: Beat the cream, confectioners' sugar, and vanilla in a small bowl until stiff peaks form. • Slice the top off one of the cakes to create a flat surface, if necessary. Place, flat side down, on a serving plate, and spread with the raspberry preserves. Cover with a layer of peach slices. Spoon the vanilla cream over the top and spread 3/4 inch (2 cm) in from the edge, using a small spatula or knife. Place the other cake on top and dust with confectioners' sugar.

Cake

1 cup (250 g) butter

1¼ cups (250 g) superfine (caster) sugar

1 teaspoon vanilla extract (essence)

4 large eggs

1⅔ cups (250 g) self-rising flour

1½ tablespoons milk

⅓ cup (90 g) raspberry preserves (jam)

8 canned peach halves, drained and sliced

Confectioners' (icing) sugar, to dust

Vanilla Cream

¾ cup (180 ml) heavy (double) cream

2 tablespoons confectioners' (icing) sugar

½ teaspoon vanilla extract (essence)

Serves: 10–12
Preparation: 90 minutes
Cooking: 45–50 minutes
Level: 2

PASSION FRUIT CREAM SPONGE

Sponge: Preheat the oven to 350°F (180°C/gas 4).
• Butter a 9-inch (23-cm) round cake pan and line
with parchment paper. • Beat the superfine sugar,
egg yolks, and orange zest in a medium bowl using
an electric mixer on high speed, until pale and
thick. • Beat the egg whites in a medium bowl using
an electric mixer on high speed until firm peaks
form. • Fold a quarter of the egg whites into the
yolk mixture. Add the flour and pour in the butter,
gently folding until incorporated. Gently fold in the
remaining whites. • Spoon the mixture into the
prepared cake pan. • Bake for 45 minutes, or until
golden brown and the sponge springs back when
lightly touched or a skewer comes out clean when
tested. • Cool the sponge in the pan for 10 minutes.
Turn out onto a rack, peel off the parchment paper,
and let cool completely. • Passion Fruit Filling: Beat
the cream and sugar in a small bowl until stiff
peaks form. Stir in the orange zest and passion fruit
pulp. • Passion Fruit Glaze: Place the confectioners'
sugar in a small bowl and add the passion fruit
pulp. Gradually pour in the water, stirring until
smooth and thick enough to spread. • Slice the
sponge in half horizontally. • Place one sponge layer
on a serving plate and spread with the passion fruit
filling. • Place the other half on top and spread with
passion fruit glaze.

Sponge

- ½ cup (100 g) superfine (caster) sugar
- 4 large egg yolks, separated
- 1 teaspoon finely grated orange zest
- ¾ cup (125 g) all-purpose (plain) flour
- ½ cup (125 g) butter, melted and cooled

Passion Fruit Filling

- ¾ cup (180 ml) heavy (double) cream
- 2 tablespoons confectioners' (icing) sugar
- 1 teaspoon finely grated orange zest
- 1 tablespoon fresh or canned passion fruit pulp

Passion Fruit Glaze

- 1⅓ cups (200 g) confectioners' (icing) sugar
- 3 tablespoons fresh or canned passion fruit pulp
- 2 tablespoons boiling water

Serves: 8–10
Preparation: 30 minutes
Cooking: 45 minutes
Level: 2

BLUEBERRY AND SOUR CREAM FILLED SPONGE

Sponge: Preheat the oven to 350°F (180°C/gas 4). • Butter a 9-inch (23-cm) round cake pan and line with parchment paper. • Beat the superfine sugar and egg yolks in a medium bowl using an electric mixer on high speed until pale and thick. • Beat the egg whites in a medium bowl with mixer on high speed until firm peaks form. • Fold a quarter of the egg whites into the yolk mixture. Add the flour and cinnamon and pour in the butter, gently folding until incorporated. Fold in the remaining whites. • Spoon the batter into the prepared cake pan. • Bake for 45 minutes, or until golden brown and the sponge springs back when lightly touched or a skewer comes out clean when tested. • Cool the sponge in the pan for 10 minutes. Turn out onto a rack, peel off the paper, and let cool completely. • Blueberry Cream Filling: Beat the cream and confectioners' sugar in a medium bowl until soft peaks form. Beat in the sour cream, lemon zest, and vanilla. Add the blueberries, stirring until well mixed. • Cinnamon Frosting: Mix the confectioners' sugar and cinnamon into a small bowl. Gradually pour in the water, stirring until smooth and the desired consistency is reached. • Split the sponge horizontally. • Place one sponge layer on a serving plate and spread with the blueberry and sour cream filling.• Place the other half on top and spread with cinnamon frosting.

Sponge

- ½ cup (100 g) superfine (caster) sugar
- 4 large eggs, separated
- ¾ cup (125 g) all-purpose (plain) flour
- 1 teaspoon ground cinnamon
- ½ cup (125 g) butter, melted and cooled

Blueberry Cream Filling

- ½ cup (125 ml) heavy (double) cream
- 2 tablespoons confectioners' (icing) sugar
- ¼ cup (60 ml) sour cream
- 1 teaspoon finely grated lemon zest
- ⅛ teaspoon vanilla extract (essence)
- 1¼ cups (300 g) blueberries

Cinnamon Frosting

- 1⅓ cups (200 g) confectioners' (icing) sugar
- 1 teaspoon cinnamon
- 2 tablespoons boiling water

Serves: 8–10
Preparation: 30 minutes
Cooking: 45 minutes
Level: 2

CHOCOLATE HAZELNUT CAKE

Cake: Preheat the oven to 350°F (180°C/gas 4).
• Butter and flour a 9-inch (23-cm) springform pan.
• Mix the flour, baking powder, and salt in a medium bowl. • Beat the butter and sugar in a large bowl with an electric mixer at medium speed until creamy. Add the egg yolks, one at a time, beating until just blended after each addition. • With mixer at high speed, beat the egg whites in a large bowl until stiff peaks form. Use a large rubber spatula to fold them into the egg yolk mixture. Gradually fold in the dry ingredients, hazelnuts, and chocolate. • Spoon the batter into the prepared pan. • Bake for 45–50 minutes, or until a toothpick inserted into the center comes out clean. • Cool the cake in the pan for 15 minutes. Loosen and remove the pan sides. Transfer to a rack and let cool completely. • Split the cake horizontally. Place one layer on a serving plate. • With mixer at high speed, beat the cream in a large bowl until stiff. • Spread the cake with the cream. Top with the remaining layer. • Frosting: Melt the chocolate in a double boiler over barely simmering water. Add the vanilla and cream.
• Spread the top of the cake with the frosting. Sprinkle with the hazelnuts.

Cake

2/3 cup (100 g) all-purpose (plain) flour

1 teaspoon baking powder

1/4 teaspoon salt

2/3 cup (150 g) butter, softened

3/4 cup (150 g) firmly packed brown sugar

4 large eggs, separated

1 cup (160 g) toasted hazelnuts, finely chopped

7 oz (200 g) dark chocolate, chopped

1 cup (250 ml) heavy (double) cream

Frosting

5 oz (150 g) dark chocolate, chopped

2 tablespoons light (single) cream

1/2 teaspoon vanilla extract (essence)

2 tablespoons hazelnuts, coarsely chopped

Serves: 6–8
Preparation: 40 minutes
Cooking: 45–50 minutes
Level: 2

CHOCOLATE WALNUT CAKE

Cake: Preheat the oven to 350°F (180°C/gas 4).
• Butter a 9-inch (23 cm) round cake pan and line with parchment paper. • Melt the chocolate in a double boiler over barely simmering water. • Dissolve the coffee in the boiling water and stir into the chocolate. • Beat the egg yolks and sugar in a medium bowl with an electric mixer on medium speed until pale and creamy. • With mixer on low, add the chocolate mixture and finely chopped walnuts. • Beat the egg whites in a small bowl with mixer on high speed until firm peaks form. • Fold a quarter of the whites into the chocolate mixture. Fold in the flour and cocoa alternately with the butter. Fold in the remaining egg whites. • Spoon the mixture into the prepared cake pan. • Bake for 25 minutes, or until golden brown and a skewer comes out clean when tested. • Let cool in the pan for 10 minutes then turn out onto a rack. Peel off the parchment paper and let cool completely. •
Chocolate Buttercream: Beat the butter and confectioners' sugar with mixer on high speed until pale and creamy. • Slice the cake in half horizontally. • Spread each round with half the chocolate buttercream. Place one round on top of the other. Frost the top and sides of the cake with the chocolate frosting. • Tope with walnut halves.

Cake

2 oz (60 g) dark chocolate, chopped

2 teaspoons freeze-dried coffee granules

1½ tablespoons boiling water

3 large eggs, separated

½ cup (100 g) firmly packed light brown sugar

⅓ cup (50 g) finely chopped walnuts

⅓ cup (50 g) all-purpose (plain) flour

2 tablespoons unsweet-ened cocoa powder

⅓ cup (90 g) butter, melted

Walnut halves, to decorate

Chocolate Buttercream

½ cup (125 g) butter,

1⅓ cups (250 g) confec-tioners' (icing) sugar

1 teaspoon coffee extract

2 tablespoons heavy (double) cream

3 oz (90 g) dark chocolate, melted

1 recipe Chocolate Frosting (see page 318)

Serves: 6–8
Preparation: 40 minutes
Cooking: 45–50 minutes
Level: 2

PEPPERMINT CREAM CAKE

Cake: Preheat the oven to 350°F (180°C/gas 4).
• Butter a 9-inch (23-cm) round cake pan. Line with parchment paper. Butter the paper. • Melt the chocolate with the water in a double boiler over barely simmering water. Set aside to cool. • Mix the flour, cocoa, baking powder, baking soda, and salt in a medium bowl. • Beat the butter and both sugars in a large bowl with an electric mixer at medium speed until creamy. • Add the eggs, one at a time, beating until just blended after each addition. • With mixer at low speed, gradually beat in the dry ingredients, alternating with the milk and chocolate mixture. • Spoon the batter into the prepared pan. • Bake for 30–40 minutes, or until a toothpick inserted into the center comes out clean. • Cool the cake in the pan for 10 minutes. Turn out onto a rack. Carefully remove the paper and let cool completely. • Peppermint Filling: With mixer at high speed, beat the confectioners' sugar and butter in a medium bowl until creamy. Stir in the milk and peppermint extract. • Chocolate Frosting: Stir together the confectioners' sugar and cocoa in a medium bowl. Beat in the butter and enough water to make a thick, spreadable frosting. • Split the cake horizontally. • Place one layer on a serving plate. Spread with the filling. Top with the remaining layer. Spread the top and sides with the chocolate frosting.

4   oz (125 g) dark chocolate, chopped

¼   cup (60 ml) water

1¼ cups (180 g) all-purpose (plain) flour

2   tablespoons unsweetened cocoa powder

1   teaspoon baking powder

1   teaspoon baking soda

¼   teaspoon salt

½   cup (125 g) butter, melted

1   cup (200 g) sugar

⅓   cup (70 g) firmly packed brown sugar

2   large eggs

⅓   cup (90 ml) milk

Peppermint Filling

3   cups (450 g) confectioners' (icing) sugar

½   cup (125 g) butter

1   tablespoon milk

½   teaspoon peppermint extract (essence)

Chocolate Frosting

2   cups (300 g) confectioners' (icing) sugar

⅓   cup (50 g) unsweetened cocoa powder

1   tablespoon butter

2   tablespoons boiling water

Serves: 8–10
Preparation: 40 min
Cooking: 30–40 min
Level: 2

BLACK FOREST CAKE

Chocolate Cake: Preheat the oven to 350°F (180°C/gas 4). • Butter a 9-inch (23-cm) round cake pan and line with parchment paper. • Mix the flour, cocoa, and salt in a medium bowl.• Melt the chocolate in a double boiler over barely simmering water, stirring until smooth. • Beat the egg yolks and brown sugar in a medium bowl with an electric mixer on medium-high speed until pale and creamy. • Add the chocolate mixture, stirring with a wooden spoon or large kitchen spoon to combine. • Beat the egg whites in a medium bowl using an electric mixer on medium-high speed until firm peaks form. • Fold a quarter of the egg whites into the chocolate mixture. • Gradually fold in the mixed dry ingredients and melted butter until well mixed. Gently fold in the remaining egg whites. • Spoon the batter into the prepared cake pan, smoothing well with a spoon. • Bake for 45 minutes, or until golden brown and the cakes spring back when lightly touched or a skewer comes out clean when tested. • Let the cake to cool in the pan for 10 minutes then turn out onto a rack. Carefully peel off the paper and let cool completely. • Vanilla Cream: Beat the cream, sugar, and vanilla in a large bowl until stiff peaks form. • When the cake is cooled completely, slice into thirds horizontally and brush each round with cherry liqueur. • To assemble the cake, place a round of cake on a serving plate. Spread the cherries evenly over the top and cover

Chocolate Cake

1⅓ cups (200 g) all-purpose (plain) flour

4 tablespoons unsweetened cocoa powder

¼ teaspoon salt

4 oz (125 g) dark chocolate, coarsely chopped

6 large eggs, separated

1 cup (200 g) firmly packed light brown sugar

¾ cup (180 g) butter, melted and cooled

¼ cup (60 ml) cherry liqueur

2 cups (500 ml) maraschino cherries, pitted + extra for decoration

3 oz (90 g) dark chocolate, coarsely grated

Large piece dark chocolate, for curls

Vanilla Cream

3½ cups (875 ml) heavy
    (double) cream

7 tablespoons
    confectioners' (icing)
    sugar

2 teaspoons vanilla
    extract (essence)

Serves: 8–10
Preparation: 45 minutes
Cooking: 45 minutes
Level: 2

with one-third of the vanilla cream. Cover with another cake round and spread with cherries and cream. Cover with the remaining cake round. • Spread the remaining vanilla cream evenly over the top and sides of the cake using a small spatula or palette knife to create a smooth finish. • Coat the sides of the cake with grated chocolate, pressing lightly with the back of a spoon to make them stick. • Make chocolate curls and shavings using a sharp vegetable peeler. Decorate the top of the cake with the chocolate curls and the extra cherries.

TIRAMISU CAKE

Cake: Preheat the oven to 350°F (180°C/gas 4).
• Butter a 9-inch (23 cm) round cake pan and line
with parchment paper. • Mix both flours in a small
bowl. • Beat the egg yolks, 1 cup (150 g) of
confectioners' sugar, and vanilla in a medium bowl
with an electric mixer on medium-high speed until
pale and thick. • Beat the egg whites in a medium
bowl until soft peaks form. Gradually add the
remaining sugar and lemon juice, beating until stiff
peaks form. • Carefully fold a quarter of the egg
whites into the yolk mixture. • Fold the flour mixture
into the yolk mixture until well incorporated. Gently
fold in the remaining whites. • Spoon the batter into
the prepared pan. • Bake for 35 minutes, or until
golden brown and the cake springs back when
lightly touched or a skewer comes out clean when
tested. • Let the cake to cool in the pan for 10
minutes then turn out onto a rack. Carefully peel off
the paper and let cool completely. • Mascarpone
Cream: Beat the cream and confectioners' sugar
until soft peaks form. Add the mascarpone and
vanilla extract, beating until combined. • Slice the
cake into thirds horizontally. • Combine the coffee
and coffee liqueur in a small bowl. • Place one
round of cake on a serving plate and brush with
one-third of the coffee mixture. Spread with one-
third of the mascarpone cream. Repeat with the
remaining rounds. • Decorate the top of the cake
with the chocolate shavings.

Cake

⅓ cup (50 g) all-purpose (plain) flour

⅓ cup (50 g) potato flour

5 large eggs, separated

1 cup (150 g) + ¼ cup (30 g) confectioners' (icing) sugar

1 teaspoon vanilla extract (essence)

1 teaspoon freshly squeezed lemon juice

⅓ cup (90 ml) very strong brewed coffee

⅓ cup (90 ml) coffee liqueur

3½ oz (100 g) dark chocolate, shaved

Mascarpone Cream

1¼ cups (300 ml) heavy (double) cream

5 tablespoons confectioners' (icing) sugar

1¼ cups (300 g) mascarpone cheese

1 teaspoon vanilla extract (essence)

Serves: 8–10
Preparation: 40 minutes
Cooking: 10 minutes
Level: 2

STICKY DATE GATEAU

Cake: Preheat the oven to 350°F (180°C/gas 4). • Butter two 9-inch (23 cm) round cake pans and line with parchment paper. • Mix the flour, cinnamon, baking powder, and salt in a large bowl. • Combine the dates, boiling water, baking soda, and chocolate in a small bowl and set aside. • Beat the butter, sugar, and vanilla in a medium bowl with an electric mixer on medium-high speed until pale and creamy. • Add the eggs one at a time, beating until combined after each addition. • With mixer on low speed, add the pecans and date mixture, beating until incorporated. • Beat in the mixed dry ingredients. • Divide the mixture in half and spoon into the prepared cake pans. • Bake for 30 minutes, or until golden brown and the cakes spring back when lightly touched or a skewer comes out clean when tested. • Allow the cakes to cool in their pans for 10 minutes then turn onto a rack. Carefully peel off the parchment paper and let cool completely. Butterscotch Buttercream: Beat the butter, confectioners' sugar, and brown sugar with an electric mixer on medium-high speed until creamy. • With mixer on low, add the butterscotch liqueur, beating until combined. • Slice the cooled cakes in half horizontally. • Divide the butterscotch buttercream into thirds and spoon onto three of the cake rounds, leaving a $3/4$-inch (2 cm) border around the edge. • Sandwich the cake layers together. • Butterscotch Frosting: Place the

Cake

2⅓ cups (350 g) all-purpose (plain) flour

1 teaspoon ground cinnamon

1 teaspoon baking powder

¼ teaspoon salt

2 cups (360 g) pitted dates

1 cup (250 ml) boiling water

½ teaspoon baking soda (bicarbonate of soda)

2 oz (60 g) dark chocolate, coarsely chopped

1 cup (250 g) butter, softened

1 cup (200 g) superfine (caster) sugar

1 teaspoon vanilla extract (essence)

3 large eggs

⅓ cup (50 g) pecans, coarsely chopped

Butterscotch Buttercream

1 cup (250 g) unsalted butter, softened

2 cups (300 g) confectioners' (icing) sugar

½ cup (100 g) firmly
    packed dark brown
    sugar

¼ cup (60 ml)
    butterscotch liqueur

Butterscotch Frosting

1⅓ cups (200 g)
    confectioners' (icing)
    sugar

¼ cup (60 ml)
    butterscotch liqueur

2 tablespoons boiling water

Caramelized Dates

¼ cup (60 ml) water

½ cup (100 g) sugar

⅓ cup (90 ml) freshly
    squeezed orange juice

½ cup (125 ml) light
    (single) cream

12 dates, pitted and halved

Serves: 8–10
Preparation: 45 minutes
Cooking: 45 minutes
Level: 2

confectioners' sugar in a small bowl. Add the butterscotch liqueur and gradually add the boiling water, stirring until the frosting is smooth and the desired consistency. • Spoon the frosting on top of the cake and spread evenly over the top and sides, using a small spatula or palette knife to create a smooth finish. • Caramelized Dates: Heat the water and sugar in a small saucepan over low heat for 5 minutes, or until the sugar has dissolved. Increase the heat to medium and boil the sugar syrup without stirring for 5–10 minutes, until it turns to caramel. • Remove from the heat and pour in the orange juice and cream, stirring to combine. • Return the saucepan to the heat and simmer for 5 more minutes, stirring until the mixture has slightly thickened. Add the dates and stir to coat in the caramel. • Set aside to cool for 30 minutes. • Decorate the top of the cake with caramelized dates.

JAFFA TORTE

Cake: Preheat the oven to 350°F (180°C/gas 4). • Butter two 9-inch (23 cm) round cake pans and line with parchment paper. • Melt the chocolate in a double boiler over barely simmering water. • Beat the egg yolks and sugar in a medium bowl with an electric mixer on medium-high speed until pale and creamy. • With mixer on low, add the orange liqueur, orange zest, and chocolate. • Beat the egg whites in a large bowl with mixer on medium-high speed until firm peaks form. • Fold a quarter of the whites into the chocolate batter. • Fold in the flour and cocoa alternately with the melted butter. Fold in the remaining egg whites. • Spoon into the prepared cake pans. • Bake for 25 minutes, or until golden brown and a skewer comes out clean when tested. • Let cool in their pans for 10 minutes then turn onto a rack. Peel off the parchment paper and let cool completely. • Slice in half horizontally and brush with orange liqueur. • Jaffa Buttercream: Beat the butter and confectioners' sugar with mixer on medium-high until pale and creamy. Stir in the orange liqueur and chocolate. • Set aside half the buttercream. Spoon the rest onto three cake rounds and sandwich together. • Place two spoonfuls of buttercream in a piping bag fitted with a star nozzle. Spread the remaining buttercream over the top and sides of the cake. Pipe a decorative pattern around the top edge of the cake. • Make chocolate curls and shavings using a vegetable peeler and decorate the top. Finish with candied orange.

Cake

4 oz (125 g) dark chocolate, chopped

6 large eggs, separated

1 cup (200 g) light brown sugar

2 tablespoons orange liqueur

2 tablespoons finely grated orange zest

1⅓ cups (200 g) all-purpose (plain) flour

¼ cup (30 g) unsweetened cocoa powder

¾ cup (180 g) butter, melted and cooled

¼ cup (60 ml) orange liqueur

Large piece dark chocolate, for curls

Candied (glacé) orange

Jaffa Buttercream

1 cup (250 g) butter

1⅓ cups (200 g) confectioners' (icing) sugar

1 tablespoon orange liqueur

8 oz (200 g) dark chocolate, melted

Serves: 8–10
Preparation: 45 minutes
Cooking: 45 minutes
Level: 2

ORANGE FRUIT GÂTEAU

Orange Gâteau: Preheat the oven to 350°F (180°C/gas 4). • Line a 10-inch (25-cm) springform pan with parchment paper. • Beat the egg yolks and water in a large bowl with an electric mixer at high speed until pale and thick. Beat in $2/3$ cup (125 g) of sugar and the lemon zest and juice. • With mixer at medium speed, beat the egg whites in a large bowl until frothy. With mixer at high speed, gradually add the remaining sugar, beating until stiff, glossy peaks form. Use a large rubber spatula to fold them into the egg yolk mixture. • Fold the flour and baking powder into the batter. • Spoon the batter into the prepared pan. • Bake for 35–40 minutes, or until a toothpick inserted into the center comes out clean. • Cool the cake in the pan for 15 minutes. Loosen and remove the pan sides. Invert onto a rack. Loosen and remove the pan bottom. Carefully remove the paper and let cool completely. • Orange Filling: Beat the egg yolks, orange zest, and sugar in a saucepan until well blended. Simmer over low heat, stirring constantly with a wooden spoon, until the mixture lightly coats a metal spoon or registers 160°F (80°C) on an instant-read thermometer. Immediately plunge the pan into a bowl of ice water and stir until the egg mixture has cooled. • Sprinkle the gelatin over the orange and lemon juices in a saucepan. Let stand 1 minute. Stir over low heat until the gelatin has completely dissolved. • Remove from the heat. Gradually fold the egg mixture into

Orange Gâteau

4 large eggs, separated

¼ cup (60 ml) hot water

1 cup (200 g) sugar

Finely grated zest and freshly squeezed juice of ½ lemon

1⅓ cups (200 g) all-purpose (plain) flour

½ teaspoon baking powder

Orange Filling

4 large egg yolks

Finely grated zest of 1 orange

½ cup (100 g) sugar

2 tablespoons unflavored gelatin

Freshly squeezed juice of 3 oranges

1 tablespoon freshly squeezed lemon juice

¾ cup (180 ml) heavy (double) cream

2 tablespoons orange liqueur

Topping

- **3 tablespoons apricot preserves**
- **¾ cup flaked almonds**
- **¼ cup (60 g) butter, softened**
- **½ cup (100 g) sugar**
- **3 oranges, thinly sliced**
- **Star fruit and candied (glacé) cherries, to decorate**

Serves: 8–10
Preparation: 1 hour
+ 3 hours to chill
Cooking: 35–45 minutes
Level: 2

the gelatin mixture. • With mixer at high speed, beat the cream in a large bowl until stiff. Use a large rubber spatula to fold the cream into the egg mixture. • Split the cake in half horizontally. Sprinkle the orange liqueur over the cake layers. • Place one layer on a serving plate and surround with the pan sides. Spread with the filling. Top with the remaining layer. • Refrigerate for 3 hours. • Remove the pan sides. • Topping: Warm the apricot preserves in a saucepan over low heat. Brush the cake with the preserves. Stick the almonds onto the sides. • Melt the butter and sugar in a saucepan over low heat. Add the orange slices and cook until the oranges begin to caramelize, about 10 minutes. • Arrange the oranges in a circle around the edge of the cake. Decorate with slices of star fruit and candied cherries.

333

STRAWBERRY CREAM GÂTEAU

Génoise: Preheat the oven to 375°F (190°C/gas 5).
• Butter a 9-inch (23-cm) springform pan. Line with parchment paper. • Mix the flour and cornstarch in a bowl. • Beat the eggs and sugar in a large heatproof bowl. Fit the bowl into a wide saucepan of barely simmering water. (Bottom of bowl should not touch the water.) Beat until the sugar has dissolved. Remove from heat and beat until cooled and tripled in volume.
• Fold in the dry ingredients. • Place 2 cups of batter in a small bowl and fold in the butter and vanilla. Fold this mixture into the remaining batter. • Spoon into the prepared pan. • Bake for 30–40 minutes, or until golden brown and a toothpick inserted into the center comes out clean. • Cool in the pan for 5 minutes. Turn out onto a rack. Carefully remove the paper and let cool completely. Filling and Topping: Soak the strawberries in the liqueur for 1 hour. • Beat the egg yolks, wine, and sugar in a double boiler over low heat until the mixture coats a metal spoon. Set aside. • Sprinkle the gelatin over the lemon juice. Let stand 1 minute. Stir the gelatin mixture into the yolk mixture. Transfer to a large bowl, cover, and refrigerate until chilled. • Fold one-third of the cream into the yolk mixture. • Drain the strawberries, reserving juice, and fold into the yolk mixture. • Split the cake horizontally.
• Butter a 9-inch (23-cm) springform pan. Place one layer in the pan. Drizzle with strawberry juice. Spread with the strawberry mixture and top with the remaining cake. Drizzle with strawberry juice. Refrigerate for 6 hours. • Remove the pan sides. Spread with the remaining cream. Top with almonds and strawberries.

Génoise
- ⅔ cup (100 g) cake flour
- ⅔ cup (100 g) cornstarch
- 6 large eggs
- ¾ cup (150 g) superfine (caster) sugar
- ⅓ cup (90 g) butter, melted and cooled
- 1 teaspoon vanilla extract (essence)

Filling and Topping
- 2 lb (1 kg) ripe strawberries, halved (reserve 12 whole berries to decorate)
- ½ cup (125 ml) orange liqueur
- 8 large egg yolks
- 1¼ cups (300 ml) dry white wine
- 1 cup (200 g) sugar
- 2 tablespoons unflavored gelatin
- 3 tablespoons freshly squeezed lemon juice
- 2 cups (500 ml) heavy (double) cream, beaten
- ½ cup (60 g) slivered almonds, toasted

Serves: 8–10
Preparation: 45 minutes + 7 hours to soak and chill
Cooking: 30–40 minutes
Level: 2

RASPBERRY HAZELNUT GÂTEAU

Hazelnut Sponge: Preheat the oven to 400°F (200°C/gas 6). • Butter a 9-inch (23-cm) springform pan. Line with parchment paper. • Beat the eggs and confectioners' sugar in a large heatproof bowl. Fit the bowl into a wide saucepan of barely simmering water. (The bottom of the bowl should not touch the water.) Beat until the sugar has dissolved. Remove from the heat and beat with an electric mixer at high speed until thick and tripled in volume. • Fold the hazelnuts and flour into the batter with a large spatula. • Spoon into the prepared pan. • Bake for 35–45 minutes, or until a toothpick inserted into the center comes out clean. • Cool in the pan for 5 minutes. Loosen and remove the pan sides. Invert onto a rack. Loosen and remove the pan bottom. Carefully remove the paper. Turn top-side up and let cool completely. • Filling and Topping: Place the raspberries, 1 cup (150 g) of confectioners' sugar, and kirsch in a large bowl. Soak for 1 hour. • Drain the raspberries, reserving the syrup. • Beat the cream cheese, remaining confectioners' sugar, and lemon zest in a large bowl with an electric mixer at medium speed until creamy. • With mixer at low speed, beat in the raspberries. • Sprinkle the gelatin over the water in a saucepan. Let stand 1 minute. Stir over low heat until the gelatin has completely dissolved. • With mixer at high speed, beat the cream in a medium

Hazelnut Sponge

8 large eggs

1 cup (150 g) confectioners' (icing) sugar

1⅓ cups (200 g) finely ground toasted hazelnuts,

1 cup (150 g) cake flour

Filling and Topping

1 lb (500 g) fresh raspberries, (reserve 20 whole to decorate)

1⅔ cups (250 g) confectioners' (icing) sugar

1 cup (250 ml) kirsch (cherry liqueur)

1 package (8 oz/250 g) cream cheese, softened

1 tablespoon finely grated lemon zest

1¼ cups (300 ml) heavy (double) cream

2 tablespoons unflavored gelatin

¼ cup (60 ml) cold water

1 cup (250 g) raspberry jelly (jam)

Serves: 8–10
Preparation: 25 minutes
 + 2 hours to soak and
 chill
Cooking: 35–45 minutes
Level: 2

bowl until stiff. Use a large rubber spatula to fold the cream and the gelatin mixture into the raspberry mixture. • Split the cake in three horizontally. Place one layer on a serving plate. Brush with the syrup. Spread with half the raspberry mixture. Top with a second layer of cake and spread with the remaining raspberry mixture. Top with the remaining layer of cake. Brush with the remaining syrup. • Heat the raspberry jelly in a saucepan over low heat until liquid. Spread over the cake. • Decorate with the raspberries. • Chill in the refrigerator for 1 hour.

339

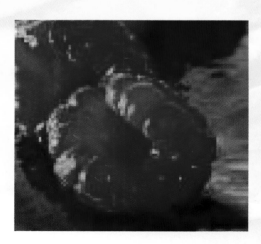

CHOCOLATE CREAM LAYER CAKE

342

Cake: Preheat the oven to 350°F (180°C/gas 4).
• Butter and flour an 8-inch (20-cm) springform pan. • Beat the egg yolks and confectioners' sugar in a large bowl with an electric mixer at high speed until pale and creamy. • Use a large rubber spatula to fold in the flour and cocoa powder. • With mixer at high speed, beat the egg whites in a large bowl until stiff peaks form. Fold into the batter, followed by the melted butter. • Spoon the batter into the prepared pan. • Bake for 35–40 minutes, or until a toothpick inserted into the center comes out clean.
• Cool the cake in the pan for 5 minutes. Loosen and remove the pan sides. Turn out onto a rack and let cool completely. • Chocolate Cream: With mixer at medium speed, beat the egg yolks, sugar, and butter in a large saucepan until pale and thick.
• Use a large rubber spatula to fold in the flour, chocolate, and vanilla. Gradually stir in the milk.
• Place over low heat, stirring constantly with a wooden spoon until the mixture lightly coats a metal spoon or registers 160°F (71°C) on an instant-read thermometer. Immediately plunge the pan into a bowl of ice water and stir until the egg mixture has cooled. • Split the cake in half horizontally. Place one layer on a serving plate. Spread with one-third of the chocolate cream. Top with the remaining layer. Spread with the remaining chocolate cream. • Sprinkle with the almonds and serve.

Cake

4   large eggs, separated
1   cup (150 g) confectioners' (icing) sugar
1   cup (150 g) all-purpose (plain) flour
⅓   cup (50 g) unsweetened cocoa powder
¼   cup (60 g) butter, melted

Chocolate Cream

2   large egg yolks
¾   cup (150 g) superfine (caster) sugar
½   cup (125 g) butter, softened
⅓   cup (50 g) all-purpose (plain) flour
3   oz (90 g) dark chocolate, grated
¼   teaspoon vanilla extract (essence)
2   cups (500 ml) milk
¼   cup (30 g) toasted almonds

Serves: 8
Preparation: 30 minutes
Cooking: 40–45 minutes
Level: 2

DEVIL'S FOOD CAKE

Cake: Preheat the oven to 350°F (180°C/gas 4).
• Butter two 9-inch (23-cm) round cake pans. Line
with parchment paper. Butter the paper. • Stir the
cocoa and water in a small bowl until smooth. • Mix
the flour, baking powder, baking soda, and salt in a
large bowl. • Beat the butter, sugar, vanilla, and liqueur
in a large bowl with an electric mixer at high speed
until creamy. • Add the eggs, one at a time, beating
until just blended after each addition. • With mixer on
low, gradually add the dry ingredients alternating with
the buttermilk and the cocoa mixture. • Spoon the
batter into the prepared pans. • Bake for 30–40
minutes, or until a toothpick inserted into the center
comes out clean. • Cool the cakes in the pans for 10
minutes. Turn out onto racks. Carefully remove the
paper and let cool completely. • Frosting: Melt the
chocolate in a double boiler over barely simmering
water. Let cool. • Beat the butter in a medium bowl
until creamy. • Beat the egg yolks in a large bowl until
pale in color. • Place the sugar and water in a medium
saucepan over low heat and stir until the sugar has
dissolved and the syrup is boiling. Wash down the
sides of the pan with a pastry brush dipped in cold
water to prevent sugar crystals from forming. Cook,
without stirring, until the syrup reaches 238°F (112°C),
or the soft-ball stage. • Remove from heat. Beat the
syrup into the egg yolks in a slow, steady stream until
cool. Gradually beat in the butter. Beat in the chocolate
and vanilla. • Place one cake on a serving plate.
Spread with one-third of the frosting. Top with the
remaining cake. Spread with the remaining frosting.

Cake

3/4 cup (120 g) unsweetened cocoa powder

1/2 cup (125 ml) boiling water

2 cups (300 g) all-purpose (plain) flour

2 teaspoons baking powder

1/2 teaspoon baking soda (bicarbonate of soda)

1/4 teaspoon salt

3/4 cup (180 g) butter

2 cups (400 g) sugar

2 teaspoons vanilla extract (essence)

1 tablespoon chocolate or coffee liqueur

2 large eggs

1 cup (250 ml) buttermilk

Frosting

8 oz (250 g) dark chocolate, chopped

1½ cups (375 g) butter

6 large egg yolks

1 cup (200 g) sugar

1/2 cup (125 ml) water

2 teaspoons vanilla extract

Serves: 8–10
Preparation: 45 minutes
Cooking 30–40 minutes
Level: 2

VIENNOIS

Cake: Preheat the oven to 300°F (150°C/gas 2). •
Butter two 8-inch (20-cm) round cake pans. Line with
parchment paper. • Mix the cocoa, flour, cornstarch,
and salt in a medium bowl. • Beat the sugar and egg
yolks in a large bowl with an electric mixer at high
speed until pale and thick. • With mixer on low,
gradually beat in the dry ingredients • With mixer on
high, beat the egg whites in a large bowl until stiff
peaks form. Fold them into the batter. • Spoon half
the batter into each of the prepared pans. • Bake for
20–25 minutes, or until springy to the touch and a
toothpick inserted into the center comes out clean. •
Cool the cakes in the pans for 10 minutes. Turn out
onto racks. Carefully remove the paper and let cool
completely. • Chocolate Frosting: bring the sugar and
cream to a boil in a saucepan over medium heat. Boil
for 1 minute, then stir in the chocolate. • Return to
medium-low heat and cook, without stirring, until the
mixture reaches 238°F (112°C), or the soft-ball stage.
Remove from the heat. • Add the butter and vanilla,
without stirring, and place the saucepan in a larger
pan of cold water for 5 minutes before stirring. • Beat
with a wooden spoon until the frosting begins to lose
its sheen, 5–10 minutes. • Let stand for 3–4 minutes,
then stir until spreadable. • Split the cakes
horizontally. Place one layer on a serving plate and
spread with frosting. Repeat with 2 more layers. Top
with the remaining layer. Spread the top and sides
with the remaining frosting. • Sprinkle the chocolate
over the top of the cake.

Cake

¼ cup (30 g) unsweetened
  cocoa powder

3 tablespoons cake flour

2 tablespoons cornstarch
  (cornflour)

¼ teaspoon salt

1½ cups (300 g) sugar

8 large eggs, separated

2 oz (60 g) dark
  chocolate, finely grated

Rich Chocolate Frosting

2 cups (400 g) sugar

1 cup (250 ml) heavy
  (double) cream

8 oz (250 g) dark
  chocolate, coarsely
  chopped

2 tablespoons butter

1 teaspoon vanilla extract
  (essence)

Serves: 8–10
Preparation: 1 hour 15
  minutes
Cooking 30–35 minutes
Level: 3

RASPBERRY SPONGE ROLL

Sponge Roll: Preheat the oven to 400°F (200°C/gas 6). • Butter and flour a 15$\frac{1}{2}$ x 10$\frac{1}{2}$-inch (38 x 21-cm) jelly-roll pan. Line with parchment paper. • Mix the flour, baking powder, and salt in a medium bowl. • Beat the egg yolks in a large bowl with an electric mixer at high speed until pale and thick. Add the sugar and vanilla and continue beating until very thick. • With mixer at low speed, gradually beat in the dry ingredients, alternating with the milk. • With mixer at high speed, beat the egg whites and cream of tartar in a large bowl until stiff peaks form. • Use a large rubber spatula to fold them into the batter. • Spoon the batter into the prepared pan. • Bake for 10–15 minutes, or until lightly browned. • Dust a clean kitchen towel with confectioners' sugar. Turn the cake out onto the towel and carefully remove the parchment paper. Roll up the cake, using the towel as a guide. Let cool. • Raspberry Filling: Chop the raspberries in a food processor until smooth. Strain to remove the seeds. • With mixer at high speed, beat the cream and sugar in a large bowl until stiff. Fold in the raspberries and pistachios. • Unroll the cake and spread with most of the filling, leaving a 1-inch (2.5-inch) border. Reroll the cake. Place on a serving dish and spoon the remaining filling along the top. Decorate with the fresh raspberries, if liked.

Sponge Roll

1 cup (150 g) cake flour

1$\frac{1}{2}$ teaspoons baking powder

$\frac{1}{4}$ teaspoon salt

3 large eggs, separated

$\frac{3}{4}$ cup (150 g) sugar

1 teaspoon vanilla extract (essence)

$\frac{1}{4}$ cup (60 ml) milk

$\frac{1}{4}$ teaspoon cream of tartar

$\frac{1}{4}$ cup (30 g) confectioners' (icing) sugar

Raspberry Filling

1 cup (200 g) fresh or frozen unsweetened raspberries, thawed

1$\frac{1}{2}$ cups (375 ml) heavy (double) cream

$\frac{1}{4}$ cup (50 g) sugar

$\frac{1}{4}$ cup pistachios, chopped

Fresh raspberries, to decorate (optional)

Serves: 8
Preparation: 45 minutes
Cooking 10–15 minutes
Level: 2

STRAWBERRY SHORTCAKE SANDWICH

Shortcake: Preheat the oven to 350°F (180°C/gas 4). • Butter two 8-inch (20 cm) round cake pans and line with parchment paper. • Beat the butter, sugar, and vanilla with an electric mixer on medium-high speed until pale and creamy. • Add the eggs one at a time, beating until just combined after each addition. • With mixer on low, gradually beat in the flour and milk until well incorporated • Divide the batter evenly between the prepared pans. • Bake for 25 minutes, or until golden brown and the cake springs back when lightly touched or a skewer comes out clean when tested. • Cool the cakes in the pans for 10 minutes then turn out onto a rack. Peel off the paper and let cool completely. Vanilla Cream: Beat the cream, confectioners' sugar, and vanilla in a small bowl until stiff peaks form. • Slice the top off one of the cakes to create a flat surface, if necessary. Place, flat side down, on a serving plate, and spread with the apricot preserves. Cover with a layer of sliced strawberries. Spoon the vanilla cream over the top, spreading ³/₄ inch (2 cm) in from the edge, using a small spatula or knife. Place the other cake on top. • Dust with confectioners' sugar and arrange the whole strawberries on top.

Shortcake

- 1 cup (250 g) butter
- 1¼ cups (250 g) superfine (caster) sugar
- 1 teaspoon vanilla extract (essence)
- 4 large eggs
- 1²/₃ cups (250 g) self-rising flour
- 1½ tablespoons milk
- ⅓ cup (90 g) apricot preserves (jam)
- 1¼ cups (300 g) strawberries, sliced
- 8 whole strawberries

  Confectioners' (icing) sugar, for dusting

Vanilla Cream

- ³/₄ cup (180 ml) heavy (double) cream
- 2 tablespoons confectioners' (icing) sugar
- ½ teaspoon vanilla extract (essence)

Serves: 8–10
Preparation: 25 minutes
Cooking 25 minutes
Level: 2

COLLARED RASPBERRY CAKE

Cake Border: Preheat the oven to 350°F (180°C/gas 4). • Line a baking sheet with parchment paper. Draw 3 parallel lines 16 inches (40 cm) long and 2 inches (5 cm) wide. • Mix the flour, cornstarch, baking powder, and salt in a medium bowl. • Beat the egg yolks and sugar in a large bowl with an electric mixer at high speed until pale and thick. • With mixer on low, gradually beat in the dry ingredients. • With mixer on high, beat the egg whites until stiff peaks form. Fold into the batter. • Place two-thirds of the batter in one bowl and the rest in another bowl. Mix the food coloring into the bowl with less batter. • Spoon the plain batter into a pastry bag fitted with a 1/2-inch (1-cm) nozzle. Using the lines as a guide, pipe two strips top and bottom leaving the central strip empty. • Spoon the green batter into a clean pastry bag. Pipe between the plain strips. • Bake for 5–8 minutes, or until the white strips are pale golden brown. • Cool in the pan for 5 minutes. Turn out onto a rack and carefully remove the paper. Let cool completely. • Prepare the shortcake (bake in two pans, following the recipe on page 350). • Split the shortcakes in half horizontally. Place one layer on a serving plate. Spread with the chantilly cream. Top with a second layer and spread with the cream. Repeat with a third layer. • Spread the top and sides of the cake with the cream. • Carefully wrap the cake border around the cake. • Decorate with the raspberries.

Cake Border

1/3 cup (50 g) all-purpose (plain) flour

1/3 cup (50 g) cornstarch (cornflour)

1/2 teaspoon baking powder

1/4 teaspoon salt

3 large eggs, separated

1/2 cup (100 g) sugar

2 tablespoons butter, melted

Green food coloring

1 recipe Chantilly Cream (see page 360)

1 recipe Shortcake (see page 350)

1 cup (150 g) fresh raspberries

Serves: 8–10
Preparation: 25 minutes
Cooking 30–35 minutes
Level: 3

CHOCOLATE ANGEL FOOD CAKE

Cake: Preheat the oven to 350°F (180°C/gas 4).
• Set out a 9½-inch (24-cm) angel food cake pan.
• Mix the confectioners' sugar, flour, cocoa, and salt in a medium bowl. • Beat the egg whites and cream of tartar in a large bowl with an electric mixer at medium speed until frothy. • With mixer at high speed, add the sugar, beating until stiff, glossy peaks form. Add the vanilla. • Use a large rubber spatula to fold in the dry ingredients. • Spoon the batter into the pan. • Bake for 40–50 minutes, or until springy to the touch and the cake shrinks from the pan sides. • Invert the cake pan over the neck of a bottle and let cool completely. • Chocolate Sauce: Melt the butter with the water in a saucepan over medium heat. Bring to a boil, stirring constantly. • Stir in the chocolate until melted. • Add the sugar, corn syrup, and salt. Bring to a boil and simmer for 5 minutes. Remove from the heat and add the vanilla. • Serve slices of cake with the berries and the warm chocolate sauce.

Cake

1½ cups (225 g) confectioners' (icing) sugar

1 cup (150 g) cake flour

¼ cup (30 g) unsweetened cocoa powder

¼ teaspoon salt

10 large egg whites

1½ teaspoons cream of tartar

1 cup (200 g) sugar

1 teaspoon vanilla extract (essence)

Fresh berries, to serve

Chocolate Sauce

½ cup (125 g) butter

⅔ cup (150 ml) water

5 oz (150 g) dark chocolate, chopped

1¼ cups (250 g) sugar

¼ cup (60 ml) light corn (golden) syrup

½ teaspoon salt

2 teaspoons vanilla extract (essence)

Serves: 8–10
Preparation: 30 minutes
Cooking: 1 hour
Level: 2

CHOCOLATE CHERRY SPONGE

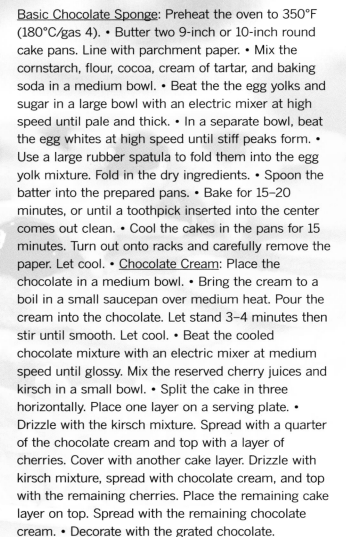

Basic Chocolate Sponge: Preheat the oven to 350°F (180°C/gas 4). • Butter two 9-inch or 10-inch round cake pans. Line with parchment paper. • Mix the cornstarch, flour, cocoa, cream of tartar, and baking soda in a medium bowl. • Beat the the egg yolks and sugar in a large bowl with an electric mixer at high speed until pale and thick. • In a separate bowl, beat the egg whites at high speed until stiff peaks form. • Use a large rubber spatula to fold them into the egg yolk mixture. Fold in the dry ingredients. • Spoon the batter into the prepared pans. • Bake for 15–20 minutes, or until a toothpick inserted into the center comes out clean. • Cool the cakes in the pans for 15 minutes. Turn out onto racks and carefully remove the paper. Let cool. • Chocolate Cream: Place the chocolate in a medium bowl. • Bring the cream to a boil in a small saucepan over medium heat. Pour the cream into the chocolate. Let stand 3–4 minutes then stir until smooth. Let cool. • Beat the cooled chocolate mixture with an electric mixer at medium speed until glossy. Mix the reserved cherry juices and kirsch in a small bowl. • Split the cake in three horizontally. Place one layer on a serving plate. • Drizzle with the kirsch mixture. Spread with a quarter of the chocolate cream and top with a layer of cherries. Cover with another cake layer. Drizzle with kirsch mixture, spread with chocolate cream, and top with the remaining cherries. Place the remaining cake layer on top. Spread with the remaining chocolate cream. • Decorate with the grated chocolate.

Basic Chocolate Sponge

- ¾ cup (120 g) cornstarch (cornflour)
- 2 tablespoons all-purpose (plain) flour
- ¼ cup (30 g) unsweetened cocoa powder
- 1 teaspoon cream of tartar
- ½ teaspoon baking soda (bicarbonate of soda)
- 4 large eggs, separated
- ¾ cup (150 g) sugar

Chocolate Cream

- 14 oz (400 g) dark chocolate, coarsely chopped
- 1 cup (250 ml) heavy (double) cream
- 1¼ cups canned sour cherries, drained (reserve the juice)
- 3 tablespoons kirsch (cherry liqueur)

   Grated chocolate, to decorate

Serves: 8–10
Preparation: 45 minutes
Cooking: 15–20 minutes
Level: 2

ALMOND ROLL WITH CARAMEL CRUNCH

Caramel Crunch: Oil a baking sheet. Cook the sugar and almonds in a saucepan over low heat, stirring constantly, until the sugar melts. Continue cooking, stirring frequently, until deep golden brown. • Pour onto the prepared baking sheet and set aside to cool, about 1 hour. • When cool, crush into small pieces. • Almond Roll: Preheat the oven to 350°F (180°C/gas 4). • Butter and flour a 15^1/2 x 10^1/2-inch (38 x 21-cm) jelly-roll pan. Line with parchment paper. • Beat the egg yolks and ^{3}/4 cup (150 g) of sugar in a large bowl with an electric mixer at high speed until pale and very thick. • With mixer on low speed, add the almonds and almond extract. • With mixer at high speed, beat the egg whites and salt in a large bowl until stiff peaks form. • Use a large rubber spatula to fold them into the almond mixture. • Spoon the batter into the prepared pan. • Bake for 15–20 minutes, or until a toothpick inserted into the center comes out clean. • Dust a clean kitchen towel with the extra 3 tablespoons of sugar. Turn the cake out onto the towel and carefully remove the paper. Roll up the cake, using the towel as a guide. Let cool. • Filling: With mixer at high speed, beat the cream in a large bowl until stiff. • Unroll the cake and spread evenly with the cream, leaving a 1-inch (2.5-cm) border. Reroll the cake. • Press the caramel crunch into the sides of the roll.

Caramel Crunch

1^1/2 cups (300 g) sugar

^{3}/4 cup (120 g) blanched whole almonds

Almond Roll

5 large eggs, separated

^{3}/4 cup (150 g) sugar + 3 tablespoons extra, to sprinkle

^{1}/3 cup (50 g) almonds, finely ground

1 teaspoon almond extract (essence)

^{1}/4 teaspoon salt

Filling

1^1/2 cups (375 ml) heavy (double) cream

Serves: 6–8
Preparation: 35 minutes + 1 hour to cool
Cooking: 20–25 minutes
Level: 2

CHOCOLATE RASPBERRY ROLL

Chocolate Roll: Preheat the oven to 375°F (190°C/ gas 5). • Butter and flour a 15^1/$_2$ x 10^1/$_2$-inch (38 x 21-cm) jelly-roll pan. Line with parchment paper. • Melt the chocolate in a double boiler over barely simmering water. Set aside to cool. • Mix the flour, baking powder, baking soda, and salt in a medium bowl. • Beat the eggs and sugar in a large bowl with an electric mixer at high speed until pale and thick. Add the vanilla. • Use a large rubber spatula to fold the dry ingredients into the egg mixture, alternating with the water. Add the chocolate. • Spoon the batter into the prepared pan. • Bake for 15–20 minutes, or until springy to the touch. • Dust a clean kitchen towel with the confectioners' sugar. Turn the cake out onto the towel and carefully remove the parchment paper. Roll up the cake, using the towel as a guide. Let cool. • Chantilly Cream: Beat the cream, confectioners' sugar, and vanilla extract with an electric mixer on high speed until stiff. • Unroll the cake and spread evenly with half the chantilly cream, leaving a 1-inch (2.5-cm) border. Sprinkle with the raspberries. • Reroll the cake. Slice and serve with the remaining chantilly passed separately.

Chocolate Roll

3 oz (90 g) dark chocolate, coarsely chopped

½ cup (75 g) all-purpose (plain) flour

½ teaspoon baking powder

½ teaspoon baking soda (bicarbonate of soda)

¼ teaspoon salt

4 large eggs

¾ cup (150 g) sugar

1 teaspoon vanilla extract (essence)

2 tablespoons cold water

2 tablespoons confectioners' (icing) sugar

Chantilly Cream

2 cups (500 ml) heavy (double) cream

2 tablespoons confectioners' (icing) sugar

1 teaspoon vanilla extract (essence)

Fresh raspberries, to fill

Serves: 6–8
Preparation: 25 minutes
Cooking: 15–20 minutes
Level: 2

LEMON ROLL

Roll: Preheat the oven to 400°F (200°C/gas 6).
• Butter and flour a 15¹/₂ x 10¹/₂-inch (38 x 21-cm)
jelly-roll pan. Line with parchment paper. • Beat the
eggs, sugar, and salt in a medium bowl with an
electric mixer at high speed until pale and very
thick. • Use a large rubber spatula to fold in the
flour. • Spoon the batter into the prepared pan.
• Bake for 8–10 minutes, or until springy to the
touch. • Dust a clean kitchen towel with the
confectioners' sugar. Turn the cake out onto the
towel and carefully remove the parchment paper.
Roll up the cake, using the towel as a guide. Let
cool. • Lemon Cream: Beat the egg and egg yolks,
¹/₂ cup (100 g) of sugar, and lemon juice in a
double boiler until well blended. Cook over low
heat, stirring constantly, until the mixture lightly
coats a metal spoon or registers 160°F (71°C) on an
instant-read thermometer. Add the butter.
Immediately plunge the pan into a bowl of ice water
and stir until cooled. • Syrup: Cook the lemon zest,
sugar, and half the water in a saucepan over
medium heat. Simmer for 3–4 minutes, until the
water is slightly reduced. • Strain the liquid and
discard the zest. Stir the remaining water and the
rum into the syrup. • Unroll the cake and brush with
the syrup. Spread evenly with the apricot preserves
and lemon cream, leaving a 1-inch (2.5-cm) border.
• Reroll the cake and refrigerate for 2 hours.

Roll

2 large eggs
¹/₃ cup (70 g) sugar
¹/₄ teaspoon salt
²/₃ cup (100 g) all-purpose
   (plain) flour
2 tablespoons
   confectioners' (icing)
   sugar
¹/₂ cup (150 g) apricot
   preserves (jam)

Lemon Cream

1 large egg + 5 egg yolks
³/₄ cup (150 g) sugar
2 tablespoons freshly
   squeezed lemon juice
¹/₄ cup (60 g) butter,
   melted

Syrup

   Zest of 1 lemon, cut into
   very thin strips
¹/₄ cup (50 g) sugar
¹/₂ cup (125 ml) water
¹/₄ cup (60 ml) rum

Serves: 6–8
Preparation: 45 minutes
   + 2 hours to chill
Cooking: 8–10 minutes
Level: 3

APRICOT GÂTEAU

Gâteau: Preheat the oven to 400°F (200°C/gas 6).
• Butter and flour a 10-inch (26-cm) springform pan.
• Mix the flour, baking powder, and salt in a large
bowl. • Beat the butter, sugar, and vanilla in a large
bowl with an electric mixer at medium speed until
creamy. • Add the eggs, one at a time, until just
blended after each addition. • With mixer at low
speed, gradually beat in the dry ingredients. • Spoon
the batter into the prepared pan. • Bake for 30–40
minutes, or until a toothpick inserted into the center
comes out clean. • Cool the cake in the pan for 10
minutes. Loosen and remove the pan sides. Invert
onto a rack. Loosen and remove the pan bottom and
let cool completely. • Filling and Topping: Mash the
apricots, sugar, and almond extract in a medium
bowl with a fork until smooth. • Place a quarter of
the apricot syrup in a saucepan. Sprinkle with the
gelatin. Let stand 1 minute. Stir over low heat until
the gelatin has completely dissolved. Stir into the
apricot mixture. Refrigerate until just beginning to
set around the edges. • Split the cake in half
horizontally. Place one layer in the cleaned
springform pan. • Add ¼ cup (60 ml) of kirsch to
the remaining syrup and drizzle over the cake.
Spread with the apricot mixture and top with the
remaining cake layer. Refrigerate for 4 hours • Heat
the preserves and remaining 1 tablespoon Kirsch in
a saucepan over low heat. • Remove the pan sides.
• Brush with the preserves. Sprinkle with the
almonds. Serve with a dollop of crème fraîche.

Gâteau

1⅔ cups (250 g) all-purpose (plain) flour

2 teaspoons baking powder

¼ teaspoon salt

1 cup (250 g) butter, softened

1¼ cups (250 g) sugar

1 teaspoon vanilla extract (essence)

4 large eggs

Filling and Topping

1 (15-oz/400-g) can apricots in syrup, drained (reserve the syrup)

2 tablespoons sugar

½ teaspoon almond extract (essence)

1½ tablespoons unflavored gelatin

5 tablespoons kirsch (cherry liqueur)

¼ cup (60 g) apricot preserves (jam)

½ cup (60 g) flaked almonds, toasted

Crème fraîche, to serve

Serves: 8–10
Preparation: 30 minutes
Cooking: 30–40 minutes
Level: 2

COCONUT LAYER CAKE

Coconut Cake: Preheat the oven to 350°F (180°C/ gas 4). • Butter two 9-inch (23-cm) round cake pans. Line with parchment paper. Butter the paper. • Mix the flour, baking powder, and salt in a large bowl. • Beat the butter, sugar, vanilla, and coconut extract in a large bowl with an electric mixer at medium-high speed until pale and creamy. • Add the eggs, one at a time, beating until just blended after each addition. • With mixer at low speed, gradually beat in the dry ingredients, alternating with the milk. Stir in the nuts by hand. • Spoon half the batter into each of the prepared pans. • Bake for 25–30 minutes, or until a toothpick inserted into the center comes out clean. • Cool the cakes in the pans for 10 minutes. Turn out onto racks. Carefully remove the paper and let cool completely. • Filling: With mixer at medium speed, beat the cream cheese, butter, and vanilla in a large bowl until smooth. Add the confectioners' sugar and coconut. • Split each cake in half horizontally. Place one layer on a serving plate. Spread with one-third of the filling. Repeat with two more layers. Place the remaining layer on top. Spread with the topping and sprinkle with the coconut. • Refrigerate for 30 minutes before serving.

Coconut Cake

2½ cups (375 g) all-purpose (plain) flour

2½ teaspoons baking powder

½ teaspoon salt

1 cup (250 g) butter, softened

2 cups (400 g) sugar

1 teaspoon vanilla extract

1 teaspoon coconut extract

4 large eggs

1 cup (250 ml) milk

½ cup (60 g) macadamia nuts or almonds, chopped

Filling

1 package (8 oz/250 g) cream cheese, softened

2 tablespoons butter

2 teaspoons vanilla extract

2 cups (300 g) confectioners' (icing) sugar

1 cup (150 g) shredded unsweetened coconut

½ recipe Chantilly Cream (see page 360)

½ cup (75 g) shredded (desiccated) coconut

Serves: 8–10
Preparation: 1 hour
Cooking: 25–30 minutes
Level: 2

VIENNESE WALNUT TORTE

Torte: Preheat the oven to 350°F (180°C/gas 4).
• Butter and flour a 9-inch (23-cm) springform pan.
• Stir together the walnuts, flour, baking powder, and salt in a medium bowl. • Beat the butter, half the sugar, and vanilla in a large bowl with an electric mixer at medium speed until creamy.
• Add the egg yolks, one at a time, beating until just blended after each addition. • With mixer at medium speed, beat the egg whites in a large bowl until frothy. With mixer at high speed, gradually beat in the remaining sugar until stiff, glossy peaks form. • Use a large rubber spatula to fold into the batter. Fold in the dry ingredients. • Spoon the batter into the prepared pan. • Bake for 50–60 minutes, or until a toothpick inserted into the center comes out clean. • Cool the cake in the pan for 10 minutes. Loosen and remove the pan sides. Invert onto a rack. Loosen and remove the pan bottom and let cool completely. • Chocolate Glaze: Melt the chocolate in a double boiler over barely simmering water. Remove from the heat and gradually stir in the butter until glossy. If needed, stir in the cream.
• Split the cake in half horizontally. Place one layer on a serving plate. Spread with the marmalade. Top with the remaining layer. Drizzle with the glaze.

Torte

2   cups (250 g) finely ground walnuts

⅓   cup (50 g) all-purpose (plain) flour

½   teaspoon baking powder

¼   teaspoon salt

1   cup (250 g) butter

1¼ cups (250 g) sugar

5   large eggs, separated

1   teaspoon vanilla extract (essence)

Chocolate Glaze

5   oz (150 g) dark chocolate, coarsely chopped

½   cup (125 g) butter, softened

2   tablespoons heavy (double) cream (optional)

⅔   cup (150 g) orange marmalade

Serves: 8–10
Preparation: 35 minutes
Cooking: 50–60 minutes
Level: 1

ALMOND BERRY SUPREME

Preheat the oven to 350°F (180°C/gas 4). • Butter one 10-inch (26-cm) and one 7-inch (18-cm) round cake pan. Line with parchment paper. • Mix the flour, almonds, baking powder, baking soda, and salt in a large bowl. • Beat the butter and sugar in a large bowl with an electric mixer at medium speed until pale and creamy. • Add the eggs, one at a time, beating until just blended after each addition. • With mixer on low, beat in the dry ingredients, alternating with the sour cream and berry fruit. • Spoon three-quarters of the batter into the larger pan. Spoon the remaining batter into the smaller pan. • Bake the larger cake for 1 hour and 30 minutes, or until a toothpick inserted into the center comes out clean. Bake the smaller cake for 60 minutes, or until a toothpick inserted into the center comes out clean. • Cool the cakes in the pans for 5 minutes. Turn out onto racks and remove the paper. Let cool. • Spread the large cake with two-thirds of the white chocolate ganache. Center the smaller cake on top. Spread with the remaining ganache. • Melt both chocolates separately in double boilers over barely simmering water. • Cut a strip of parchment paper 2½ inches (5 cm) tall long enough to wrap around the smaller cake. Cut another strip 3½ inches (8 cm) tall long enough to wrap around the larger cake. Spread the short strip with the white chocolate. Spread the long strip with the dark chocolate. Wrap the smaller strip around the top layer of cake. Wrap the larger strip around the bottom layer. Set aside. Carefully remove the paper. • Decorate with the fruit.

3 cups (450 g) all-purpose (plain) flour

2 cups (200 g) finely ground almonds

2 teaspoons baking powder

½ teaspoon baking soda (bicarbonate of soda)

½ teaspoon salt

2 cups (500 g) butter

4 cups (400 g) sugar

12 large eggs

1¼ cups (300 ml) sour cream

1 cup (120 g) fresh raspberries

1 cup (120 g) fresh blackberries

1½ recipes White Chocolate Ganache (see page 252)

5 oz (150 g) white chocolate, coarsely chopped

10 oz (300 g) dark chocolate, coarsely chopped

2 cups (250 g) mixed fresh berries

Serves: 16–20
Preparation: 1 hour
Cooking: 90 minutes
Level: 3

WHITE CHOCOLATE MOUSSE CAKE WITH LEMON AND KIWI

372

Mousse: Melt the white chocolate in a double boiler over barely simmering water. Set aside to cool. • Beat the cream cheese and sugar in a large bowl with an electric mixer at medium speed until smooth. • Add the white chocolate. • Sprinkle the gelatin over the orange juice in a saucepan. Let stand 1 minute. Stir over low heat until the gelatin has completely dissolved. Set aside to cool for 30 minutes. • Beat the cooled orange juice into the cream cheese mixture. • With mixer at high speed, beat the cream in a medium bowl until stiff. • Use a rubber spatula to fold the cream into the cream cheese mixture. • Trim the rounded top off the cake. • Place the cake in a 9-inch (23-cm) springform pan. Pour the mousse over the cake and refrigerate for 6 hours. • Lemon Topping: Stir the lemon juice and sugar in a saucepan over low heat until the sugar has dissolved. Remove from the heat and stir in the gelatin until dissolved. Set aside to cool. • Pour the topping over and refrigerate for 6 hours, or until set. • Loosen and remove the pan sides. Decorate with the kiwi fruit.

Mousse

6 oz (180 g) white chocolate, coarsely chopped

2 (3-oz packages/180 g) cream cheese, softened

¼ cup (50 g) sugar

4 teaspoons unflavored gelatin

⅓ cup (90 ml) freshly squeezed orange juice

1½ cups (375 ml) heavy (double) cream

1 9-inch (23-cm) Butter Cake (see page 230)

Lemon Topping

½ cup (125 ml) freshly squeezed lemon juice

¼ cup (50 g) sugar

1 teaspoon unflavored gelatin

2 kiwi fruit, peeled and sliced

Serves: 8–10
Preparation: 1 hour
+ 12 hours to chill
Cooking: 25–30 minutes
Level: 2

BIRTHDAY FRUIT AND ICE CREAM CAKE

374

Leave the ice cream at room temperature for 10 minutes to soften. • Wrap two pieces of cardboard with foil and place a butter cake on each. Slice the domed tops off the cakes. Cut around the inside of each cake leaving a 1/2-inch (1-cm) shell on the sides and bottom. Scoop out the insides of the cake. • Fill the hollow centers of the cakes with the ice cream, packing it down firmly. Brush the cake with the jam and place one cake over the other, open-side down, to create a closed circle. Press together firmly and wrap in plastic wrap (cling film) or aluminum foil and freeze overnight. • Remove the foil and place the cake on a serving plate. Brush with a layer of apricot preserves. Working quickly, stick slices of kiwi all over the surface of the cake. Top with strawberries. Brush the fruit with more apricot preserves. • Serve immediately or return to the freezer.

1 quart (1 liter) favorite flavor ice cream

2 recipes Butter Cake (see page 230)

¼ cup (jam or preserves (raspberry, strawberry, or apricot are good choices), stirred until liquid

½ cup (125 ml) apricot preserves (jam), warm

12 strawberries, cut in half

3 kiwi fruit, peeled and thinly sliced

Serves: 8–10
Preparation: 1 hour
  + 12 hours to freeze
Cooking: 25–30 minutes
Level: 1

CAPPUCCINO SWEETHEART

Truffles: Melt the chocolate with the cream in a double boiler over barely simmering water. Set aside to cool. • Dissolve the coffee in the liqueur and stir into the chocolate mixture. Refrigerate for 1 hour, or until thick. • Roll teaspoonfuls of the chocolate mixture into round truffles and place on a dish lined with parchment paper. This should yield about 12 truffles. Cover and refrigerate until firm. • Coffee Buttercream: Melt the white chocolate with the cream in a double boiler over barely simmering water. Set aside to cool. • Beat the butter in a large bowl with an electric mixer at high speed until creamy. Gradually beat in the confectioners' sugar. • Beat in the chocolate mixture and dissolved coffee. • Split the cake horizontally. Place one layer on a serving plate and spread with a quarter of the buttercream. Place the remaining layer on top. Spread all over with the remaining buttercream. • Press the hazelnuts into the sides of the cake and arrange the truffles on top. Dust with the cocoa.

■■■*This cake makes a wonderful Valentine's Day gift.*

Truffles

4 oz (125 g) dark chocolate, chopped

3 tablespoons heavy (double) cream

2 teaspoons freeze-dried coffee granules

½ tablespoon coffee liqueur

Coffee Buttercream

10 oz (300 g) white chocolate, chopped

⅔ cup (150 ml) heavy (double) cream

1¾ cups (430 g) butter

1 cup (150 g) confectioners' (icing) sugar

1 tablespoon freeze-dried coffee granules dissolved in 1 tablespoon boiling water, cooled

1 cup (100 g) hazelnuts, toasted and chopped

¼ cup (30 g) unsweetened cocoa powder, to dust

1 Butter Cake (see page 230), baked in a 9-inch (23-cm) heart-shaped cake pan

Serves: 8–10
Preparation: 1 hour
  + 1 hour to chill
Cooking: 25–30 minutes
Level: 3

RED VELVET CAKE

Cake: Preheat the oven to 350°F (180°C/gas 4).
• Butter two 9-inch round cake pans. Line with parchment paper. Butter the paper. • Combine the flour, cocoa, baking powder, baking soda, and salt in a large bowl. • Beat the butter, sugar, and vanilla in a large bowl with an electric mixer at medium-high speed until pale and creamy. • Add the eggs, one at a time, beating until just blended after each addition. • With mixer at low speed, gradually beat in the dry ingredients, alternating with the buttermilk, food coloring, and vinegar. • Spoon half the batter into each of the prepared pans. • Bake for 25–30 minutes, or until a toothpick inserted into the center comes out clean. • Cool the cakes in the pans for 10 minutes. Turn out onto racks. Carefully remove the paper and let cool completely. • Cream Cheese Frosting: With mixer at medium speed, beat the cream cheese, butter, and vanilla in a large bowl until creamy. Gradually beat in the confectioners' sugar until fluffy. • Place one cake on a serving plate. Spread with one-third of the frosting. Place the other cake on top. Spread with the remaining frosting.

Cake

2 cups (300 g) all-purpose (plain) flour

½ cup (75 g) unsweetened cocoa powder

1 teaspoon baking powder

½ teaspoon baking soda (bicarbonate of soda)

¼ teaspoon salt

½ cup (125 g) butter, softened

1½ cups (300 g) sugar

1 teaspoon vanilla extract (essence)

3 large eggs

1 cup (250 ml) milk

2 tablespoons red food coloring

1 tablespoon white vinegar

Cream Cheese Frosting

1 package (8 oz/250 g) cream cheese, softened

½ cup (125 g) butter, softened

1 teaspoon vanilla extract

3 cups (450 g) con-fectioners' (icing) sugar

Serves: 8–10
Preparation: 35 minutes
Cooking: 25–35 minutes
Level: 1

PINEAPPLE MERINGUE CAKE

Cake: Preheat the oven to 350°F (180°C/gas 4).
• Butter and flour two 8-inch (20-cm) springform pans. • Combine the flour, baking powder, and salt in a medium bowl. • Beat the butter, sugar, and vanilla in a large bowl with an electric mixer at medium speed until creamy. • Add the egg yolks, one at a time, beating until just blended after each addition. • With mixer at low speed, gradually beat in the dry ingredients, alternating with the milk.
• Spoon the batter into the prepared pans. •
Topping: With mixer at medium speed, beat the egg whites, vanilla, and rum extract in a large bowl until soft peaks form. With mixer at high speed, gradually add the sugar, beating until stiff, glossy peaks form. Stir in the macadamia nuts. • Drop spoonfuls of the meringue over the unbaked batter in the pans, spreading it out. • Bake for 25–30 minutes, or until a toothpick inserted into the center comes out clean. • Cool the cakes in the pans for 10 minutes. Loosen and remove the pan sides. Transfer to racks, meringue-side up, and let cool completely. • Pineapple Cream Filling: With mixer at high speed, beat the cream, confectioners' sugar, and vanilla in a large bowl until stiff. Fold in the pineapple. • Place one cake, meringue-side up, on a serving plate. Spread with half the filling and top with the remaining cake. Spread with the remaining filling. • Refrigerate for 1 hour before serving.

1⅓ cups (200 g) all-purpose (plain) flour

1½ teaspoons baking powder

¼ teaspoon salt

⅓ cup (90 g) butter, softened

¾ cup (150 g) sugar

1 teaspoon vanilla extract

3 large egg yolks

½ cup (125 ml) milk

Topping

3 large egg whites

1 teaspoon vanilla extract

½ teaspoon rum extract

½ cup (100 g) sugar

½ cup (50 g) macadamia nuts, chopped

Pineapple Cream Filling

1 cup (250 ml) heavy (double) cream, chilled

2 tablespoons con-fectioners' (icing) sugar

1 teaspoon vanilla extract

1 (8 oz/250 g) can crushed pineapple, drained

Serves: 6–8
Preparation: 40 minutes
   + 1 hour to chill
Cooking: 25–30 minutes
Level: 2

LEMON MERINGUE SPONGE

Meringue: Preheat the oven to 275°F (120°C/gas 1).
• Line two large baking sheets with parchment paper and mark out three 9-inch (23 cm) circles.
• Beat the egg whites in a large bowl with an electric mixer at medium speed until frothy.
• With mixer at high speed, gradually add the superfine sugar, beating until stiff, glossy peaks form. • Spread one-third of the meringue onto each parchment round. • Bake for 50–60 minutes, or until crisp. Turn the oven off and leave the meringues in the oven with door ajar until cool. Remove from the oven and carefully remove the paper. • Lemon Syrup: Stir the sugar, lemon juice, and water in a saucepan over medium heat until the sugar has dissolved. Set aside to cool. • With mixer at high speed, beat the cream, confectioners' sugar, and vanilla in a medium bowl until stiff. • Place one cake on a serving plate. Drizzle with the syrup and spread with lemon curd. Top with a meringue round, trimming the edges if needed. Spread the meringue with lemon curd and top with another cake layer. Repeat, using all the lemon curd and lemon syrup. Place the remaining layer on top.
• Spread the top of the cake with the cream. Sprinkle with the almonds.

Meringue

4 large egg whites

1 cup (200 g) superfine (caster) sugar

2 9-inch Génoises (see page 336), baked in four 9-inch (23-cm) cake pans

Lemon Syrup

½ cup (100 g) sugar

¼ cup (60 ml) freshly squeezed lemon juice

2 tablespoons water

½ cup (125 ml) heavy (double) cream

2 tablespoons confectioners' (icing) sugar

½ teaspoon vanilla extract (essence)

3 cups (450 ml) Lemon Curd

½ cup (50 g) flaked (slivered) almonds

Serves: 12–16
Preparation: 1 hour
 + 1 hour to cool
Cooking: 1 hour
Level: 2

PORTUGUESE MERINGUE CAKE

Cake: Preheat the oven to 325°F (160°C/gas 3).
• Butter a 9-inch (23-cm) springform pan. Line with parchment paper. Butter the paper. • Mix the flour and salt in a medium bowl. • Beat the eggs, egg yolks, and sugar in a large bowl with an electric mixer at high speed until pale and very thick.
• Gradually fold the dry ingredients into the batter.
• Spoon the batter into the prepared pan. • Bake for 40–50 minutes, or until a toothpick inserted into the center comes out clean. • Cool the cake in the pan for 5 minutes. Loosen and remove the pan sides. Invert onto a rack. Loosen and remove the pan bottom. Carefully remove the paper and let cool completely. • Syrup: Bring the sugar and water to a boil in a saucepan over medium heat. Simmer for 5 minutes, stirring constantly. Remove from the heat and stir in the walnuts and caramel flavoring.
• Preheat the oven to 350°F (180°C/gas 4). • Slice the cake in three horizontally. Place one layer in a 10-inch (24-cm) springform pan. • Spoon one-third of the syrup over the cake. Repeat with the remaining 2 layers and the syrup. • Meringue: Beat the egg whites, sugar, water, and cream of tartar with an electric mixer at high speed until stiff, glossy peaks form. • Spread the meringue over the cake. • Bake for 8–10 minutes, or until lightly browned. • Cool the cake completely in the pan on a rack.

Cake

- 1¼ cups (180 g) all-purpose (plain) flour
- ¼ teaspoon salt
- 3 large eggs + 5 large egg yolks
- ¾ cup (150 g) sugar

Syrup

- 1½ cups (300 g) sugar
- 1 cup (250 ml) water
- 1 cup (100 g) walnuts, coarsely chopped
- 3 tablespoons caramel flavoring

Meringue

- 5 large egg whites
- ¼ cup (50 g) sugar
- 5 teaspoons water
- ¼ teaspoon cream of tartar

Serves: 8–10
Preparation: 35 minutes
Cooking: 50–60 minutes
Level: 2

MERINGUE WITH CHOCOLATE FILLING

<u>Meringue</u>: Preheat the oven to 275°F (120°C/gas 1) • Line a baking sheet with parchment paper and mark two 9-inch (23-cm) circles on the paper. • Beat the egg whites in a large bowl with an electric mixer at medium speed until frothy. • With mixer at high speed, gradually beat in the confectioners' sugar until stiff, glossy peaks form. • Spoon the mixture into a pastry bag with a plain 1/2-inch (1-cm) nozzle and pipe into two spiral disks, starting at the center and filling each 9-inch (23-cm) circle. • Bake for 60–70 minutes, or until crisp and dry. Turn off the oven and leave the door ajar until the meringues are completely cool, about 1 hour. • <u>Chocolate Pastry Cream</u>: Beat the egg yolks and sugar until pale and thick. • Bring the milk to a boil with the salt and vanilla, then stir it into the egg and sugar. • Cook over low heat, stirring constantly with a wooden spoon, until the mixture lightly coats a metal spoon. • Melt the chocolate in a double boiler over barely simmering water. • Stir the chocolate into the hot pastry cream. • Press parchment paper directly on the surface to prevent a skin from forming. Refrigerate for 30 minutes, or until chilled. <u>Cream Topping</u>: With mixer at high speed, beat the cream, sugar, and vanilla in a small bowl until stiff. • Place a layer of meringue on a serving plate. Spread with the chocolate pastry cream. Top with the remaining meringue layer. • Spread with the cream and decorate with the strawberries.

Meringue

5 large egg whites

1½ cups (225 g) confectioners' (icing) sugar

Chocolate Pastry Cream

5 large egg yolks

2/3 cup (125 g) sugar

1/3 cup (50 g) cornstarch (cornflour)

2 cups (500 ml) milk

Pinch of salt

1 teaspoon vanilla extract (essence)

8 oz (250 g) dark chocolate, chopped

Cream Topping

3/4 cup (180 ml) heavy (double) cream

1 tablespoon sugar

½ teaspoon vanilla extract (essence)

10 ripe strawberries, halved

Serves: 8–10
Preparation: 1 hour
    + 1 hour to cool
Cooking: 60–70 minutes
Level: 2

BANANA VACHERIN

Preheat the oven to 275°F (120°C/gas 1). • Line a baking sheet with parchment paper and mark two 9-inch (23-cm) circles on the paper. • Beat the egg whites in a large bowl with an electric mixer at medium speed until frothy. • With mixer at high speed, gradually add the brown sugar, beating until stiff, glossy peaks form. • Add the vanilla. • Spoon the mixture into a pastry bag fitted with a 1/2-inch (1-cm) nozzle and pipe the mixture into two spiral disks, starting at the center of the drawn circles and filling each circle. • Bake for 50–60 minutes, or until crisp. Turn off the oven and leave the door ajar until the meringues are completely cool, about 1 hour. • Carefully remove the paper. • About 1 hour before serving, beat the cream and confectioners' sugar in a large bowl with mixer at high speed until stiff. • Place two-thirds of the cream in a separate bowl and fold in the bananas (reserve a few slices to decorate). • Place a meringue layer on a serving plate. Spread with half the cream. Top with the remaining layer and spread with the remaining cream. • Decorate with the banana slices.

5   large egg whites

1½ cups (300 g) firmly packed light brown sugar

1   teaspoon vanilla extract (essence)

1½ cups (375 ml) heavy (double) cream

2   tablespoons confectioners' (icing) sugar

2   medium ripe bananas, peeled and very thinly sliced

Serves: 6–8
Preparation: 30 minutes + 1 hour to cool
Cooking: 50–60 minutes
Level: 1

■■■Brighten this sweet layer cake up with a fruit coulis. Tangy fruits, such as kiwi fruit, raspberries, or black currants will liven up the flavor as well.

CHOCOLATE CREAM DACQUOISE

Dacquoise: Preheat the oven to 300°F (150°C/gas 2).
• Line a large baking sheet with parchment paper and mark out three 9-inch (23 cm) circles. • Beat the egg whites and salt in a large bowl with an electric mixer at medium speed until frothy. With mixer at high speed, gradually add the sugar, beating until stiff, glossy peaks form. • Use a large rubber spatula to fold in the almonds and cornstarch. • Spoon the meringue into a pastry bag fitted with a ¹/₂-inch (1-cm) plain tip. Pipe the meringue in a spiral to fill the rounds. • Bake for 80–90 minutes, or until crisp.
• Cool for 10 minutes. Transfer to racks. Remove the paper and let cool completely. • Chocolate Cream: Melt the chocolate in a double boiler over barely simmering water. Let cool. • Beat the butter in a bowl with an electric mixer at medium speed until creamy.
• With mixer at high speed, beat the egg yolks in a large bowl until pale and thick. • Stir the sugar and water in a saucepan over medium heat until the sugar has dissolved and the syrup is boiling. Cook, without stirring, until it reaches 238°F (112°C), or the soft-ball stage. • Remove from the heat and slowly beat the syrup into the egg yolks. Gradually beat in the butter, followed by the chocolate and vanilla. Beat until cool.
• Place one dacquoise on a serving plate and spread with one-third of the chocolate cream. Top with another dacquoise and spread with one-third of the chocolate cream. Place the remaining dacquoise on top. Spread with the remaining chocolate cream.
• Decorate with the hazelnuts.

Dacquoise

6 large egg whites
¹/₈ teaspoon salt
1¹/₂ cups (300 g) sugar
1¹/₂ cups (300 g) almonds, finely ground
1 tablespoon cornstarch (cornflour)

Chocolate Cream

8 oz (250 g) dark chocolate, chopped
1¹/₂ cups (375 g) butter, softened
6 large egg yolks
1 cup (200 g) sugar
¹/₂ cup (125 ml) water
2 teaspoons vanilla extract (essence)
Toasted hazelnuts, to decorate

Serves: 8–10
Preparation: 45 minutes
Cooking: 80–90 minutes
Level: 2

COFFEE CREAM DACQUOISE

Dacquoise: Preheat the oven to 300°F (150°C/gas 2).
• Line a large baking sheet with parchment paper and
mark out two 9-inch (23-cm) circles. • Beat the egg
whites and salt in a large bowl with an electric mixer
at medium speed until frothy. With mixer at high
speed, gradually add the sugar, beating until stiff,
glossy peaks form. • Use a large rubber spatula to
fold in the almonds and cornstarch. • Spoon the
meringue into a pastry bag fitted with a ¹/₂-inch
(1-cm) plain tip. Pipe the meringue in a spiral to fill
the rounds. • Bake for 80–90 minutes, or until crisp.
• Cool the meringues for 10 minutes. Transfer onto
racks. Carefully remove the paper and let cool
completely. • Coffee Buttercream: Stir the coffee and
sugar in a saucepan over medium heat until the sugar
has dissolved. • Cook, without stirring, until the
mixture reaches 238°F (112°C), or the soft-ball stage.
• Beat the egg yolks in a double boiler with an electric
mixer at high speed until pale. • Gradually beat the
syrup into the beaten yolks. • Place over barely
simmering water, stirring constantly with a wooden
spoon, until the mixture lightly coats a metal spoon.
• Place the pan in a bowl of ice water and stir until
cooled. • Beat the butter in a large bowl until creamy.
Beat into the egg mixture. • Place one round of
dacquoise on a serving plate. Spread with the
buttercream. Cover with the other round. • Dust with
the confectioners' sugar and stick the almonds all
around the sides. • Refrigerate for 30 minutes
before serving.

Dacquoise

4 large egg whites
¹/₈ teaspoon salt
1 cup (200 g) sugar
1 cup (200 g) finely ground hazelnuts
1 tablespoon cornstarch (cornflour)

¹/₃ cup (50 g) confectioners' (icing) sugar
¹/₄ cup (30 g) flaked toasted almonds

Coffee Buttercream

¹/₂ cup (125 ml) very strong lukewarm coffee
³/₄ cup (150 g) sugar
3 large egg yolks
1 cup (250 g) butter, softened

Serves: 8–10
Preparation: 1 hour + 30 minutes to chill
Cooking: 80–90 minutes
Level: 2

RED FRUIT DACQUOISE

Hazelnut Meringue Disks: Preheat the oven to 300°F (150°C/gas 2). • Line a large baking sheet with parchment paper and mark out two 9-inch (23-cm) circles. • Beat the egg whites and salt in a large bowl with an electric mixer at medium speed until frothy. With mixer at high speed, gradually add the sugar, beating until stiff, glossy peaks form. • Use a large rubber spatula to fold in the hazelnuts and cornstarch. • Spoon the meringue into a pastry bag fitted with a 1/2-inch (1-cm) plain tip. Pipe the meringue in a spiral to fill the rounds. • Bake for 80–90 minutes, or until crisp. • Cool the meringues for 10 minutes. Transfer onto racks. Carefully remove the paper and let cool completely. • Choux Pastry: Prepare the pastry following the instructions on page 526. • Preheat the oven to 425°F (210°C/gas 7). • Line a baking sheet with parchment paper and draw a 9-inch (23-cm) circle on the paper. • Spoon the choux pastry into a pastry bag fitted with a plain 1/2-inch (1-cm) nozzle and pipe the mixture into a spiral disk, starting at the center of the drawn circle and filling it. • Bake for 15–20 minutes, or until golden brown. Cool the pastry completely in the pan on a rack. • Red Fruit Filling: Beat the cream cheese, sugar, and lemon zest and juice in

Hazelnut Meringue Disks

- 4 large egg whites
- 1/8 teaspoon salt
- 1 cup (200 g) sugar
- 1 cup (200 g) finely ground hazelnuts
- 1 tablespoon cornstarch (cornflour)

- 1/2 recipe Choux Pastry (see page 526)

Red Fruit Filling

- 2 cups (500 g) cream cheese, softened
- 1/2 cup (100 g) sugar
  Finely grated zest and juice of 1 lemon
- 2 tablespoons unflavored gelatin
- 1/4 cup (60 ml) cold water
- 1 cup (250 ml) heavy (double) cream
- 3 cups (450 g) mixed red fruit, such as raspberries or red currants

Topping

½ cup (125 ml) heavy (double) cream

1 tablespoon sugar

½ cup (60 g) slivered almonds

Confectioners' (icing) sugar, to dust

Raspberries, to decorate

Serves: 8–10
Preparation: 90 minutes + 1 hour to chill
Cooking: 1 hour 35–50 minutes
Level: 3

a large bowl with an electric mixer at high speed.
• Sprinkle the gelatin over the water in a small saucepan. Let stand 1 minute. Simmer over low heat until the gelatin has completely dissolved. Let cool.
• With mixer at high speed, beat the cream in a large bowl until stiff peaks form. • Fold the gelatin mixture, cream, and the fruit into the cream cheese mixture. • Place one meringue disk on a serving plate. Surround with 9-inch (23-cm) springform pan sides. Spoon in half the filling and place the remaining meringue disk on top. Spoon in the remaining filling and top with the pastry circle. Refrigerate for 1 hour, or until set. • Topping: With mixer at high speed, beat the cream and sugar in a large bowl until stiff peaks form. • Remove the pan sides. Spread the sides with the cream and press in the almonds. Dust with the confectioners' sugar and decorate with the raspberries.

PINE NUT AND PRALINE MERINGUE TORTE

Meringue Disks: Preheat the oven to 275°F (140°C/gas 1). • Line two large baking sheets with parchment paper and mark each one with two 9-inch (23 cm) circles. • Beat the egg whites in a medium bowl with an electric mixer on medium speed until soft peaks form. Gradually add the sugar, beating with mixer on high speed until thick and glossy. • Fold in the pine nuts and lemon zest. • Spoon the mixture onto the prepared baking sheets and spread using a spatula or the back of a spoon. • Bake for 1 hour, or until crisp. Remove from the oven, leave to cool for 10 minutes, and then transfer to racks to cool completely, about 1 hour. • Pine Nut Praline: Line a baking sheet with parchment paper. • Cook the sugar and water in a small heavy based saucepan on medium heat until melted and a golden caramel color. Remove from the heat, add the pine nuts, and pour onto the prepared baking sheet. • Allow the praline to cool and set hard. • Pine Nut Praline Cream: Beat the cream and confectioners' sugar until soft peaks form. Add the lemon zest and vanilla extract, beating until combined. • Grind half the praline mixture using a food processor and fold into the cream. • Spread each meringue disk with a quarter of the pine nut praline cream. Place the disks one on top of the other. Coarsely chop the remaining praline and scatter over the top layer.

Meringue Disks

6 large egg whites

1¾ cups (350 g) superfine (caster) sugar

1¾ cups (315 g) pine nuts, lightly toasted

1 teaspoon finely grated lemon zest

Pine Nut Praline

1½ cups (300 g) sugar

3 tablespoons water

1 cup (180 g) pine nuts, lightly toasted

Pine Nut Praline Cream

2 cups (500 ml) heavy (double) cream

4 tablespoons confectioners' (icing) sugar

1 teaspoon finely grated lemon zest

1 teaspoon vanilla extract (essence)

Serves: 8–12
Preparation: 45 minutes + 1 hour to cool
Cooking: 1 hour
Level: 2

SPICED ORANGE MERINGUE TORTE

Meringue Disks: Preheat the oven to 275°F (140°C/gas 1). • Line two large baking sheets with parchment paper and mark each one with two 9-inch (23 cm) circles. • Beat the egg whites in a medium bowl using an electric mixer on medium-high speed until soft peaks form. Gradually add the sugar, beating with mixer on high speed until the meringue is thick and glossy. • Fold in the ground almonds, orange zest, cinnamon, nutmeg, and cloves. • Spoon the mixture onto the prepared baking sheets and spread using a spatula or the back of a spoon. • Bake for 1 hour, or until crisp. Leave to cool for 10 minutes and then transfer to racks to cool completely. • Spiced Orange Cream: Beat the cream and confectioners' sugar until thick. Add the crème fraiche, orange zest, cinnamon, and cloves, beating until combined. • Spread a quarter of the spiced orange cream onto each meringue disk. Place the disks one on top of the other. Arrange the candied orange slices decoratively around the outside edge of the top layer.

Meringue Disks

- 6 large egg whites
- 1¾ cups (350g) superfine (caster) sugar
- 2½ cups (250 g) ground almonds
- 1 tablespoon finely grated orange zest
- 2 teaspoons ground cinnamon
- 1 teaspoon ground nutmeg
- ½ teaspoon ground cloves
- 4 candied (glacé) orange slices, halved

Spiced Orange Cream

- 1½ cups (375 ml) heavy (double) cream
- 5 tablespoons confectioners' (icing) sugar
- ½ cup (125 ml) crème fraiche
- 1 tablespoon finely grated orange zest
- ½ teaspoon ground cinnamon
- ⅛ teaspoon ground cloves

Serves: 8–10
Preparation: 30 minutes
Cooking: 1 hour
Level: 2

CHOCOLATE ALMOND DACQUOISE

Prepare the chocolate sponge. • <u>Meringue Disks</u>: Preheat the oven to 300°F (150°C/gas 2). • Butter three 8-inch (20-cm) round cake pans. Line with parchment paper. • Beat the egg whites in a large bowl with an electric mixer at medium speed until frothy. With mixer at high speed, gradually beat in the sugar until stiff and glossy. • Fold in the almonds and almond extract. • Spoon into the prepared pans. • Bake for 60–70 minutes, or until pale gold and crisp. • Cool in the pans for 10 minutes. Turn out onto racks. Carefully remove the paper and let cool completely.
• <u>Rich Chocolate Frosting</u>: Bring the sugar and 1 cup (250 ml) of cream to a boil in a saucepan over medium heat. Boil for 1 minute, then remove from the heat. • Stir in the chocolate. • Return to medium heat and cook, without stirring, until the mixture reaches 238°F (112°C), or the soft-ball stage. Remove from the heat. • Add the butter and vanilla, without stirring, and place the saucepan in a larger pan of cold water for 5 minutes before stirring. • Beat with a wooden spoon until the frosting begins to lose its sheen, 5–10 minutes. Stir in 1 tablespoon cream. Do not let the frosting harden too much before adding the cream.
• Let stand for 3–4 minutes, then stir until spreadable. Add more cream, 1 teaspoon at a time, if it is too stiff.
• Split the sponge cake into three layers. Spread one with one-third of the frosting. Top with a meringue disk, followed by a cake layer. Spread with half the remaining frosting. Top the remaining meringue disk and cake. Finish with a layer of frosting.

1 **Basic Chocolate Sponge cake (see page 356)**

Meringue Disks

3 **large egg whites**

½ **cup (100 g) superfine (caster) sugar**

¾ **cup (75 g) almonds, finely ground**

2 **teaspoons almond extract (essence)**

Rich Chocolate Frosting

2 **cups (400 g) sugar**

1 **cup (250 ml) heavy (double) cream + 1–2 tablespoons as needed**

8 **oz (250 g) dark chocolate, coarsely chopped**

2 **tablespoons butter**

1 **teaspoon vanilla extract (essence)**

Serves: 8–10
Preparation: 1 hour + time to prepare the sponge
Cooking: 60–70 minutes
Level: 3

RASPBERRY AND COCONUT MERINGUE TORTE

Meringue Disks: Preheat the oven to 275°F (140°C/gas 1). • Line two large baking sheets with parchment paper and mark each one with two 9-inch (23 cm) circles. • Beat the egg whites in a medium bowl using an electric mixer on medium-high speed until soft peaks form. Gradually add the sugar, beating with mixer on high speed until the meringue is thick and glossy. • Fold in the coconut. • Spoon the mixture onto the prepared baking sheets and spread using a spatula or the back of a spoon. • Bake for 1 hour, or until crisp. Remove from the oven, leave to cool for 10 minutes, and then transfer to racks to cool completely. •
Raspberry Cream: Beat the cream and sugar together until thickened. • Fold in the raspberry liqueur, cinnamon, melted chocolate, and half the raspberries. • Place meringue disk on a serving plate and spread with a quarter of the raspberry cream. Repeat with the other meringue disks and cream. Top with the remaining raspberries and coconut shavings.

Meringue Disks

6 large egg whites

1¾ cups (350 g) superfine (caster) sugar

2 cups (250 g) shredded (desiccated) coconut, lightly toasted

Raspberry Cream

2 cups (500 ml) heavy (double) cream

4 tablespoons confectioners' (icing) sugar

1 tablespoon raspberry liqueur

½ teaspoon ground cinnamon

3 oz (90 g) white chocolate, melted

1½ cups (300 g) fresh raspberries

¼ cup (30 g) shaved coconut, lightly toasted

Serves: 8–10
Preparation: 30 minutes
Cooking: 1 hour
Level: 2

PLUM AND HAZELNUT MERINGUE TORTE

Meringue Disks: Preheat the oven to 275°F (140°C/gas 1). • Line two large baking sheets with parchment paper and mark each one with two 9-inch (23 cm) circles. • Beat the egg whites in a medium bowl with an electric mixer on medium-high speed until soft peaks form. Gradually add the sugar, beating with mixer on high speed until the meringue is thick and glossy. • Fold in the ground hazelnuts and cinnamon. • Spoon the mixture onto the prepared baking sheets and spread using a spatula or the back of a spoon. • Bake for 1 hour, or until crisp. Remove from the oven, leave to cool for 10 minutes, and then transfer to racks to cool completely. • Vanilla Cream: Beat the cream and confectioners' sugar in a large bowl until soft peaks form. Add the crème fraîche and vanilla extract, beating until combined. • Place meringue disk on a serving plate and spread with a quarter of the vanilla cream. Top with a quarter of the plum slices. Repeat with the other disks. • Serve as soon as possible after assembling, before the meringue begins to dissolve.

Meringue Disks

6 large egg whites

1¾ cups (350 g) superfine (caster) sugar

2½ cups (250 g) ground hazelnuts

1 teaspoon ground cinnamon

16 canned or stewed plums, pitted, halved, and sliced

Vanilla Cream

1¾ cups (430 ml) heavy (double) cream

4 tablespoons confectioners' (icing) sugar

¼ cup (60 ml) crème fraîche

1 teaspoon vanilla extract (essence)

Serves: 6–8
Preparation: 45 minutes
Cooking: 1 hour
Level: 2

GINGER AND LIME TORTE

Ginger and Lime Curd: Heat the sugar, ginger, and lime juice and zest in a small saucepan over medium heat, stirring until the sugar has dissolved. • Whisk the eggs yolks in a double boiler and gradually pour in the hot ginger and lime mixture. Strain through a fine mesh sieve and then return to the double boiler over simmering water. • Cook, stirring continuously, until the mixture thickens and coats the back of a wooden spoon. Do not allow it to boil. • Remove from the heat and add the butter cubes, one at a time, beating until incorporated. • Pour the ginger and lime curd into a medium bowl, cover with plastic wrap (cling film) and refrigerate for 1 hour, or until chilled and set. • Meringue Disks: Preheat the oven to 275°F (140°C/gas 1).• Line two large baking sheets with parchment paper and mark each one with two 9-inch (23 cm) circles. • Beat the egg whites in a medium bowl with an electric mixer on medium-high speed until soft peaks form. Gradually add the sugar, beating until the meringue mixture is thick and glossy. • Add the ground almonds, ginger, and lime zest, stirring with a wooden spoon to combine. • Spoon the mixture onto the prepared baking sheets and spread using a spatula or the back of a spoon. • Bake for 1 hour, or until crisp. Let cool for 10 minutes then transfer to racks to cool completely, about 1 hour. • Place meringue disk on a serving plate and spread with one-third of the ginger and lime curd. Repeat with two more disk. Cover with the remaining meringue disk and dust with confectioners' sugar.

Ginger and Lime Curd

- 1¾ cups (350 g) superfine (caster) sugar
- 2 tablespoons candied (glacé) ginger, finely chopped
- 1 cup (250 ml) freshly squeezed lime juice, strained
- 2 teaspoons finely grated lime zest
- 7 large egg yolks
- 1¼ cups (300 g) butter, cubed

  Confectioners' (icing) sugar, for dusting

Meringue Disks

- 6 large egg whites
- 1¾ cups (350 g) superfine (caster) sugar
- 2½ cups (250 g) ground almonds
- 1 tablespoon candied (glacé) ginger, finely chopped
- 1 tablespoon finely grated lime zest

Serves: 6–8
Preparation: 40 minutes + 2 hours to chill and cool
Cooking: 1 hour
Level: 2

PIES AND TARTS

PORTUGUESE CUSTARD TARTS

Butter a 12-cup muffin pan. • Cut twelve pastry rounds, fit into the prepared muffin pans and refrigerate. • <u>Filling</u>: Heat the sugar and water in a medium saucepan over medium-low heat, stirring until the sugar dissolves. • Combine the cornstarch, custard powder, and $1/4$ cup (60 ml) of milk in a medium bowl, stirring until smooth. Add the remaining milk, egg yolks, and vanilla, stirring until combined. • Pour the egg mixture into the sugar syrup and cook over low heat, stirring until thickened. • Transfer the custard into a medium bowl, cover with parchment paper, and refrigerate until cool. • Preheat the oven to 425°F (220°C/gas 7). • Spoon the custard filling into the prepared pastry bases. • Bake for 30 minutes, or until custard is set and the tops have browned slightly. • Allow the tarts to cool a little in the pans before transferring to a rack. Serve warm.

2   sheets pre-rolled puff pastry

Filling

1   cup (200 g) sugar
$1/3$ cup (90 ml) water
3   tablespoons cornstarch (cornflour)
1   tablespoon custard powder
2   cups (500 ml) milk
4   large egg yolks, lightly beaten
1   teaspoon vanilla extract (essence)

Serves: 6–12
Preparation: 30 minutes + 1 hour to chill
Cooking: 45 minutes
Level: 1

NEENISH TARTS

Pastry: Butter 18 barquette molds, small tartlet pans, or shallow patty tins. • Place the flour and salt in a food processor with the metal blade. Add the butter and process until it resembles coarse crumbs. • Combine the egg yolk and water in a small bowl and gradually add to the butter mixture, pulsing briefly until a dough forms. • Transfer to a lightly floured work surface and shape into two disks. Wrap the disks in plastic wrap (cling film) and refrigerate for 1 hour. • Roll out the pastry on a lightly floured surface to $1/8$ inch (3 mm) thick. • Cut out 18 rounds large enough to line the molds. Fit into the molds and refrigerate for 30 minutes. • Preheat the oven to 400°F (200°C/gas 6). • Prick the pastry in the pans with a fork. Bake for 10 minutes, or until lightly golden. • Filling: Blend the flour and milk in a small saucepan until smooth. Simmer over medium heat, stirring constantly, until it comes to a boil. Remove from the heat and stir in the egg yolks one at a time. • Transfer to a small bowl, cover with plastic wrap (cling film), and refrigerate until cool. • Beat the butter, sugar, and vanilla in a small bowl with an electric mixer until pale and creamy. • Gradually add the cooled egg mixture, beating until smooth. • Spoon the mixture into the pastry shells. • Frosting: Place the confectioners' sugar and milk in a small heatproof bowl and stir over a pan of barely simmering water until smooth. Transfer half the frosting to a small bowl and stir in the cocoa. • Spread the white frosting over one half of each tart. Let set then spread the other half with chocolate frosting.

Pastry

- 2⅔ cups (400 g) all-purpose (plain) flour
- ¼ teaspoon salt
- ¾ cup (180 g) butter, cubed
- 1 large egg yolk
- ¼ cup (60 ml) iced water

Filling

- 1 tablespoon all-purpose (plain) flour
- ½ cup (125 ml) milk
- 2 large egg yolks
- ¼ cup (60 g) butter
- 2 tablespoons superfine (caster) sugar
- ¼ teaspoon vanilla extract (essence)

Frosting

- 1 cup (150 g) confectioners' (icing) sugar
- 2 tablespoons milk
- 1 tablespoon unsweetened cocoa powder

Serves: 6–12
Preparation: 40 minutes + 90 minutes to chill
Cooking: 45 minutes
Level: 2

WHITE CHOCOLATE AND STRAWBERRY TARTLETS

Pastry: Combine the flour, sugar, and almonds in a medium bowl. • Cut in the butter with a pastry blender (or pulse in a food processor) until the mixture resembles fine crumbs. • Mix in the yolks, zest, and rum and draw together with your hands into a smooth dough. • Place on a sheet of plastic wrap (cling film) large enough to fully enclose it when rolled into a log. • Roll the dough into a log about 2 inches (5 cm) in diameter on the wrap. • Seal and chill in the refrigerator for at least 2 hours. • Preheat the oven to 375°F (190°C/gas 5). Set out eight (4-inch/10-cm) tartlet pans with removable bottoms. • Unwrap the log and slice $\frac{1}{8}$-inch (3-mm) thick disks. • Press the disks into the bottom and sides of the pans, overlapping to cover the pans completely. Make the edges slightly thicker than the base. • Prick with a fork and bake for 15 minutes, or until golden. Let cool on a rack. • Cream Filling: Stir the chocolate, water, and $\frac{1}{2}$ cup (125 ml) of cream in a small saucepan over low heat until the chocolate has melted. • Remove from the heat and stir in the liqueur. Let cool. • Beat the remaining cream in a bowl with an electric mixer until soft peaks form. • Fold spoonfuls of cream into the chocolate mixture. • Chill in the refrigerator for 20 minutes. • Strawberry Glaze: Warm the preserves with the liqueur in a small saucepan over low heat. • Brush the pastry crusts with half this mixture. • Spread with the filling and top with strawberries. • Re-heat the remaining preserves and brush over the strawberries. Chill in the refrigerator for 2–4 hours, until the cream has set.

Pastry

- $1\frac{2}{3}$ cups (250 g) all-purpose (plain) flour
- $\frac{1}{3}$ cup (75 g) superfine (caster) sugar
- $\frac{1}{2}$ cup (50 g) ground almonds
- $\frac{3}{4}$ cup (180 g) butter
- 2 large egg yolks, beaten
- 1 teaspoon orange zest, finely grated
- 1 teaspoon rum

Cream Filling

- 8 oz (250 g) white chocolate, chopped
- 2 tablespoons water
- $1\frac{1}{2}$ cups (375 ml) heavy (double) cream
- 3 tablespoons kirsch or Grand Marnier

Strawberry Glaze

- $\frac{1}{2}$ cup (120 g) strawberry preserves (jam)
- 1 tablespoon kirsch or Grand Marnier
- 2 cups (300 g) strawberries, sliced

Serves: 8
Preparation: 1 hour
+ 4–6 hours to chill
Cooking: 30 minutes
Level: 2

RASPBERRY TARTLETS

Pastry: Place the flour and salt in a medium bowl. Cut in the butter with a pastry blender until the mixture resembles fine crumbs. Add the zest and bind together with the egg and enough lemon juice to form a smooth dough. • Press the dough into a disk, wrap in plastic wrap (cling film), and chill in the refrigerator for at least 30 minutes. • Butter 12 small fluted tartlet pans. • Roll out the pastry on a lightly floured surface to 1/4 inch (5 mm) thick. • Cut out 12 disks. Line the pans with the pastry and chill for 30 minutes. • Preheat the oven to 400°F (200°C/gas 6). • Prick the pastry with a fork and line with baking parchment. Fill with baking beans and bake for 10 minutes. Remove the lining and beans, and return the pastry to the oven for a 5–10 minutes, until golden brown. Let cool. • Filling: Chop the raspberries in a food processor until puréed. • Transfer to a large bowl and stir in the confectioners' sugar, liqueur, lemon zest and juice, ricotta, and yogurt. • Sprinkle the gelatin over the water in a saucepan. Let stand 1 minute. Stir over low heat until the gelatin has completely dissolved. • Stir the gelatin into the raspberry mixture and refrigerate until thickened. • Beat the cream in a medium bowl with an electric mixer until stiff. Fold the cream into the raspberry mixture. • Spoon the raspberry mixture into the tartlets cases. • Decorate with the extra raspberries. • Refrigerate for 1 hour before serving.

Pastry

- 2 cups (300 g) all-purpose (plain) flour
- 1/4 teaspoon salt
- 2/3 cup (150 g) butter
- 1 large egg, beaten

  Finely grated zest and juice of 1 lemon

Filling

- 2 cups (300 g) raspberries + 12 extra, to decorate
- 2/3 cup (100 g) confectioners' (icing) sugar
- 1/2 cup (125 ml) raspberry liqueur

  Finely grated zest and juice of 1 lemon
- 2/3 cup (150 g) fresh ricotta cheese, drained
- 1 cup (250 ml) plain yogurt
- 1 1/2 tablespoons unflavored gelatin
- 1/4 cup (60 ml) cold water
- 1 1/2 cups (325 ml) heavy (double) cream

Serves: 6
Preparation: 45 minutes + 2 hours to chill
Cooking: 15–20 minutes
Level: 2

PINEAPPLE AND STRAWBERRY TARTLETS

Pastry: Place the flour and salt in a medium bowl. Cut in the butter with a pastry blender until the mixture resembles fine crumbs. Add the zest and bind together with the egg and enough lemon juice to form a smooth dough. • Press the dough into a disk, wrap in plastic wrap (cling film), and chill in the refrigerator for at least 30 minutes. • Butter 12 small fluted tartlet pans. • Roll out the pastry on a lightly floured surface to ¼ inch (5 mm) thick. • Cut out 12 disks. Line the pans with the pastry and chill for 30 minutes. • Preheat the oven to 400°F (200°C/gas 6). • Prick the pastry with a fork and line with baking parchment. Fill with baking beans and bake for 10 minutes. Remove the lining and beans and return the pastry to the oven for a 5–10 minutes, or until golden brown. Let cool. Vanilla Custard: Combine the milk and cream in a heavy saucepan. Bring the mixture to simmering point over low heat. • Beat the egg yolks, sugar, and vanilla in a large bowl with an electric mixer on high speed. Pour in one-third of the cream mixture. Gradually beat in the remaining cream mixture. • Rinse out and dry the pan, and return the mixture to it. Simmer over low heat, stirring constantly, until the custard thickens and just reaches simmering point. Remove from the heat and strain through a fine-mesh sieve into a chilled bowl. Let cool, stirring occasionally. • Topping: Spread each tartlet with apricot preserves. • Fill each one with custard and top with a pineapple chunk and a piece of strawberry. • Dust with the confectioners' sugar.

Pastry

- 2 cups (300 g) all-purpose (plain) flour
- ¼ teaspoon salt
- ⅔ cup (150 g) unsalted butter
- 1 large egg, beaten

  Finely grated zest and juice of 1 lemon

Vanilla Custard

- 1 cup (250 ml) milk
- 1 cup (250 ml) heavy (double) cream
- 1 teaspoon vanilla extract (essence)
- 5 large egg yolks
- 2 tablespoons superfine (caster) sugar

Topping

- ½ cup (150 g) apricot preserves (jam)
- 24 canned pineapple chunks, drained
- 3 fresh strawberries, sliced
- ⅓ cup (50 g) confectioners' (icing) sugar, to dust

Serves: 6
Preparation: 45 minutes + 1 hour to chill
Cooking: 35–40 minutes
Level: 2

LEMON CURD TARTLETS

Pastry: Mix the flour and salt in a medium bowl. • Beat the butter and sugar in a large bowl with an electric mixer at high speed until creamy. • Add the egg yolk, lemon zest, and lemon extract, beating until just blended. • Mix in the dry ingredients. • Cover with plastic wrap (cling film) and refrigerate for 30 minutes. • Preheat the oven to 350°F (180°C/gas 4). • Set out two 12-cup mini muffin pans. • Form the dough into balls the size of walnuts and press into the cups. • Prick all over with a fork. • Bake for 12–15 minutes, or until just golden. • Transfer to racks to cool. • Lemon Curd: Stir the sugar, lemon juice, and zest in a small saucepan over medium heat until the sugar dissolves. • Beat the eggs yolks in a heatproof bowl and gradually add the hot lemon mixture. Strain the mixture through a fine-mesh sieve. • Return to the heatproof bowl and place over a saucepan of simmering water. Cook, stirring continuously, until the mixture coats the back of a wooden spoon. Do not allow the mixture to boil. • Remove from the heat and add the butter cubes, one at a time, stirring until fully combined. • Cover the mixture with parchment paper and refrigerate for 1 hour, or until cooled. • Spoon the lemon curd into the tartlet cases just before serving.

Pastry

- 2 cups (300 g) all-purpose (plain) flour
- ¼ teaspoon salt
- ½ cup (125 g) butter, softened
- ½ cup (100 g) sugar
- 1 large egg yolk
  Finely grated zest of 1 lemon
- ½ teaspoon lemon extract (essence)

Lemon Curd

- ⅓ cup (70 g) superfine (caster) sugar
- ¼ cup (60 ml) freshly squeezed lemon juice
- 2 teaspoons finely grated lemon zest
- 3 large egg yolks
- ¼ cup (60 g) unsalted butter, cubed

Serves: 8–12
Preparation: 30 minutes + 90 minutes to chill
Cooking: 30 minutes
Level: 1

PECAN TARTLETS

Pastry: Preheat the oven to 350°F (180°C/gas 4).
• Butter a 12-cup mini-muffin pan. • Place the flour, salt, and baking powder in a medium bowl. Cut in the butter and cream cheese until the mixture resembles fine crumbs. Stir in enough water to form a firm dough. • Wrap in plastic wrap (cling film) and refrigerate for 30 minutes. • Roll out the dough on a lightly floured surface to $1/8$ inch (3 mm) thick. • Use a 2-inch (5-cm) fluted cookie cutter to cut out 12 dough rounds. Press the dough rounds into the prepared cups. • Filling: With mixer at high speed, beat the eggs in a large bowl until frothy. • Beat in the brown sugar, butter, vanilla, and salt. • Stir in the pecans. • Spoon the filling into the cups. • Bake for 15–20 minutes, or until a toothpick inserted into the center comes out clean. • Transfer to racks and let cool completely.

Pastry

1 cup (150 g) all-purpose (plain) flour

$1/8$ teaspoon salt

$1/8$ teaspoon baking powder

3 oz (90 g) cold cream cheese

$1/2$ cup (125 g) cold butter

1 tablespoon ice water

Filling

2 large eggs

$1/2$ cup (100 g) firmly packed dark brown sugar

2 tablespoons butter, melted

$1/2$ teaspoon vanilla extract (essence)

$1/8$ teaspoon salt

1 cup (100 g) coarsely chopped pecans

Serves: 6
Preparation: 30 minutes
+ 30 minutes to chill
Cooking: 15–20 minutes
Level: 1

MAIDS OF HONOR

Lightly dust the work surface with confectioners' sugar. • Dampen two 12-cup muffin pans with water using a brush. • Roll out the pastry to ⅛ inch (3 mm) thick (or just unroll if using ready rolled pastry). • Cut out 18–20 pastry rounds with a 3-inch (8-cm) plain cutter. • Line the pans with the pastry rounds. Chill in the refrigerator until the filling is ready. • Preheat the oven to 400°F (200°C/gas 6). • Filling: Combine the curd cheese, sugar, lemon zest and juice, brandy (if using), and almonds in a bowl. • Beat the egg and yolk in a separate bowl and stir into the mixture. • Grate in a little fresh nutmeg. Mix until well blended. • Divide the filling among the prepared pastry cases, about a tablespoon for each one. • Bake for 20–25 minutes, or until the pastries have puffed up and are golden brown. • Transfer to a rack to cool a little. • Serve while still slightly warm.

■ ■ ■ *Legend has it that these little curd tartlets come from the 16th-century kitchens at Hampton Court Palace, near London, where the recipe was locked away in an iron chest. King Henry VIII loved the sweet pastries and named them "maids of honor" after the ladies in waiting who served them to him. It is said that the maid who invented the recipe was not allowed to leave the Palace and had to bake the pastries for the king alone. The tartlets were traditionally made with mashed potatoes and renneted milk.*

Confectioners' (icing) sugar, to dust

8 oz (250 g) frozen puff pastry, thawed

Filling

8 oz (250 g) curd cheese or ricotta, drained

3 tablespoons superfine (caster) sugar

Finely grated zest of 1 lemon

2 tablespoons freshly squeezed lemon juice

1 teaspoon brandy, optional

½ cup (50 g) ground almonds

1 large egg

1 large egg yolk

Pinch of freshly grated nutmeg

Serves: 10–15
Preparation: 30 minutes + 30 minutes to chill
Cooking: 15–20 minutes
Level: 1

MINI MINCE PIES

<u>Pastry</u>: Place the flour in a medium bowl and cut in the butter with a pastry blender until it resembles coarse bread crumbs. • Stir in the sugar and almonds. • Add the extract to 3 tablespoons of milk, and pour onto the dry ingredients. Mix to a dough, adding a little more milk if needed. (Alternatively, pulse the ingredients in a food processor until the mixture comes together.) • Shape the dough into a disk and wrap in plastic wrap (cling film) • Chill in the refrigerator for at least 30 minutes. • Preheat the oven to 400°F (200°C/gas 6). • Place the hazelnuts on a baking sheet and roast for 5–6 minutes, until just beginning to brown. Leave to cool on a plate. • Lightly butter three 12-cup mini-muffin pans. (If you only have 1 or 2 pans, make the pies in batches. Chill and re-roll the pastry between batches.) • Place the pastry on a floured work surface. Cut in half or divide into thirds. • Place a large sheet of parchment paper on top and roll to $1/8$ inch (3 mm) thick. • Cut out 36 circles with a $2^1/2$-inch (6-cm) fluted cookie cutter. • Line the pans with the rounds. Fill each case one with a teaspoon of mince-meat. • Bake the pies for 10–12 minutes, or until the pastry is golden and crisp. • Cool in the pans for 5 minutes before transferring to racks. • <u>Topping</u>: Mix the sugar with enough lemon juice to make a smooth paste. Spoon over the pies and top with a hazelnut.

■ ■ ■ *Mince pies are a Christmas speciality in Britain. The mincemeat filling can be bought in jars or you can make your own. Nowadays there's no meat in it.*

Pastry

$1^1/3$ cups (200 g) all-purpose (plain) flour

$1/2$ cup (125 g) unsalted butter, slightly chilled and diced

$1/4$ cup (50 g) superfine (caster) sugar

$1/4$ cup (30 g) ground almonds

$1/4$ teaspoon almond extract (essence)

5 tablespoons (75 ml) milk

Filling

14 -oz (400 g) jar of mincemeat or 1 recipe homemade mincemeat (see facing page)

Topping

$3/4$ cup (100 g) hazelnuts

8 tablespoons confectioners' (icing) sugar

2 tablespoons freshly squeezed lemon juice

Serves: 12
Preparation: 45 minutes + 30 minutes to chill + 24–48 hours for homemade mincemeat
Cooking: 15–20 minutes
Level: 2

Homemade Mincemeat

- ½ cup (100 g) raisins
- ½ cup (100 g) golden raisins (sultanas)
- ½ cup (100 g) currants
- ½ cup (50 g) candied (glacé) peel, finely chopped
- ⅓ cup (30 g) blanched almonds, finely chopped
- ⅓ cup (30 g) hazelnuts, finely chopped
- ½ cup (100 g) firmly-packed dark brown sugar
- 1½ oz (45 g) shredded vegetable suet or apple substitute (see note right)
- ½ cooking apple, peeled, cored, and grated
- Finely chopped rind of ½ lemon
- Freshly squeezed juice of ½ lemon
- Finely chopped rind of ½ orange
- Freshly squeezed juice of ½ orange
- ¼ teaspoon nutmeg
- ¼ teaspoon ground cinnamon
- ½ teaspoon pumpkin pie spice (all-spice)
- 3 tablespoons brandy, rum, or whisky

Homemade Mincemeat: Mix all the ingredients in a large bowl. Cover with aluminum foil and refrigerate for 24–48 hours. Stir the mincemeat again before filling the pies.

■ ■ ■ *This mixture of fruit and spices is quick and easy to make. No cooking is involved and unlike bought mincemeat you can add the spices and flavorings you like and replace any ingredients with something more to your taste or requirements.*
Vegetable suet can be replaced with stewed apple. Peel, core, and slice 2 apples and cook with 1 tablespoon each of water, sherry, butter, and granulated sugar over medium heat for 10 minutes, until pulpy.

CHRISTMAS MINCE PIE

Mincemeat Filling: Peel and core the apples and cut in small cubes. Place the apples in a large bowl. Add the all the other filling ingredients and stir using a wooden spoon until combined. Cover the bowl with plastic wrap (cling film) and refrigerate for 48 hours, stirring occasionally, to allow to the flavors to infuse. • Pastry: Pulse the flour, salt, and butter in a food processor until the mixture resembles fine crumbs. Add the confectioners' sugar and pulse again. • Combine the egg yolk and water in a small bowl and gradually add to the flour mixture until it combines to form a dough. • Transfer to a lightly floured work surface and shape into two disks. Wrap in plastic wrap (cling film) and refrigerate for 1 hour. • Roll out the pastry on a lightly floured work surface to $1/8$ inch (3 mm) thick. • Line a deep 10-inch (26-cm) pie pan with one of the disks, pressing it firmly around the edges of the pan. Place the other disk on a plate and refrigerate both for 30 minutes. • Preheat the oven to 400°F (200°C/gas 6). • Remove the pie base from the refrigerator and spoon in the mincemeat filling. Cover with the rolled lid and pinch the edges together to seal. • Bake for 25–30 minutes, or until the pastry is golden. • Remove from the oven and let cool completely. Dust with confectioners' sugar just before serving.

Mincemeat Filling

1   lb (500 g) apples

2½ cups (450 g) raisins

2½ cups (450 g) currants

1⅓ cups (240 g) golden raisins (sultanas)

1   cup (100 g) candied peel

1¼ cups (190 g) blanched almonds, chopped

2   cups (400 g) sugar

¼   cup (60 ml) brandy

     Finely grated zest and juice of 2 lemons

2   teaspoons finely grated orange zest

½   teaspoon cinnamon

½   teaspoon ground nutmeg

¼   teaspoon ground cloves Confectioners' (icing) sugar, to dust

Pastry

2⅔ cups (400 g) all-purpose (plain) flour

½   teaspoon salt

¾   cup (180 g) butter, cubed

2   tablespoons confec-tioners' (icing) sugar

1   large egg yolk

¼   cup (60 ml) iced water

Serves: 10–12
Preparation: 45 minutes
   + 49 hours to chill
Cooking: 25–30 minutes
Level: 2

MERRY BERRY PIES

434

Pastry: Mix the flour and sugar in a large bowl.
• Cut in the butter with a pastry blender until the mixture resembles coarse crumbs. • Stir in enough water to form a smooth dough. • Bring together with both hands and knead lightly. It may need a little more water if crumbly, or flour if sticky.
• Shape into a ball and wrap in plastic wrap (cling film). • Refrigerate for 30 minutes. • Filling: Toss the berries and plums with the sugar and cornstarch in a bowl. • Preheat the oven to 400°F (200°C/gas 6). Lightly butter a baking sheet. • Dust a work surface with flour and roll the pastry out into sheets 1/4 inch (5 mm) thick. • Cut out four 8-inch (20 cm) rounds with a pastry cutter or cut around a small plate. • Brush the pastry bases with a little egg white and sprinkle with the ground almonds or semolina to to stop them from becoming soggy. • Divide the berry mixture among the rounds, spooning it into the center. • Fold the edges of the pastry as far as they will go, partially enclosing the filling and pinching the corners to seal. • Whisk the egg yolk with the milk in a small bowl and brush over the pies. Sprinkle with the sugar. • Bake for 20–25 minutes, or until the pastry is golden brown and the juices from the fruit are bubbling out slightly. • Serve hot.

■ ■ ■ *If time is at a premium, you can make these pies with sheets of ready-made short-crust pastry.*

Pastry

2 cups (300 g) pastry flour

3 tablespoons superfine (caster) sugar

2/3 cup (180 g) butter, chilled and diced

3 tablespoons iced water

Filling

1 cup (200 g) gooseberries, topped and tailed

2 cups (300 g) blackberries or blueberries

4 big red or yellow plums (about 10 oz/300 g), pitted and quartered

1/2 cup (100 g) superfine (caster) sugar

1 tablespoon cornstarch (cornflour)

1 large egg, separated

1 tablespoon ground almonds or semolina

1 tablespoon milk

2 tablespoons sugar, to sprinkle

Serves: 4
Preparation: 30 minutes + 30 minutes to chill
Cooking: 20–25 minutes
Level: 2

PINE NUT TART

Sweet Tart Pastry: Mix the flour, salt, and confectioners' sugar in a medium bowl. Cut in the butter with a pastry blender or pulse the mixture in a food processor until it resembles fine bread crumbs. • Add the egg yolk and knead or pulse briefly until the ingredients come together. Add the water and knead or pulse to obtain a smooth dough. • Press into a log, wrap in plastic wrap (cling film) and chill in the refrigerator for at least 30 minutes. • Preheat the oven to 325°F (170°C/gas 3). Lightly grease a 9-inch (23-cm) tart pan with removable base. • Roll out the pastry on a lightly floured work surface to 1/8 inch (3 mm) thick. Fit into the tart pan and refrigerate for 30 minutes. • Remove the tart from the refrigerator, cover with a piece of parchment paper and fill with pie weights or dried beans. • Bake for 25 minutes, or until light golden brown. Leave to cool while you prepare the filling. • Leave the oven at the same heat. • Pine Nut Filling: Heat the corn syrup and lemon juice in a small saucepan over low heat until liquid. • Beat the butter, sugar, vanilla, and lemon zest in a medium bowl with an electric mixer on medium-high speed until pale and creamy. • Add the eggs one at a time, beating until just combined after each addition. • Stir in the pine nuts with a wooden spoon. • Spoon the filling into the tart case and bake for 40 minutes, or until set.

Sweet Tart Pastry

1½ cups (225 g) all-purpose (plain) flour

¼ teaspoon salt

⅓ cup (50 g) confectioners' (icing) sugar

½ cup (125 g) cold butter, cut in small cubes

1 large egg yolk

2 tablespoons water, as required

Pine Nut Filling

½ cup (125 ml) light corn (golden) syrup

1 tablespoon freshly squeezed lemon juice

½ cup (125 g) butter, softened

½ cup (100 g) firmly packed light brown sugar

½ teaspoon vanilla extract (essence)

1 teaspoon finely grated lemon zest

3 large eggs, lightly beaten

1½ cups (270 g) pine nuts, lightly toasted

Serves: 6–8
Preparation: 30 minutes + 1 hour to chill
Cooking: 65 minutes
Level: 1

LEMON AND LIME MERINGUE PIE

Prepare the pastry and bake following the instructions on page 436. Leave to cool while you prepare the filling and topping. • Filling and Topping: Preheat the to 375°F (190°C/gas 5).
• Combine ¼ cup (50 g) of superfine sugar with the lemon juice, lime juice, and both zests in a small saucepan over medium heat until the sugar has dissolved. • Beat the egg yolks in a heatproof bowl and gradually add the hot citrus liquid.
• Strain the mixture through a fine mesh sieve, return to the heatproof bowl and place over a saucepan of barely simmering water. Cook, stirring continuously, until the mixture thickens to coat the back of a wooden spoon. Do not allow the mixture to boil. • Remove from the heat and stir in the butter cubes one at a time, until fully combined.
• Pour the hot citrus mixture into the prepared tart base and set aside. • To make the meringue, beat the egg whites with an electric mixer on high speed until soft peaks form. Gradually add the remaining sugar a little at a time, beating until the meringue is thick and glossy. Stir in the vanilla. • Spoon the meringue topping over the citrus filling, using a spatula to create wave-like peaks. • Bake for 10 minutes, or until the meringue is light golden brown. • Cool to room temperature before serving.

1 recipe Sweet Tart Pastry (see page 436)

Filling and Topping

½ cup (100 g) superfine (caster) sugar

2 tablespoons freshly squeezed lime juice

3 tablespoons freshly squeezed lemon juice

1 teaspoon finely grated lime zest

1 teaspoon finely grated lemon zest

3 large eggs, separated

¼ cup (60 g) cold unsalted butter, cubed

¼ teaspoon vanilla extract (essence)

Serves: 6–8
Preparation: 30 minutes
  + 1 hour to chill
Cooking: 35 minutes
Level: 1

RASPBERRY AND FRANGIPANE TART

440

Prepare the pastry and bake following the instructions on page 436. Leave to cool while you prepare the filling. • Leave the oven on at the same temperature. • <u>Frangipane Filling</u>: Process the sugar, butter, flour, ground almonds, eggs, and vanilla in a food processor on medium speed for 2 minutes, or until a smooth, paste-like mixture is formed. • Spoon the frangipane mixture into the tart case and smooth the top using a spatula or the back of the spoon. Press the raspberries decoratively into the top of the tart. • Bake for 40 minutes, or until the frangipane is golden brown. • Remove from the oven and let cool to room temperature in the pan. • Dust with confectioners' sugar just before serving.

1   recipe Sweet Tart Pastry
    (see page 436)

Frangipane Filling

½   cup (100 g) superfine
    (caster) sugar

⅓   cup (90 g) unsalted
    butter, softened

⅓   cup (50 g) all-purpose
    (plain) flour

1½ cups (150 g) ground
    almonds

2   large eggs

1   teaspoon vanilla extract
    (essence)

1   cup (150 g) fresh
    raspberries

    Confectioners' (icing)
    sugar, to dust

Serves: 6–8
Preparation: 30 minutes
    + 1 hour to chill
Cooking: 65 minutes
Level: 1

CUSTARD TART

<u>Sweet Tart Pastry (with lemon)</u>: Mix the flour, salt, and confectioners' sugar in a medium bowl. Cut in the butter with a pastry blender or pulse the mixture in a food processor until it resembles fine bread crumbs. • Add the egg yolk and lemon zest and knead or pulse briefly until the ingredients come together. Add the water and knead or pulse to obtain a smooth dough. • Press into a log, wrap in plastic wrap (cling film) and chill in the refrigerator for at least 30 minutes. • Preheat the oven to 325°F (170°C/gas 3). Lightly grease a 9-inch (23-cm) tart pan with a removable base. • Roll out the pastry on a lightly floured work surface to $1/8$ inch (3 mm) thick. Fit into the tart pan and refrigerate for 30 minutes. • Remove the tart from the refrigerator, cover with a piece of parchment paper and fill with pie weights or dried beans. • Bake for 25 minutes, or until light golden brown. • Whisk the egg white in a small bowl using a fork. Remove the pie weights or beans and brush the egg white over the tart base using a pastry brush and bake for 5 more minutes. • Set aside on a rack. • <u>Custard Filling</u>: Preheat the oven to 350°F (180°C/gas 4). • Whisk the eggs, yolks, sugar, cream, and milk in a medium bowl until combined. Pour the egg mixture into the prepared pastry shell. • Bake for 50 minutes, or until just set. • Remove from the oven and sprinkle the top with freshly ground nutmeg. • Allow the tart to cool in the pan then refrigerate for at least 1 hour before serving.

Sweet Tart Pastry (with lemon)

$1\frac{1}{2}$ cups (225 g) all-purpose (plain) flour

$1/4$ teaspoon salt

$1/3$ cup (50 g) confectioners' (icing) sugar

$1/2$ cup (125 g) cold unsalted butter, cut in small cubes

1 large egg, separated

$1/2$ teaspoon finely grated lemon zest

2 tablespoons water, as required

Custard Filling

2 large eggs, + 2 large egg yolks

3 tablespoons superfine (caster) sugar

2 cups (500 ml) heavy cream

$1\frac{1}{2}$ cups (375 ml) milk

1 teaspoon ground nutmeg

Serves: 6–8
Preparation: 30 minutes + 2 hours to chill
Cooking: 1 hour 20 minutes
Level: 1

COCONUT AND MANGO TART

Prepare the pastry and bake following the instructions on page 436. Leave to cool while you prepare the filling. • Coconut and Mango Filling: Preheat the oven to 325°F (170°C/gas 3). • Beat the eggs and sugar with an electric mixer on medium-high speed until light and fluffy. • Stir in the mascarpone, coconut milk, and coconut with a wooden spoon until well combined. • Pour the filling into the prepared tart case. Arrange the mango slices decoratively on the top. • Bake for 40 minutes, or until golden brown. • Remove from the oven and allow to cool and set for 1 hour before serving.

1　recipe Sweet Tart Pastry (see page 436)

Coconut and Mango Filling

2　large eggs

1　cup (200 g) superfine (caster) sugar

½　cup (125 g) mascarpone cheese

½　cup (125 ml) coconut milk

2½ cups (560 g) shredded (desiccated) coconut

2　fresh or canned mango, sliced lengthwise

Serves: 6–8
Preparation: 30 minutes + 2 hours to cool and chill
Cooking: 65 minutes
Level: 1

BAKEWELL TART

Prepare the pastry and bake following the instructions on page 436. Leave to cool while you prepare the filling. • Frangipane Filling: Preheat the oven to 325°F (170°C/gas 3). • Process the sugar, butter, flour, ground almonds, eggs, and almond extract in a food processor on medium speed for 2 minutes, or until a smooth, paste-like mixture is formed. • Spread the strawberry preserves over the baked tart base and spoon the frangipane mixture on top, smoothing the surface with a spatula or the back of a spoon. • Bake for 30 minutes. Remove from the oven, spread with flaked almonds and bake for 10 more minutes, or until the frangipane and almonds are golden brown. • Remove from the oven and let cool to room temperature in the pan.

1   recipe Sweet Tart Pastry
    (see page 436)

Frangipane Filling

½   cup (100 g) superfine
    (caster) sugar

⅓   cup (80 g) unsalted
    butter, softened

⅓   cup (50 g) all-purpose
    (plain) flour

1½ cups (150 g) ground
    almonds

2   large eggs

1   teaspoon almond
    extract (essence)

⅓   cup (110 g) strawberry
    preserves (jam)

½   cup (50 g) flaked
    almonds

Serves: 6–8
Preparation: 30 minutes +
    2 hours to cool and chill
Cooking: 70 minutes
Level: 1

CHOCOLATE AND HAZELNUT TART

448

Sweet Chocolate Tart Pastry: Mix the flour, salt, confectioners' sugar, and cocoa in a medium bowl. Cut in the butter with a pastry blender or pulse the mixture in a food processor until it resembles fine bread crumbs. • Add the egg yolk and knead or pulse briefly until the ingredients come together. Add the water and knead or pulse to obtain a smooth dough. • Press into a log, wrap in plastic wrap (cling film) and chill in the refrigerator for at least 30 minutes. • Preheat the oven to 325°F (170°C/gas 3). Lightly grease a 9-inch (23-cm) tart pan with removable base. • Roll out the pastry on a lightly floured work surface to $1/8$ inch (3 mm) thick. Fit into the tart pan and refrigerate for 30 minutes. • Remove the tart from the refrigerator, cover with a piece of parchment paper and fill with pie weights or dried beans. • Bake for 25 minutes. • Remove the parchment paper and pastry weights and bake for 10 more minutes, or until the center is cooked through and light golden. Leave to cool while you prepare the filling. • Chocolate Hazelnut Filling: Melt the chocolate and cream in a double boiler over barely simmering water, stirring occasionally until smooth. • Stir in the hazelnuts. • Pour the filling into the prepared tart case and refrigerate for 1 hour until set. • Dust with cocoa just before serving.

Sweet Chocolate Tart Pastry

1⅓ cups (225 g) all-purpose (plain) flour

¼ teaspoon salt

⅓ cup (50 g) confectioners' (icing) sugar

¼ cup (30 g) unsweetened cocoa powder

½ cup (125 g) cold unsalted butter, cut in small cubes

1 large egg yolk

2 tablespoons water, as required

Chocolate Hazelnut Filling

12 oz (300 g) dark chocolate, coarsely chopped

1¼ cups (300 ml) heavy (double) cream

½ cup (100 g) hazelnuts, lightly toasted and coarsely chopped

Cocoa, for dusting

Serves: 6–8
Preparation: 30 minutes + 1 hour to chill
Cooking: 70 minutes
Level: 1

BLACKBERRY AND CUSTARD PIE

Pie Crust Pastry: Pulse the flour, salt, and butter in a food processor until the mixture resembles fine crumbs. Add the confectioners' sugar and pulse again. • Combine the egg yolk and water in a small bowl and gradually add to the flour mixture until it combines to form a dough. • Transfer to a lightly floured work surface and shape into two disks. Wrap in plastic wrap (cling film) and refrigerate for 1 hour. • Roll out the pastry on a lightly floured work surface to $1/8$ inch (3 mm) thick. • Line a 9-inch (23-cm) pie pan with one of the disks, pressing it firmly around the edges of the pan. Place the other disk on a plate and refrigerate both for 30 minutes. • Preheat the oven to 400°F (200°C/gas 6). • Filling: Place the blackberries and cinnamon in a medium bowl, stirring to combine. Pour into the prepared pie pan. Cover with the pastry lid, make a hole in the top with a small sharp knife and press down with your fingers around the edges to seal. • Cut off any excess pastry, brush with milk, and sprinkle with raw sugar. • Bake for 30 minutes. • Custard: Beat the egg yolks and sugar in a medium bowl using an electric mixer on high speed until pale and creamy. • Heat the cream in a small saucepan over medium heat until almost boiling. Pour the hot cream into the egg mixture, beating to combine. • Remove the pie from the oven and slowly pour in the custard through the hole in the top. Reserve any remaining custard for serving. • Bake for 10 minutes or until the pastry is golden brown. • Serve hot.

Pie Crust Pastry

$2^2/_3$ cups (400 g) all-purpose (plain) flour

$1/2$ teaspoon of salt

$3/4$ cup (180 g) cold butter, cubed

2 tablespoons confectioners' (icing) sugar

1 large egg yolk

$1/4$ cup (60 ml) iced water + extra, as required

Blackberry Filling

2 cups (300 g) fresh or frozen blackberries

1 teaspoon ground cinnamon

Milk, to glaze

Raw sugar, to sprinkle

Custard

3 large egg yolks

$2/3$ cup (125 g) sugar

$1^1/4$ cups (300 ml) heavy (double) cream

Serves: 6–8
Preparation: 30 minutes + 90 minutes to chill
Cooking: 70 minutes
Level: 2

PECAN TART

452

Prepare the pastry and bake following the instructions on page 436. Leave to cool while you prepare the filling. • <u>Pecan Filling</u>: Preheat the oven to 325°F (170°C/gas 3). • Beat the eggs, sugar, corn syrup, butter, and vanilla in a medium bowl until well combined. • Stir in the pecans using a wooden or large kitchen spoon. • Pour the filling into the prepared tart case. • Bake for 35–40 minutes, or until just set. The filling may still be a little wobbly but will set once cooled. • Serve at room temperature.

1 recipe Sweet Tart Pastry (see page 436)

Pecan Filling

3 large eggs

¼ cup (50 g) firmly packed light brown sugar

⅔ cup (150 ml) light corn (golden) syrup

⅓ cup (80 g) butter, melted

1 teaspoon vanilla extract (essence)

2 cups (250 g) pecans, lightly toasted

Serves: 6–8
Preparation: 30 minutes + 1 hour to chill
Cooking: 60–65 minutes
Level: 1

RICOTTA AND PLUM TART

454

Prepare the pastry and bake following the instructions on page 436. Leave to cool while you prepare the filling. • Ricotta and Plum Filling: Preheat the oven to 325°F (170°C/gas 3). • Beat the mascarpone, ricotta, sugar, honey, and vanilla in a medium bowl using an electric mixer on medium speed until smooth. • Beat in the eggs, egg yolk, and flour until well combined. Pour into the prepared tart case. Place the plum quarters around the tart decoratively. • Bake for 30–40 minutes, of until the filling is light golden brown but still slightly wobbly. • Remove from the oven and glaze with apricot jam. Serve warm.

1   recipe Sweet Tart Pastry
    (see page 436)

Ricotta and Plum Filling

¾ cup (180 g) mascarpone

1   cup (250 g) ricotta

½ cup (100 g) sugar

⅓ cup (80 ml) honey

1   teaspoon vanilla extract
    (essence)

2   large eggs + 1 large egg
    yolk

1   tablespoon all-purpose
    (plain) flour

12 ripe plums, pitted and
    quartered

2   tablespoons apricot
    preserves (jam), melted

Serves: 6–8
Preparation: 30 minutes
    + 1 hour to chill
Cooking: 60–65 minutes
Level: 1

BLUEBERRY PIE

Prepare the pie crust pastry. Wrap in plastic wrap (cling film) and refrigerate for 1 hour. • Roll out the pastry on a lightly floured work surface to ⅛ inch (3 mm) thick. • Line a 9-inch (23-cm) pie pan with one of the disks, pressing it firmly around the edges of the pan. Place the other disk on a plate and refrigerate both for 30 minutes. • Preheat the oven to 400°F (200°C/gas 6). • Blueberry Filling: Combine the blueberries, ground almonds, sugar, and lemon zest in a medium bowl. • Pour into the prepared pie pan and cover with the pastry lid, pressing down with your fingers around the edges to seal. Cut off any excess pastry, brush with milk, and sprinkle with raw sugar. • Bake for 40 minutes, or until the pastry is golden brown. • Serve warm.

1   recipe Pie Crust Pastry
    (see page 450)

Blueberry Filling

3   cups (600 g) fresh or
    frozen blueberries

⅓   cup (30 g) ground
    almonds

¼   cup (50 g) sugar

2   teaspoons finely grated
    lemon zest

    Milk, to glaze

    Raw sugar, to sprinkle

Serves: 6–8
Preparation: 30 minutes
   + 90 minutes to chill
Cooking: 40 minutes
Level: 1

APPLE AND STRAWBERRY PIE

Prepare the pie crust pastry. Wrap in plastic wrap (cling film) and refrigerate for 1 hour. • Roll out the pastry on a lightly floured work surface to 1/8 inch (3 mm) thick. • Line a 9-inch (23-cm) pie pan with one of the disks, pressing it firmly around the edges of the pan. Place the other disk on a plate and refrigerate both for 30 minutes. • Apple and Strawberry Filling: Preheat the oven to 400°F (200°C/gas 6). • Peel, core, and thinly slice the apples. • Cook the apples in a large saucepan over medium heat for 5 minutes. • Add the strawberries, brown sugar, orange zest, and cinnamon and simmer for 10 more minutes, or until they begin to soften. • Remove from the heat and pour the filling into the prepared pie pan. Cover with the pastry lid, pressing down with your fingers around the edges to seal. Cut off any excess pastry, brush with milk and sprinkle with raw sugar. • Bake for 40 minutes, or until the pastry is golden brown. • Dust with confectioners' sugar and serve warm.

1 recipe Pie Crust Pastry (see page 450)

Apple and Strawberry Filling

1½ lb (750 g) tart apples, such as Granny Smiths

2 cups (300 g) fresh or frozen strawberries, halved

⅓ cup (70 g) light brown sugar

1 teaspoon finely grated orange zest

1 teaspoon ground cinnamon

Milk, to glaze

Raw sugar, to sprinkle

Confectioners' (icing) sugar, to dust

Serves: 6–8
Preparation: 30 minutes + 90 minutes to chill
Cooking: 40 minutes
Level: 1

APRICOT AND ALMOND TART

460

Prepare the pastry and bake following the instructions on page 436. Leave to cool while you prepare the filling. • Apricot and Almond Filling: Preheat the oven to 325°F (170°C/gas 3). • Process the sugar, butter, flour, ground almonds, eggs, and vanilla extract in a food processor on medium speed for 2 minutes, or until a smooth, paste-like mixture is formed. • Spoon the almond mixture into the tart case and smooth using a spatula or the back of a spoon. Arrange the apricot halves cut side facing down decoratively around the tart, starting from the outside perimeter and working into the middle. • Bake for 40 minutes, or until golden brown. • Remove from the oven and allow to cool to room temperature in the pan.

1 recipe Sweet Tart Pastry (see page 436)

Apricot and Almond Filling

½ cup (100 g) superfine (caster) sugar

⅓ cup (90 g) unsalted butter, softened

⅓ cup (50 g) all-purpose (plain) flour

1½ cups (150 g) ground almonds

2 large eggs, beaten

1 teaspoon vanilla extract (essence)

6 ripe apricots, halved and pitted

Serves: 6–8
Preparation: 30 minutes + 2 hours to cool and chill
Cooking: 65 minutes
Level: 1

CREAM CHEESE AND BLUEBERRY TART

462

Prepare the pastry and bake following the instructions on page 436. Leave to cool while you prepare the filling. • Cream Cheese and Blueberry Filling: Preheat the oven to 325°F (170°C/gas 3). • Beat the egg yolks and sugar with an electric mixer on medium-high speed until pale and creamy. • Add the cream cheese, vanilla, and cinnamon, mixing until smooth. • Use a wooden spoon to stir in the bread crumbs and blueberries until incorporated. • Beat the egg whites in a medium bowl with mixer on medium-high speed until firm peaks form. • Fold the whites into the cream cheese mixture. Spoon into the prepared tart case. • Bake for 45 minutes, or until golden brown. • Remove from the oven and let cool to room temperature in the pan.

1 recipe Sweet Tart Pastry (see page 436)

Cream Cheese and Blueberry Filling

4 large eggs, separated

½ cup (100 g) superfine (caster) sugar

1⅓ cups (330 g) cream cheese, softened

½ teaspoon vanilla extract (essence)

1 teaspoon ground cinnamon

1¼ cups (75 g) fresh bread crumbs

1 cup (125 g) fresh or frozen blueberries

Serves: 6–8
Preparation: 30 minutes + 2 hours to cool and chill
Cooking: 1 hour
Level: 1

PLUM AND AMARETTI CRUNCH TART

464

Prepare the pastry and bake following the instructions on page 436. Leave to cool while you prepare the filling and topping. • Plum Filling: Preheat the oven to 375°F (190°C/gas 5). • Combine the ground almonds, brown sugar, orange zest, and mascarpone cheese in a medium bowl, stirring with a wooden spoon. Add the plum halves, stirring to coat in the mascarpone mixture. Spoon into the prepared tart base. • Amaretti Crunch Topping: Combine all the topping ingredients in a medium bowl and rub together using your finger tips until combined into a lumpy mixture. • Sprinkle the topping over the plum-filled tart. • Bake for 40 minutes, or until the topping is golden brown. • Remove from the oven and allow to cool to room temperature in the pan.

1 recipe Sweet Tart Pastry (see page 436)

Plum Filling

2 tablespoons ground almonds

1 tablespoon dark brown sugar

1 teaspoon orange zest

½ cup (125) mascarpone cheese

12 plums, halved and pitted

Amaretti Crunch Topping

¼ cup (60 g) butter, softened

3 tablespoons firmly packed light brown sugar

1 cup (125 g) crushed amaretti cookies

⅓ cup (50 g) flaked almonds

3 tablespoons shredded (desiccated) coconut

1 teaspoon ground cinnamon

Serves: 6–8
Preparation: 40 minutes + 2 hours to cool and chill
Cooking: 1 hour
Level: 1

PASSION FRUIT TART

466

Prepare the pastry and bake following the instructions on page 436. • Remove the parchment paper and pastry weights and bake for 10 more minutes, or until the center is cooked through and light golden. Set aside and leave to cool a little while you prepare the filling. • <u>Passion Fruit Curd</u>: heat the sugar, passion fruit pulp, orange juice and zest in a small saucepan over medium heat, stirring until the sugar has dissolved. • Beat the eggs yolks in a heatproof bowl and gradually pour in the hot passion fruit mixture. Strain through a fine mesh sieve. • Return to the heatproof bowl and place over a saucepan of barely simmering water. Cook, stirring continuously, until the mixture thickens and coats the back of a wooden spoon. Do not allow the mixture to boil. • Remove from the heat and add the butter cubes, one at a time, whisking until fully incorporated. • Pour the passion fruit curd into the prepared tart case and smooth using a spatula or the back of a spoon. • Refrigerate the tart for 1 hour, or until cooled and set.

1 recipe Sweet Tart Pastry (see page 436)

Passion Fruit Curd

1¾ cups (350 g) superfine (caster) sugar

1¼ cups (300 ml) passion fruit pulp, strained

1 tablespoon freshly squeezed orange juice

1 teaspoon finely grated orange zest

7 large egg yolks

1¼ cups (300 g) unsalted butter, cubed

Serves: 6–8
Preparation: 30 minutes + 2 hours to chill
Cooking: 35 minutes
Level: 2

MOCHACCINO TART

Prepare the pastry and bake following the instructions on page 448. • Remove the parchment paper and pastry weights and bake for 10 more minutes, or until the center is cooked through. Leave to cool while you prepare the filling and topping. • <u>Mocha Filling</u>: Melt the chocolate, cream, coffee liqueur, and coffee granules in a double boiler over barely simmering water, stirring occasionally until smooth. • Pour the filling into the prepared tart case and refrigerate for 1 hour, or until set. • <u>Topping</u>: Beat the cream, mascarpone, and confectioners' sugar until soft peaks form. Spoon the cream mixture on top of the tart and dust with cocoa.

1 recipe Sweet Chocolate Tart Pastry (see page 448)

Mocha Filling

12 oz (300 g) dark chocolate, coarsely chopped

1¼ cups (300 ml) heavy (double) cream

3 tablespoons coffee liqueur

2 teaspoons freeze-dried coffee granules

Topping

¾ cup (180 ml) heavy (double) cream

¼ cup (60 g) mascarpone cheese

2 tablespoons confectioners' (icing) sugar

Unsweetened cocoa powder, to dust

Serves: 8–10
Preparation: 30 minutes + 2 hours to chill
Cooking: 35 minutes
Level: 1

CHERRY TART

Prepare the pastry and bake following the instructions on page 436. Leave to cool while you prepare the filling and topping. • Cherry Filling: Preheat the oven to 375°F (190°C/gas 5). • Beat the sour cream, cream cheese, lemon zest, egg yolks, brown sugar, cinnamon, and liqueur together in a medium bowl until smooth. • Pour the sour cream mixture into the prepared tart base and arrange the cherries on top. • Bake for 40 minutes, or until golden brown and set. • Remove from the oven and allow to cool to room temperature in the pan.

1 recipe Sweet Tart Pastry (see page 436)

Cherry Filling

1 cup (250 ml) sour cream

3 oz (90 g) cream cheese, softened

1 teaspoon finely grated lemon zest

2 large egg yolks

⅓ cup (70 g) firmly packed light brown sugar

½ teaspoon ground cinnamon

1 tablespoon cherry liqueur

1 pound (500 g) sour cherries, pitted

Serves: 6–8
Preparation: 30 minutes + 2 hours to cool and chill
Cooking: 65 minutes
Level: 1

RASPBERRY AND CUSTARD TART

Prepare the pastry and bake following the instructions on page 436. Leave to cool while you prepare the filling and topping. • <u>Pastry Cream</u>: Preheat the oven to 450°F (230°C/gas 8). • Heat the milk and cinnamon stick in a small saucepan over medium heat and bring to a boil. Decrease heat to low, cover, and simmer gently for 15 minutes. • Strain the milk through a fine mesh sieve into a pitcher (jug). • Beat the egg yolks, sugar, and cornstarch in a medium bowl until combined. • Gradually pour in the hot milk, stirring with a wooden spoon until incorporated. • Pour the custard into a small saucepan and simmer over low heat, stirring continuously with a wooden spoon until thickened. • Remove from the heat, stir in the butter and set aside to cool a little. • Pour the custard into the prepared tart case and scatter with the raspberries. • Bake for 10 minutes. • Remove from the oven and allow to cool and set in the pan.

1   recipe Sweet Tart
    Pastry (see page 436)

Pastry Cream

1   cup (250 ml) milk
½   cinnamon stick
2   large egg yolks
¼   cup (50 g) sugar
2   tablespoons cornstarch
    (cornflour)
2   teaspoons butter

2   cups (300 g) fresh
    raspberries

Serves: 6–8
Preparation: 30 minutes +
    2 hours to cool and chill
Cooking: 35 minutes
Level: 2

GINGER AND LIME CURD TART

474

Prepare the pastry and bake following the instructions on page 436. • Remove the parchment paper and pastry weights and bake for 10 more minutes, or until the center is cooked through and light golden. Set aside and leave to cool a little while you prepare the filling. • <u>Ginger and Lime Curd</u>: Heat the sugar, ginger, lime juice and zest in a small saucepan over medium heat, stirring until the sugar has dissolved. • Beat the eggs yolks in a heatproof bowl and gradually pour in the hot ginger and lime mixture. • Strain through a fine mesh sieve and then return to the heatproof bowl. Place over a saucepan of barely simmering water. Cook, stirring continuously, until the mixture thickens and coats the back of a wooden spoon. Do not allow the mixture to boil. • Remove from the heat and add the butter cubes, one at a time, whisking until fully incorporated. • Pour the ginger and lime curd into the prepared tart case and smooth using a spatula or the back of a spoon. • Refrigerate the tart for 1 hour, or until cooled and set.

1 recipe Sweet Tart Pastry (see page 436)

Ginger and Lime Curd

1¾ cups (350 g) superfine (caster) sugar

2 tablespoons candied (glacé) ginger, finely chopped

1¼ cups (300 ml) freshly squeezed lime juice, strained

2 teaspoons finely grated lime zest

7 large egg yolks

1¼ cups (300 g) butter, cubed

Serves: 6–8
Preparation: 30 minutes + 2 hours to chill
Cooking: 35 minutes
Level: 2

STRAWBERRY TART

Prepare the pastry and bake following the instructions on page 436. Leave to cool while you prepare the filling and topping. • Strawberry Filling: Preheat the oven to 375°F (190°C/gas 5). • Spoon the strawberry preserves into the prepared tart case, spreading evenly with a spatula. • Sprinkle the almonds over the top. • Bake for 10 minutes, or until the preserves are bubbling and the almonds are golden brown. • Remove from the oven and allow to cool to room temperature in the pan.

1 recipe Sweet Tart Pastry (see page 436)

Strawberry Filling

1 cup (300 g) whole fruit strawberry preserves (jam)
½ cup (80 g) flaked almonds

Serves: 6–8
Preparation: 25 minutes
+ 1 hour to chill
Cooking: 35 minutes
Level: 1

■ ■ ■ *This is an easy tart to make. If liked, substitute the strawberry preserves with the same quantity of raspberry or apricot preserves (jam).*

CRÈME BRÛLÉE TART

Prepare the pastry and bake following the instructions on page 436. Leave to cool while you prepare the filling. • Vanilla Custard Filling: Preheat the oven to 325°F (170°C/gas 3). • Beat the egg yolks and 1/3 cup (70 g) sugar in a medium bowl until pale and creamy. • Heat the cream, milk, and vanilla pod and seeds in a small saucepan over medium-high heat and bring to a boil. • Gradually pour the hot cream mixture into the egg yolks, whisking until incorporated. • Strain the custard through a fine mesh sieve and discard the vanilla pod. • Pour the custard into the prepared tart case. • Bake for 40 minutes, or until set. • Remove from the oven and allow to cool to room temperature in the pan. Refrigerate for 1 hour, or until chilled and set. • Preheat the broiler (grill) to high. Remove the tart from the refrigerator and sprinkle the top with the remaining sugar. • Cover the pastry edges with foil to prevent them from burning. • Place the tart on the highest shelf underneath the grill and cook for 1 minute, or until the sugar melts and turns golden brown.

1 recipe Sweet Tart Pastry (see page 436)

Vanilla Custard Filling

5 large egg yolks

1/3 cup (70 g) superfine (caster) sugar + 2 tablespoons

1¼ cups (300 ml) heavy (double) cream

2/3 cup (150 ml) milk

1 vanilla pod, split lengthwise and seeds scraped out

Serves: 6–8
Preparation: 35 minutes + 3 hours to cool and chill
Cooking: 65 minutes
Level: 2

PEACH PIE

Prepare the pie crust pastry. Wrap in plastic wrap (cling film) and refrigerate for 1 hour. • Roll out the pastry on a lightly floured work surface to $^1/_8$ inch (3 mm) thick. • Line a 9-inch (23-cm) pie pan with one of the disks, pressing it firmly around the edges of the pan. Place the other disk on a plate and refrigerate both for 30 minutes. • <u>Peach Filling</u>: Preheat the oven to 400°F (200°C/gas 6). • Combine the sugar, flour, ground almonds, and cinnamon in a medium bowl. Add the peach slices, pour in the lemon juice, and toss to coat. • Spoon the filling into the prepared pie pan and dot with butter. • Place the remaining piece of pastry on top, pressing down with your fingers around the edges to seal. Cut off any excess pastry, brush with the beaten egg, and sprinkle with raw sugar. Cut a crisscross in the center of the pie lid to allow steam to be released during baking. • Bake for 40 minutes, or until the pastry is golden brown. • Serve warm with a dollop of whipped cream or crème fraîche.

1 recipe Pie Crust Pastry (see page 450)

Peach Filling

$^1/_3$ cup (70 g) sugar

2 tablespoons all-purpose (plain) flour

2 tablespoons ground almonds

1 teaspoon ground cinnamon

2 lb (1 kg) peaches, peeled, pitted, and sliced

1 tablespoon freshly squeezed lemon juice

1 tablespoon butter

1 large egg, lightly beaten

Raw sugar, to sprinkle

Whipped cream or crème fraîche, to serve

Serves: 8–10
Preparation: 40 minutes + 90 minutes to chill
Cooking: 40 minutes
Level: 2

RAISIN PIE

Prepare the pie crust pastry. Wrap in plastic wrap (cling film) and refrigerate for 1 hour. • Roll out the pastry on a lightly floured work surface to $1/8$ inch (3 mm) thick. • Line a 9-inch (23-cm) pie pan with one of the disks, pressing it firmly around the edges of the pan. Place the other disk on a plate and refrigerate both for 30 minutes. • Raisin Filling: Preheat the oven to 400°F (200°C/gas 6). • Place the raisins and water in a medium saucepan over medium heat and simmer for 10 minutes. • Combine the sugar, cornstarch, cinnamon, and orange juice and zest in a small bowl, stirring to make a paste. • Decrease the raisin heat to low and gradually add the cornstarch mixture. Simmer for 2 more minutes, stirring until thickened. • Remove from the heat and add the butter, stirring to incorporate. • Pour the raisin filling into the prepared pie pan and place the remaining piece of pastry on top, pressing down with your fingers around the edges to seal. Cut off any excess pastry and decorate with pastry shapes made from the excess dough if desired. Brush with the beaten egg and sprinkle with raw sugar. • Prick with a fork several times to allow steam to be released during baking. Dust with cinnamon. • Bake for 40 minutes, or until the pastry is golden brown. • Serve warm.

1   recipe Pie Crust Pastry (see page 450)

Raisin Filling

2½ cups (450 g) raisins

1½ cups (375 ml) water

½   cup (100 g) firmly packed light brown sugar

2   tablespoons cornstarch (cornflour)

1   teaspoon ground cinnamon + extra, to dust

3   tablespoons freshly squeezed orange juice

1   teaspoon finely grated orange zest

1½ tablespoons butter, cubed

1   large egg, lightly beaten

Serves: 8–10
Preparation: 30 minutes + 90 minutes to chill
Cooking: 55 minutes
Level: 2

FRUITS OF THE FOREST PIE

484

Prepare the pie crust pastry. Wrap in plastic wrap (cling film) and refrigerate for 1 hour. • Roll out the pastry on a lightly floured work surface to 1/8 inch (3 mm) thick. • Line a 9-inch (23-cm) pie pan with one of the disks, pressing it firmly around the edges of the pan. Place the other disk on a plate and refrigerate both for 30 minutes. • Berry Filling: Preheat the oven to 400°F (200°C/gas 6). • Combine the blueberries, blackberries, raspberries, sugar, flour, cinnamon, nutmeg, and lemon zest in a medium bowl, stirring to combine. • Pour the berry filling into the prepared pie pan and cover with the pastry lid, pressing down with your fingers around the edges to seal. Cut off any excess pastry and decorate with pastry shapes made from the excess dough if desired. Make a few small slits to allow steam to be released during baking. Brush with the beaten egg and sprinkle with raw sugar. • Bake for 40 minutes, or until the pastry is golden brown. • Serve warm.

1   recipe Pie Crust Pastry (see page 450)

Berry Filling

2   cups (300 g) fresh or frozen blueberries

2   cups (300 g) fresh or frozen blackberries

2   cups (300 g) fresh or frozen raspberries

1/3 cup (70 g) sugar

3   tablespoons all-purpose (plain) flour

1   teaspoon ground cinnamon

1/2 teaspoon ground nutmeg

2   teaspoons finely grated lemon zest

1   large egg, lightly beaten

    Raw sugar, to sprinkle

Serves: 6–8
Preparation: 30 minutes + 90 minutes to chill
Cooking: 40 minutes
Level: 2

BLACK DORIS PLUM PIE

486

Prepare the pie crust pastry. Wrap in plastic wrap (cling film) and refrigerate for 1 hour. • Roll out the pastry on a lightly floured work surface to $1/8$ inch (3 mm) thick. • Line a 9-inch (23-cm) pie pan with one of the disks, pressing it firmly around the edges of the pan. Place the other disk on a plate and refrigerate both for 30 minutes. • Plum Filling: Preheat the oven to 400°F (200°C/gas 6).
• Combine the brown sugar, flour, and cinnamon in a medium bowl. Add the plum slices and lemon juice, stirring to coat. • Spoon the filling into the prepared pie pan and dot with butter. • Cut the remaining piece of pastry into $2/3$-inch (1.5-cm) strips and lay them on top of the plums in a lattice pattern, pressing down with your fingers around the edges to seal. Cut off any excess pastry and brush with the beaten egg. • Bake for 40 minutes, or until the pastry is golden brown. • Serve warm.

1 recipe Pie Crust Pastry (see page 450)

Plum Filling

$1/3$ cup (70 g) firmly packed dark brown sugar

3 tablespoons all-purpose (plain) flour

1 teaspoon ground cinnamon

2 lb (1 kg) plums, pitted, and sliced

1 tablespoon freshly squeezed lemon juice

1 tablespoon butter

1 large egg, lightly beaten

Raw sugar, to sprinkle

Serves: 6–8
Preparation: 40 minutes
+ 90 minutes to chill
Cooking: 40 minutes
Level: 2

APPLE AND DATE PIE

488

Prepare the pie crust pastry. Wrap in plastic wrap (cling film) and refrigerate for 1 hour. • Roll out the pastry on a lightly floured work surface to ⅛ inch (3 mm) thick. • Line a 9-inch (23-cm) pie pan with one of the disks, pressing it firmly around the edges of the pan. Place the other disk on a plate and refrigerate both for 30 minutes. • Apple and Date Filling: Preheat the oven to 400°F (200°C/gas 6). • Combine the sugar, flour, orange zest, and cinnamon in a medium bowl. • Peel, core, and slice the apples. • Add the apple slices, dates, and walnuts to the sugar mixture. Pour in the orange juice and toss to coat. • Spoon the filling into the prepared pie pan and dot with butter. • Place the remaining piece of pastry on top, pressing down with your fingers around the edges to seal. Cut off any excess pastry and decorate with pastry shapes made from the excess dough if desired. • Brush with the beaten egg and sprinkle with raw sugar. Pierce the pie lid with a sharp knife here and there to allow steam to be released during baking. • Bake for 40 minutes, or until the pastry is golden brown. • Serve warm.

1 recipe Pie Crust Pastry (see page 450)

Apple and Date Filling

¼ cup (50 g) sugar

1 tablespoon all-purpose (plain) flour

1 teaspoon finely grated orange zest

1 teaspoon ground cinnamon

1½ lb (750 g) tart apples, such as Granny Smith

1 cup (180 g) pitted and chopped dates

¼ cup (30 g) walnuts, coarsely chopped

2 tablespoons freshly squeezed orange juice

1 tablespoon butter

1 large egg, lightly beaten

Raw sugar, to sprinkle

Serves: 6–8
Preparation: 40 minutes + 90 minutes to chill
Cooking: 40 minutes
Level: 2

APRICOT AND COCONUT PIE

490

Prepare the pie crust pastry. Wrap in plastic wrap (cling film) and refrigerate for 1 hour. • Roll out the pastry on a lightly floured work surface to 1/8 inch (3 mm) thick. • Line a 9-inch (23-cm) pie pan with one of the disks, pressing it firmly around the edges of the pan. Place the other disk on a plate and refrigerate both for 30 minutes. • Apricot and Coconut Filling: Preheat the oven to 400°F (200°C/gas 6). • Place the apricots and water in a medium saucepan over medium heat and simmer for 10 minutes. • Combine the sugar, cornstarch, cinnamon, and orange juice and zest in a small bowl, stirring to make a paste. • Decrease the apricot heat to low and gradually add the cornstarch mixture. Simmer for 2 more minutes, stirring until thickened. • Remove from the heat and add the butter and coconut, stirring to incorporate. • Pour the apricot filling into the prepared pie pan and place the remaining piece of pastry on top, pressing down with your fingers around the edges to seal. Cut off any excess pastry and decorate with pastry shapes made from the excess dough if desired. • Brush with the beaten egg and sprinkle with raw sugar. Prick with a fork several times to allow steam to be released during baking. • Bake for 40 minutes, or until the pastry is golden brown. • Serve warm.

1   recipe Pie Crust Pastry
    (see page 450)

Apricot and Coconut Filling

2½ cups (450 g) dried
    apricots

1¼ cups (300 ml) water

½   cup (100 g) sugar

2   tablespoons cornstarch
    (cornflour)

1   teaspoon ground
    cinnamon

3   tablespoons freshly
    squeezed orange juice

1   teaspoon finely grated
    orange zest

1   tablespoon butter,
    cubed

1   cup (125 g) shredded
    (desiccated) coconut

1   large egg, lightly beaten

Serves: 6–8
Preparation: 30 minutes
  + 90 minutes to chill
Cooking: 55 minutes
Level: 2

PEAR, CHOCOLATE, AND GINGER PIE

492

Prepare the pie crust pastry. Wrap in plastic wrap (cling film) and refrigerate for 1 hour. • Roll out the pastry on a lightly floured work surface to $1/8$ inch (3 mm) thick. • Line a 9-inch (23-cm) pie pan with one of the disks, pressing it firmly around the edges of the pan. Place the other disk on a plate and refrigerate both for 30 minutes. • Pear, Chocolate, and Ginger Filling: Preheat the oven to 400°F (200°C/gas 6). • Combine the sugar, orange zest, cinnamon, ginger, and chocolate in a medium bowl. Add the pear slices and toss to coat. • Spoon the filling into the prepared pie pan and place the remaining piece of pastry on top, pressing down with your fingers around the edges to seal. Cut off any excess pastry and decorate with pastry shapes made from the excess dough if desired. • Make a few small slits with a sharp knife to allow steam to be released during baking. • Brush with the beaten egg and sprinkle with raw sugar. • Bake for 40 minutes, or until the pastry is golden brown. • Serve warm.

1 recipe Pie Crust Pastry (see page 450)

Pear, Chocolate, and Ginger Filling
1/4 cup (50 g) sugar
1 teaspoon finely grated orange zest
1/2 teaspoon ground cinnamon
2 tablespoons candied (glacé) ginger, finely chopped
3 oz (90 g) dark chocolate, coarsely chopped
2 lb (1 kg) pears, peeled, cored, and sliced
1 large egg, lightly beaten
Raw sugar, to sprinkle

Serves: 6–8
Preparation: 35 minutes + 90 minutes to chill
Cooking: 40 minutes
Level: 2

PUMPKIN PIE

Prepare the pie crust pastry. Wrap in plastic wrap (cling film) and refrigerate for 1 hour. • Roll out the pastry on a lightly floured work surface to $1/8$ inch (3 mm) thick. • Line a 9-inch (23-cm) pie pan with one of the disks, pressing it firmly around the edges of the pan. Place the other disk on a plate and refrigerate both for 30 minutes. • Pumpkin Filling: Preheat the oven to 350°F (180°C/gas 4). • Combine all the filling ingredients in a medium bowl, stirring with a wooden or large kitchen spoon to combine. • Pour the filling into the prepared tart base and place the remaining piece of pastry on top, pressing down with your fingers around the edges to seal. Cut off any excess pastry and make a few small slits with a sharp knife to allow steam to be released during baking. • Bake for 45–55 minutes, until the pastry is golden brown and the filling has set in the center. • Serve warm or at room temperature with a dollop of whipped cream or crème fraîche.

1 recipe Pie Crust Pastry (see page 450)

Pumpkin Filling

$1^{3}/_{4}$ cups (400 g) canned or fresh pumpkin purée

3 large eggs, lightly beaten

½ cup (100 g) firmly packed light brown sugar

1 cup (250 ml) heavy (double) cream

1 tablespoon all-purpose (plain) flour

1 teaspoon ground cinnamon

¼ teaspoon ground ginger

¼ teaspoon ground nutmeg

⅛ teaspoon ground clove

Whipped cream or crème fraîche, to serve

Serves: 6–8
Preparation: 30 minutes + 90 minutes to chill
Cooking: 45–55 minutes
Level: 2

COCONUT CREAM TART

Prepare the pastry and bake following the instructions on page 436. • Remove the parchment paper and pastry weights and bake for 10 more minutes, or until the center is cooked through and light golden. Set aside and leave to cool a little while you prepare the filling. • Coconut Cream Filling: Place the half-and-half and coconut cream in a medium saucepan over medium-low heat and bring to a boil. • Beat the eggs, sugar, flour, and vanilla in a medium bowl until combined. • Pour the hot cream into the egg mixture, whisking until incorporated. • Add the shredded coconut, stirring with a wooden spoon to combine. • Pour the filling into the prepared pie base. Chill for 3 hours, or until set. • Topping: Beat the cream, vanilla, and confectioners' sugar in a medium bowl, until firm peaks form. Spoon the cream onto the set tart, using a spatula or the back of a spoon to create decorative peaks. Sprinkle the top with shaved coconut or slivered almonds.

1 recipe Sweet Tart Pastry (see page 436)

Coconut Cream Filling

2 cups (500 ml) half-and-half

1 cup (250 ml) coconut cream

2 large eggs

3/4 cup (150 g) sugar

1/2 cup (75 g) all-purpose (plain) flour

1 teaspoon vanilla extract (essence)

3/4 cup (90 g) shredded (desiccated) coconut

Topping

1 cup (250 ml) heavy (double) cream

1/4 teaspoon vanilla extract (essence)

2 tablespoons confectioners' (icing) sugar

2 tablespoons shaved coconut or slivered almonds, lightly toasted

Serves: 6–8
Preparation: 30 minutes
  + 4 hours to chill
Cooking: 35 minutes
Level: 2

MAPLE, WALNUT, AND APPLE PIE

Prepare the pie crust pastry. Wrap in plastic wrap (cling film) and refrigerate for 1 hour. • Roll out the pastry on a lightly floured work surface to $1/8$ inch (3 mm) thick. • Line a 9-inch (23-cm) pie pan with one of the disks, pressing it firmly around the edges of the pan. Place the other disk on a plate and refrigerate both for 30 minutes. • Maple, Walnut, and Apple Filling: Preheat the oven to 400°F (200°C/gas 6). • Beat the eggs, sugar, maple syrup, butter, and vanilla in a medium bowl until combined. • Add the apples and toasted walnuts, stirring until well combined. • Pour the filling into the prepared pie pan and place the remaining piece of pastry on top, pressing down with your fingers around the edges to seal. Cut off any excess pastry and make a few small slits with a sharp knife to allow steam to be released during baking. • Brush with the beaten egg. • Bake for 40 minutes, or until the pastry is golden brown. • Serve warm.

1 recipe Pie Crust Pastry (see page 450)

Maple, Walnut, and Apple Filling

3 large eggs

$1/4$ cup (50 g) firmly packed light brown sugar

$2/3$ cup (150 ml) maple syrup

$1/3$ cup (90 g) butter, melted

$1/2$ teaspoon vanilla extract (essence)

3 tart apples, such as Granny Smiths, peeled, cored, and sliced

$2 1/2$ cups (180 g) walnuts, lightly toasted

1 large egg, lightly beaten

Serves: 6–8
Preparation: 30 minutes + 90 minutes to chill
Cooking: 40 minutes
Level: 2

499

PASTRIES

PUFF-PASTRY PRETZELS

<u>Chocolate Pastry</u>: Place the flour, sugar, almonds, and cocoa in a mound on a work surface. • Dot the butter over the dry ingredients. • Use a pastry blender to cut in the butter. • Make a well in the center, add the egg and vanilla, then knead with your hands into a firm dough. • Shape into a disk and wrap in plastic wrap (cling film). Chill in the refrigerator for 30 minutes. • Preheat the oven to 400°F (200°C/gas 6). Line two baking sheets with parchment paper. • Dust a work surface with flour and roll out the puff pastry to about $1/8$-inch (3 mm) thick. Cut into rectangles, each measuring 12 inches (30 cm) in length. • Roll out the chocolate pastry to the same thickness and size to fit the puff-pastry rectangles. • Lightly beat the egg white with a fork and brush over the puff pastry rectangles. • Place the chocolate rectangles on top and press together lightly. • Cut lengthwise into $2/3$-inch (1.5-cm) wide strips. • Twirl each strip like a rope and form into a pretzel shape by crossing one end over the other to form a circle and bringing the ends down to the opposite edge of the circle. Press lightly to seal. • Place the pretzels 2 inches (5 cm) apart on the prepared baking sheets. • Beat the egg yolk in a small bowl and brush over the pretzels. • Bake for 20–25 minutes, until golden brown. • Let cool on a rack before serving.

Chocolate Pastry

1 cup (150 g) all-purpose (plain) flour

$1/3$ cup (70 g) sugar

$3/4$ cup (75 g) ground almonds

2 tablespoons unsweetened cocoa powder

$2/3$ cup (125 g) butter, chilled and diced

1 medium egg

1 teaspoon vanilla extract (essence)

To Assemble

10 oz (300 g) puff pastry, thawed if frozen

1 large egg, separated

Serves: 6–8
Preparation: 50 minutes
  + 30 minutes to chill
Cooking: 25 minutes
Level: 2

CHERRY AND ALMOND STRUDEL

Filling: Beat the eggs and sugar in a large bowl with an electric mixer at high speed until pale and creamy. • With mixer on low, beat in the cheese until well blended. • Fold in the cherries and almonds. Set aside. • Preheat the oven to 375°F (190°C/gas 5) and butter a large baking sheet. • To Assemble: mix the bread crumbs and cinnamon in a small bowl. • Put the melted butter in a separate bowl. • Phyllo pastry usually comes in blocks of 8 x 12-inch (20 x 30-cm) sheets. Keep unused sheets covered with a damp tea towel to prevent them from drying out. • Place 1 sheet before you on the work surface, stretching it out lengthways away from you. • Brush generously with melted butter and sprinkle lightly with the bread crumb mixture. • Add another sheet and repeat the buttering, sprinkling, and layering until all 6 sheets are before you in a neat pile. Brush the top sheet and sprinkle with the remaining bread crumbs. • Place the filling along the short end nearest to you. • Roll up, away from you, tucking in the sides. • Carefully lift the roll, using spatulas to help you, and place on the baking sheet. • Brush more butter over the top. • Make 5 diagonal slashes with a serrated knife, cutting through the top layer of the pastry to the filling. • Bake for 30–35 minutes, until crisp, basting with butter from time to time. • Five minutes before the end of baking time, sprinkle the strudel with confectioners' sugar. • Leave on the sheet for 5 minutes, then transfer to a rack. • Cut into portions with a serrated knife. • Serve warm or at room temperature.

Filling

2   small eggs

½ cup (100 g) superfine (caster) sugar

1   lb (500 g) ricotta cheese (drained) or quark

1½ lb (750 g) pitted morello cherries, drained

¾ cup (75 g) ground almonds

½ cup (50 g) blanched almonds, toasted and coarsely chopped

To Assemble

½ cup (40 g) fresh bread crumbs

½ teaspoon ground cinnamon

½ cup (110 g) melted butter, for brushing

6   phyllo pastry sheets, thawed if frozen

1   tablespoon confectioners' (icing) sugar, to dust

Serves: 6
Preparation: 40 minutes
Cooking: 35 minutes
Level: 2

PLUM PUFFS

Preheat the oven to 400°F (200°C/gas 6). • Dampen a baking sheet with water using a brush. • Lightly dust a work surface with flour and roll out the pastry into a 12-inch (30-cm) square about $\frac{1}{8}$-inch (3 mm) thick. • Cut into six 4 x 6-inch (10 x 15-cm) rectangles and place on the baking sheet about 1 inch (2.5 cm) apart. Prick each rectangle all over with a fork, leaving a 1 inch-(2-cm)-border around the edge. Chill in the refrigerator for 15 minutes while you prepare the topping. • Place the marzipan, crème fraîche, and orange juice in a food processor and blend until smooth. • Halve the plums, remove the pits (stones), and cut each half into thick slices. • Spread the marzipan mixture among the pastry rectangles, leaving a 1-inch (2.5-cm) border uncovered around the edges. • Arrange the plum slices cut-side down and overlapping on top. Sprinkle with almonds, if using. • Bake for 20–25 minutes, until puffed up and golden. • Serve warm or at room temperature.

1 lb (500 g) puff pastry, thawed if frozen

6 oz (180 g) marzipan, softened

2 tablespoons crème fraîche

2 tablespoons freshly squeezed orange juice

6 large plums

2 tablespoons almond flakes (optional)

Serves: 6
Preparation: 20 minutes
Cooking: 20–25 minutes
Level: 1

SWEET ALMOND PASTRY

<u>Pastry</u>: Prepare the pastry following the instructions on page 346. Chill in the refrigerator for 30 minutes. • <u>Filling</u>: Peel the apples, then core and cut into small chunks. • Mix in a bowl with the brown sugar, lemon juice, and cinnamon. • Brush a 10-inch (25-cm) tart pan a removable bottom with butter. • Take the pastry out of the refrigerator and lightly dust a work surface with the confectioners' sugar. • Roll out the pastry to $1/4$-inch (5-mm) thick and line the pan. • Prick the base all over with a fork and spread the apples evenly over the top. • Preheat the oven to 350°F (180°C/gas 4).• <u>Almond Topping</u>: Beat the butter, sugar, and vanilla in a bowl with an electric mixer at high speed until pale and creamy. • Add the eggs, one at a time, beating until just combined after each addition. • With mixer on low, gradually beat in the almonds and flour. • Cover the apples evenly with the mixture. • Sprinkle with the flaked almonds and sugar. • Bake for 45–50 minutes, or until golden brown. • Let cool in the pan.

1 recipe Sweet Tart Pastry (see page 346)

1 teaspoon melted butter, to brush the pan

Filling

3 large Cox apples

2 tablespoons brown sugar

3 tablespoons freshly squeezed lemon juice

Pinch of cinnamon

1 tablespoon confec- tioners' (icing) sugar

Almond Topping

$1/2$ cup (120 g) butter

$1/2$ cup (120 g) superfine (caster) sugar

$1/2$ teaspoon vanilla extract

2 large eggs

$1^{1}/4$cups (120 g) ground almonds

1 tablespoon all-purpose (plain) flour

2 tablespoons flaked almonds, for sprinkling

1 tablespoon light brown sugar, to sprinkle

Serves: 6–8
Preparation: 35 minutes
  + 30 minutes to chill
Cooking: 45–50 minutes
Level: 1

GAZELLE HORNS

■ ■ ■ *These Moroccan pastries are served at weddings. They are said to be natural aphrodisiacs.*

Pastry: Combine the flour and salt in a large bowl. • Stir in the oil, orange blossom water, and water. • Mix well and knead for 10 minutes into a soft, elastic dough. • Wrap in plastic wrap (cling film) and chill in the refrigerator for 30–40 minutes while you are making the filling. • Filling: Grind the almonds in a food processor until medium-finely ground. • Add the sugar and process the mixture again. • Add the eggs and orange blossom water and process into a dense paste. • Shape into rolls about 2 inches (6 cm) long and ½ inch (1 cm) in diameter and form into crescent shapes. • Place the crescents on parchment paper or an oiled plate and set aside. • Oil a large baking sheet. Preheat the oven to 400°F (200°C/gas 6).
• To Assemble: Lightly flour a work surface and roll the dough to ⅛ inch (3 mm) thick, or even thinner if possible. • Cut into long 2½-inch (7-cm) wide strips. • Arrange the almond crescents down the middle of each strip. Leave a 1½-inch (3-cm) gap between each crescent. • Cut the dough at an equal distance between each crescent. • Brush the dough edges with a little water and fold over the almond crescents. Press to seal, enclosing and re-shaping the curved almond paste filling to look like gazelle horns. • Cut away any overlapping pastry. • Place the horns on the baking sheet with a spatula. • Prick each one twice with a fork, making sure they retain their shape. • Bake for 10–15 minutes, until light golden. Let cool. • Sprinkle the pastries with a few drops of orange blossom water and dust with confectioners' sugar.

Pastry
1⅔ cups (250 g) all-purpose (plain) flour
½ teaspoon salt
2 tablespoons sunflower oil
⅓ cup (90 ml) orange blossom water
⅓ cup (90 ml) water

Filling
1½ cups (250 g) blanched almonds
1¼ cups (250 g) superfine (caster) sugar
2 small eggs
⅓ cup (90 ml) orange blossom water
1 tablespoon sunflower oil, to brush baking sheet

Glaze
1 tablespoon orange blossom water, to sprinkle
2 tablespoons confectioners' (icing) sugar, to dust

Serves: 12
Preparation: 1 hour + 30–40 minutes to chill
Cooking: 10–15 minutes
Level: 3

MA'AMOUL LEBANESE ALMOND PASTRIES

Pastry: Place the semolina in a large bowl and pour in the butter. • Mix well, cover, and leave to rest for 6 hours, or overnight, at room temperature. • Next day, stir in the rosewater and orange blossom water and mix into a dough. • Preheat the oven to 350°F (180°C/gas 4) and lightly oil two baking sheets. • Filling: Combine all the filling ingredients in a bowl and mix well. • Take a heaped teaspoonful of the dough, shape it into a ball, and make a hollow in the center with your finger. • Stuff a little of the filling into the hollow and seal the opening. • Shape into balls or ovals. • Place the pastries on the prepared sheets and bake for 10–15 minutes, until pale golden brown. • Leave to cool on racks until firm. • When completely cooled, dust with confectioners' sugar.

Pastry

- 1 lb (500 g) fine semolina
- 1 cup (250 g) butter, melted
- ½ cup (125 ml) rosewater
- ½ cup (125 ml) orange blossom water

Filling

- ⅔ cup (50 g) ground almonds
- ⅓ cup (30 g) shelled walnuts, crushed
- ⅓ cup (30 g) shelled pistachio, crushed
- 1 tablespoon granulated sugar
- 1 tablespoon orange blossom water

Glaze

- Confectioners' (icing) sugar, to dust

Serves: 10–12
Preparation: 1 hour
  + 6 hours to rest
Cooking: 15 minutes
Level: 2

■ ■ ■ *Traditionally, these pastries are filled with nuts or dates and served with small cups of hot cardamom-flavored Arabic coffee.*

ALMOND BOWS

Preheat the oven to 400°F (200°C/gas 6). • Brush a large baking sheet with melted butter and sprinkle with cold water. • <u>Filling</u>: Place the marzipan, apricot preserves, and butter in a medium bowl and beat with an electric mixer until smooth. • Roll the pastry out into a large rectangle measuring 14 x 20 inches (35 x 50 cm). • Working from the short side, spread the almond filling on the bottom half of the pastry and fold the top half over it toward you. Your rectangle will now measure 10 x 14 inches (25 x 35 cm). • Cut the filled pastry into 10 x $2/3$-inch (25 x 1.5-cm) strips with a sharp knife.• Loosely knot each strip into a bow. • Place on the prepared baking sheet and brush with evaporated milk. • Sprinkle with almonds, if liked, and bake for 15 minutes, or until puffed up and golden. • Transfer to a rack to cool. • Dust with the confectioners' sugar just before serving.

Filling

8 oz (250 g) marzipan, softened

1 tablespoon apricot preserves (jam)

$1/4$ cup (60 g) unsalted butter, softened

10 oz (300 g) puff pastry, thawed if frozen

Glaze

$3/4$ cup (180 g) evaporated milk or cream

2 tablespoons toasted almonds, coarsely chopped (optional)

2 tablespoons confectioners' (icing) sugar, to dust

Serves: 8–10
Preparation: 20 minutes
Cooking: 15 minutes
Level: 1

PALMIERS

Dust a work surface with confectioners' sugar. • Roll
the pastry out into a 5 x 5-inch (12 x 12-cm) square.
Roll the square out to a 10 x 5-inch (24 x 12-cm)
rectangle, and fold lengthwise into thirds. Give the
pastry rectangle one-quarter turn and roll out to a 10
by 5-inch (25 by 13-cm) rectangle again. Fold the
pastry into thirds. • Place on a plate and chill the
pastry in the refrigerator for 30 minutes. • Sprinkle
the surface with confectioners' sugar and roll out into
a 12-inch (30-cm) square about $1/8$ inch (3 mm) thick.
• Trim the edges with a sharp knife and cut the
square down the middle to make two 12 x 6-inch (30
x 15-cm) wide strips. • With the long edge facing you
and working from the short side, bring the two ends
of a strip halfway toward the center, so they meet in
the middle. • Fold them over lengthways to give you a
strip of 4 layers. • Repeat with the other strip. • Wrap
in plastic wrap (cling film) and chill in the refrigerator
for 30 minutes. • Butter two baking sheets and
sprinkle with cold water. • Remove the pastry bands
from the refrigerator, unwrap, and roll in the
confectioner's sugar. Cut each one into thin slices,
about $1/4$ inch (5 mm) wide and 3 inches (8 cm)
across. • Place cut-side down on the sheet in rows
$2^1/2$ inches (6 cm) apart. • Preheat the oven to 425°F
(220°C/gas 7). • Bake for 5–6 minutes, turn the
palmiers and bake for 5–6 more minutes, or until
golden and crisp. • Transfer to a rack with a spatula.
Let cool completely. • Serve on the same day they
are made.

8 oz (250 g) puff pastry,
   thawed if frozen

$2/3$ cup (100 g)
   confectioners' sugar

Serves: 8–10
Preparation: 1 hour
Cooking: 10–12 minutes
Level: 2

MINI NUT AND CHOCOLATE STRUDELS

Filling: Mix the nuts, sugar, and chocolate in a bowl. Sprinkle with the liqueur and stir in the orange juice. Set aside. • Lightly butter two baking sheets. • To Assemble: Mix the sugar and almonds in a small bowl. • Put the melted butter in a separate bowl. • Phyllo pastry usually comes in blocks of 8 x 12-inch (20 x 30-cm) sheets. Cut the block in half across the width, so each phyllo sheet is a 6 x 8-inch (15 x 20 cm) rectangle. (Keep the unused sheets covered with a damp tea towel to prevent the pastry from drying out.) • Place one rectangle before you on the work surface stretching out lengthways away from you. • Brush generously with melted butter. • Place another rectangle on top and brush with more butter. • Sprinkle with a little of the sugar and almond mix. • Spread 1 tablespoon of the filling along the short end nearest to you. • Fold the end over the filling and fold in the long edges. • Roll up away from you. • Place on the sheet, seam-side down. • Continue with the remaining phyllo sheets until all the filling is used up. • Preheat the oven to 325°F (170°C/gas 3). • Brush each mini strudel with the remaining butter and sprinkle with the sugar and almond mix. • Bake for 20 minutes, or until golden brown and crisp. • Leave on the sheets for 3 minutes. Remove to racks and dust with confectioners' sugar. Let cool. • Melt the chocolate in a double boiler over barely simmering water. • Fit a pastry bag with a plain writing nozzle and pipe zigzag lines over the strudels. • Leave to set.

Filling

1½ cups (150 g) hazelnuts, finely chopped

3 tablespoons light brown sugar

2 oz (60 g) dark chocolate, finely chopped

1 tablespoon orange liqueur

2 tablespoons freshly squeezed orange juice, strained

To Assemble

2 tablespoons sugar

4 tablespoons ground almonds

¼ cup (60 g) unsalted butter melted, for brushing

5 sheets phyllo pastry, thawed if frozen

Glaze

1 tablespoon confectioners' sugar, to dust

2 oz (60 g) dark chocolate, for piping

Serves: 10–12
Preparation: 40 minutes
Cooking: 20 minutes
Level: 2

RASPBERRY DOUBLE-DECKERS

Filling: Beat the cream in a large chilled bowl with an electric mixer on high speed until stiff. • Beat the mascarpone, Cointreau, and confectioners' sugar in a separate bowl until smooth. • Fold the mascarpone mixture into the cream. • Cover and chill in the refrigerator. • Put a piping bag fitted with a medium, fluted nozzle in the refrigerator • Generously dust a work surface with confectioners' sugar and roll out the pastry to $^1/_8$ inch (3 mm) thick. • Cut out 8 circles with a plain 3$^1/_2$-inch (9-cm) pastry cutter. • Butter a large baking sheet and brush with cold water. • Place the pastry rounds on the sheet, spacing 2 inches (5 cm) apart, and chill for 20 minutes. • Preheat the oven to 425°F (220°C/gas 7). • Bake the pastry rounds for 10 minutes, until golden and puffed up. • Transfer immediately with a palette knife to a rack and leave to cool. • Shortly before serving, make an indentation with a small sharp knife in the middle of four of the pastry rounds. • Fill each hole with cream and top with raspberries. Spoon the remaining cream into the chilled pastry bag and pipe a cream border around the rim of each of the four remaining pastry rounds. Place a decorated pastry round on top of a plain filled one. • Pipe a cream rosette on top and decorate with raspberries. • Lightly dust with confectioners' sugar.

■ ■ ■ *Bake the pastry only 1 or 2 hours before serving, and fill the double-deckers at the last moment.*

Filling

1$^1/_4$ cups (300 ml) heavy (double) cream

$^2/_3$ cup (150 g) mascarpone cheese

3 tablespoons Cointreau or lemon juice

2 tablespoons confectioners' sugar

1 cup (120 g) fresh raspberries

12 oz (350 g) puff pastry, thawed if frozen

5 tablespoons confectioners' sugar, for worktop and dusting

Serves: 4
Preparation: 25 minutes + 20 minutes to chill
Cooking: 10 minutes
Level: 2

BLACKBERRY AND APPLE STRUDEL

Preheat the oven to 425°F (220°C/gas 7). • Butter a large baking sheet. • <u>Filling</u>: Sauté the apples in 2 tablespoons of butter in a large frying pan over medium heat for 5 minutes. Stir in the blackberries and sugar and simmer, stirring often, for 8–10 minutes. Stir in the apricots, pecans, and cinnamon. Drain any juice and set aside to cool. • Lay the sheets of dough out flat and cover with a damp kitchen towel. (This will stop them from drying out.) • Brush the first sheet with melted butter. Sprinkle with some bread crumbs. Top with another sheet and brush with butter. Repeat with 4 more sheets, finishing with a phyllo layer. • Spread the blackberry mixture over the pastry and carefully roll it up. • Use spatulas to transfer to the baking sheet. Place seam-side down. Brush with the remaining butter. • Bake for 20–25 minutes, or until lightly browned. • Serve warm.

Filling

2 tart cooking apples (Granny Smiths are ideal), peeled, cored, and thinly sliced

1½ cups (200 g) fresh blackberries

¾ cup (150 g) sugar

½ cup (60 g) dried apricots, finely chopped

1 cup (150 g) pecans, toasted and coarsely chopped

1 teaspoon ground cinnamon

6 sheets phyllo dough, thawed if frozen

½ cup (125 g) + 2 tablespoons butter, melted

¼ cup (30 g) fine dry bread crumbs

Serves: 6–8
Preparation: 30 minutes
Cooking: 20–25 minutes
Level: 1

PINEAPPLE STRUDEL

Preheat the oven to 400°F (200°C/gas 6). • Butter a large baking sheet. • Lay the sheets of dough out flat and cover with a damp kitchen towel. (This will stop them from drying out.) • Brush the first sheet with butter. Top with a second sheet and brush with butter. Repeat with three more sheets. • Mix the apples, pineapple, cornstarch, pumpkin pie spice, vanilla, and honey in a large bowl. • Spread the pastry with the pineapple mixture, leaving a 1-inch (2.5-cm) border all around. • Cover with the remaining sheet of dough. Brush with butter. Carefully roll up the strudel. • Use spatulas to help transfer to the baking sheet. • Bake for 20–30 minutes, or until lightly browned. • Serve warm.

6   sheets phyllo dough, thawed if frozen

½   cup (125 g) butter, melted

3   apples, peeled, cored, and thinly sliced

8   oz (250 g) crushed pineapple, drained

1   tablespoon cornstarch (cornflour)

2   teaspoons pumpkin pie spice (all-spice)

1   teaspoon vanilla extract (essence)

3   tablespoons honey

Serves: 6–8
Preparation: 30 minutes
Cooking: 20–30 minutes
Level: 2

CHOCOLATE ÉCLAIRS

<u>Choux Pastry</u>: Place the water, butter, sugar, and salt in a large pan over medium-low heat. When the mixture boils, remove from the heat and add the flour all at once. Use a wooden spoon to stir vigorously until a smooth paste forms. Return to low heat and stir constantly until the mixture pulls away from the pan sides. Remove from the heat and let cool for 5 minutes. • Add 5 eggs, one at a time, until just blended after each addition. The batter should be shiny and stiff enough to hold its shape if dropped onto a baking sheet. Add another egg if the pastry is too stiff. • Preheat the oven to 425°F (210°C/gas 7). • Line a baking sheet with parchment paper. • Place the choux pastry in a pastry bag fitted with a $^3/_4$-inch (1.5-cm) tip and pipe ten 4-inch (10-cm) strips of pastry onto the baking sheet. • Lightly beat an egg with the water and brush over the pastry. Run the tines of a fork down the tops of the éclairs to encourage them to crack evenly during baking. • Bake for 15 minutes. Reduce the oven temperature to 400°F (200°C/gas 6) and bake for 15 minutes more. Remove from the oven and turn off the heat. Use the point of a sharp knife to make a few small cuts along the sides of the éclairs to release steam. Return the éclairs to the oven and leave the door slightly ajar for 10 minutes. • Transfer to racks to cool. • <u>Vanilla Pastry Cream</u>: Beat the egg yolks and sugar in a large bowl with an electric mixer on high speed until pale and

Choux Pastry

2   cups (500 ml) water

$^2/_3$ cup (150 g) unsalted butter, cut up

1   tablespoon sugar

$^1/_4$ teaspoon salt

$1^2/_3$ cups (250 g) all-purpose (plain) flour

6   large eggs + 1 extra, as required

1   teaspoon water

Vanilla Pastry Cream

5   large egg yolks

$^3/_4$ cup (150 g) sugar

$^1/_3$ cup (50 g) all-purpose (plain) flour

2   cups (500 ml) milk

    Pinch of salt

1   teaspoon vanilla extract (essence)

$^1/_2$ cup (125 ml) heavy (double) cream

Simple Chocolate Frosting

2   cups (300 g) confectioners' (icing) sugar

$^1/_4$ cup (30 g) unsweetened cocoa powder

2   tablespoons butter, softened

1 teaspoon vanilla extract
   (essence)

   **About 2 tablespoons
   boiling water**

Serves: 10
Preparation: 1 hour + 90
   minutes to cool and chill
Cooking: 30 minutes
Level: 3

thick. Stir in the flour, salt, and vanilla. • Bring the milk to a boil, then stir it into the egg mixture. • Simmer over low heat, stirring constantly with a wooden spoon, until the mixture thickens, about 10 minutes. • Remove from the heat and let cool, about 1 hour. • Beat the cream with an electric mixer at high speed until stiff. Fold into the cooled pastry cream. • <u>Simple Chocolate Frosting</u>: Stir the confectioners' sugar and cocoa in a double boiler. Add the butter, vanilla, and enough of the water to make a firm paste. Stir over simmering water until the frosting is thick and spreadable, about 3 minutes. • <u>To Assemble</u>: Just before serving, place the pastry cream in a pastry bag fitted with a 1/4-inch (5 mm) tip. Make a slit in the side of each éclair and fill with filling. • Spread the top of each éclair with the frosting. Refrigerate for 15 minutes.

COFFEE ÉCLAIRS

Prepare the choux pastry and the èclairs following the instructions for chocolate éclairs (see page 526) up to the stage when the éclairs have cooled. • Using a sharp knife, carefully slit each éclair in half lengthwise but without completeing detaching the two halves. • Coffee Cream Filling: Beat the cream, sugar, and coffee granules in a large bowl with an electric mixer at high speed until stiff. • Coffee Frosting: Place the confectioners' sugar in a small bowl and stir in the dissolved coffee. • To Assemble: Just before serving, place the pastry cream in a pastry bag fitted with a $1/4$-inch (5-mm) tip. Make a slit in the side of each éclair and fill with filling. • Spread the top of each éclair with the frosting. Refrigerate for 15 minutes. • If liked, decorate the tops with a little melted chocolate.

1   recipe Choux Pastry (see page 526)

Coffee Cream Filling

$2^1/2$ cups (575 ml) heavy (double) cream

$1/3$ cup (75 g) sugar

1   tablespoon freeze-dried coffee granules

Coffee Frosting

$1^1/2$ cups (225 g) confectioners' sugar

1   tablespoon freeze-dried coffee granules, dissolved in 1 tablespoon boiling water

Melted chocolate, to decorate (optional)

Serves: 10
Preparation: 1 hour + 90 minutes to cool and chill
Cooking: 30 minutes
Level: 3

ZABAGLIONE THOUSAND-LAYER CAKE

<u>Zabaglione</u>: Beat the egg yolks and sugar in a double boiler with an electric mixer at high speed until pale and very thick. • Gradually add the Marsala. • Place over barely simmering water and cook, beating constantly, until very thick, 10–15 minutes. Set aside to cool. Chill in the refrigerator for 2 hours. • Preheat the oven to 400°F (200°C/gas 6). • Line two baking sheets with parchment paper. • Unfold or unroll the pastry on a lightly floured work surface. Roll into four equal squares. • Place on the prepared baking sheets and prick all over with a fork. • Bake for 15–20 minutes, or until golden brown. • Sprinkle each piece of pastry with 1 tablespoon of confectioners' sugar and return to the oven to caramelize, about 5 minutes. • Cool the pastry on racks. • Use a large rubber spatula to fold the whipped cream and crumbled meringues into the chilled zabaglione. • Place one pastry layer on a serving plate and spread with one-third of the zabaglione. Sprinkle with raspberries and almonds. Repeat this layering process with two more pastry layers. Top with the remaining pastry and dust with confectioners' sugar.

Zabaglione

4 large egg yolks

¼ cup (50 g) sugar

½ cup (125 ml) dry Marsala wine or dry sherry

1 lb (500 g) fresh or frozen puff pastry, thawed if frozen

1 cup (150 g) confectioners' (icing) sugar

1 cup (250 ml) heavy (double) cream, whipped

1 cup (100 g) meringues, crumbled

1 cup (200 g) fresh raspberries

⅔ cup flaked almonds, toasted

Serves: 8–10
Preparation: 20 minutes
  + 2 hours to chill
Cooking: 25–35 minutes
Level: 2

WHITE CHOCOLATE THOUSAND-LAYER CAKE

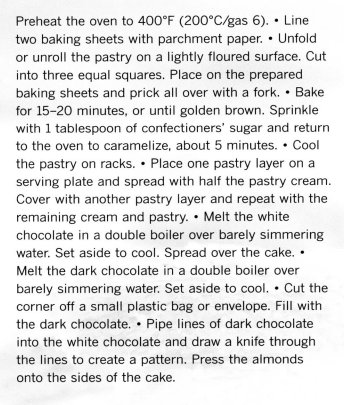

Preheat the oven to 400°F (200°C/gas 6). • Line two baking sheets with parchment paper. • Unfold or unroll the pastry on a lightly floured surface. Cut into three equal squares. Place on the prepared baking sheets and prick all over with a fork. • Bake for 15–20 minutes, or until golden brown. Sprinkle with 1 tablespoon of confectioners' sugar and return to the oven to caramelize, about 5 minutes. • Cool the pastry on racks. • Place one pastry layer on a serving plate and spread with half the pastry cream. Cover with another pastry layer and repeat with the remaining cream and pastry. • Melt the white chocolate in a double boiler over barely simmering water. Set aside to cool. Spread over the cake. • Melt the dark chocolate in a double boiler over barely simmering water. Set aside to cool. • Cut the corner off a small plastic bag or envelope. Fill with the dark chocolate. • Pipe lines of dark chocolate into the white chocolate and draw a knife through the lines to create a pattern. Press the almonds onto the sides of the cake.

1 lb (500 g) fresh or frozen puff pastry, thawed if frozen

3 tablespoons confectioners' sugar

1 recipe Vanilla Pastry Cream (see page 526)

8 oz (250 g) white chocolate, coarsely chopped

2 oz (60 g) dark chocolate, coarsely chopped

1 cup (120 g) flaked almonds

Serves: 10–12
Preparation: 45 minutes
Cooking: 10–15 minutes
Level: 2

ALMOND AND WALNUT BAKLAVA

Preheat the oven to 400°F (200°C/gas 6). • Butter a large jelly-roll pan. • Lay the sheets of dough out flat and cover with a damp kitchen towel. (This will stop them from drying out.) • Mix the almonds, walnuts, cinnamon, and cloves in a large bowl. • Fit one phyllo sheet in the pan and brush with butter. Fit another sheet on top and brush with butter. Place another 3 sheets on top, brushing each one with butter. Sprinkle with the nut mixture. Cover with the remaining sheets of pastry, brushing each one with butter. • Cut the baklava into squares and drizzle with the remaining butter. • Bake for about 30 minutes, or until golden brown. • Syrup: Place all the ingredients in a medium saucepan and bring to a boil. Simmer over low heat for 10–15 minutes, or until deep golden brown and syrupy. • Drizzle the syrup over the baklava after removing it from the oven. • Let rest for at least 4 hours before serving.

10 sheets phyllo pastry, thawed if frozen

3 cups (350 g) chopped almonds

3 cups (350 g) chopped walnuts

1 tablespoon ground cinnamon

1 teaspoon ground cloves

2/3 cup (180 g) butter, melted

Syrup

2¼ cups (450 g) sugar

1¼ cups (300 ml) water

1/3 cup (90 g) honey

2 teaspoons freshly squeezed lemon juice

½ teaspoon vanilla extract (essence)

Serves: 10–12
Preparation: 45 minutes + 4 hours to rest
Cooking: 50 minutes
Level: 2

PISTACHIO BAKLAVA

Preheat the oven to 350°F (180°C/gas 4). • Butter a large jelly-roll pan. • Lay the sheets of phyllo out flat and cover with waxed paper and a damp kitchen towel. (This will stop them from drying out.) • Butter a baking sheet. • Process 4 cups (600 g) of almonds with the pistachios, confectioners' sugar, orange-flower water, and cardamom in a food processor until very finely chopped. • Place a phyllo sheet in the prepared pan and brush with butter. Cover with 6 more sheets, brushing each one with butter. • Spread with the almond mixture and top with the remaining 5 sheets of pastry, brushing each one with butter. • Use a knife to cut into diamond shapes. Sprinkle with the remaining almonds and brush with butter. • Bake for about 50 minutes, or until browned. • Heat the honey in a saucepan until liquid. Drizzle the honey over the baklava. • Cut into diamonds and rest overnight.

12 sheets phyllo dough, thawed if frozen

5 cups (750 g) almonds

2 cups (300 g) pistachios

1 cup (150 g) confectioners' (icing) sugar

3 tablespoons orange-flower water or rose water

1 teaspoon ground cardamom

1 cup (250 g) butter, melted

1 cup (150 g) whole almonds

1¼ cups (300 ml) honey

Serves: 10–12
Preparation: 2 hours
    + 12 hours to rest
Cooking: 50 minutes
Level: 2

PEACH PUFF

Preheat the oven to 400°F (200°C/gas 6). • Set out a baking sheet. • Mix the peaches, almonds, pistachios, amaretti crumbs, sugar, and vanilla in a large bowl. • Roll the pastry out on a lightly floured work surface in a $1/8$-inch (3 mm) thick rectangle. Prick all over with a fork. Place the pastry on the prepared sheet. • Spoon the peach mixture into the center. Fold the pastry over and tuck in the ends to seal. Turn seam-side down on the baking sheet. Cut slashes into the top of the pastry. • Brush with the beaten egg and dust with the confectioners' sugar. • Bake for about 40 minutes, or until golden brown. • Serve warm.

1   lb (500 g) peaches, peeled, pitted, and cut into cubes

1   cup (100 g) slivered almonds

½   cup (50 g) pistachios, chopped

3   amaretti cookies, lightly crushed

2   tablespoons sugar

1   teaspoon vanilla extract (essence)

1   lb (500 g) fresh or frozen puff pastry, thawed if frozen

1   large egg, lightly beaten

Confectioners' (icing) sugar, to dust

Serves: 6–8
Preparation: 30 minutes
Cooking: 40 minutes
Level: 1

CINNAMON APPLE PUFF

Preheat the oven to 400°F (200°C/gas 6). Butter a jelly-roll pan. • Set aside one-quarter of the pastry and roll the remainder out on a lightly floured surface into a rectangle large enough to line the base and sides of the pan. Fit into the jelly-roll pan, pressing up the sides. Prick all over with a fork. • Stir the applesauce, sugar, lemon zest, and cinnamon in a large bowl. Spread evenly over the pastry. • Roll out the remaining dough and cut into long strips. Arrange the strips over the apple filling in a lattice pattern, sealing them to the pastry sides. Brush the egg yolk over the pastry. • Bake for about 30 minutes, or until golden brown. • Serve warm.

1 lb (500 g) fresh or frozen puff pastry, thawed if frozen

2 cups (500 ml) unsweetened applesauce

⅓ cup (70 g) sugar

1 tablespoon finely grated lemon zest

1 teaspoon ground cinnamon

1 large egg yolk, lightly beaten

Serves: 8–10
Preparation: 30 minutes
Cooking: 30 minutes
Level: 1

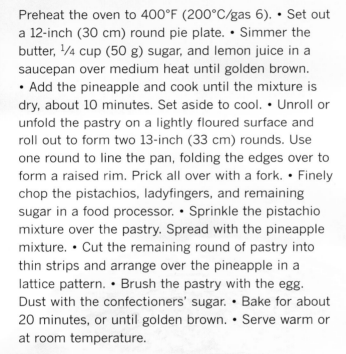

PINEAPPLE AND PISTACHIO PUFF

544

Preheat the oven to 400°F (200°C/gas 6). • Set out a 12-inch (30 cm) round pie plate. • Simmer the butter, $1/4$ cup (50 g) sugar, and lemon juice in a saucepan over medium heat until golden brown. • Add the pineapple and cook until the mixture is dry, about 10 minutes. Set aside to cool. • Unroll or unfold the pastry on a lightly floured surface and roll out to form two 13-inch (33 cm) rounds. Use one round to line the pan, folding the edges over to form a raised rim. Prick all over with a fork. • Finely chop the pistachios, ladyfingers, and remaining sugar in a food processor. • Sprinkle the pistachio mixture over the pastry. Spread with the pineapple mixture. • Cut the remaining round of pastry into thin strips and arrange over the pineapple in a lattice pattern. • Brush the pastry with the egg. Dust with the confectioners' sugar. • Bake for about 20 minutes, or until golden brown. • Serve warm or at room temperature.

1   **tablespoon butter**
$1/3$ **cup (70 g) sugar**
2   **tablespoons freshly squeezed lemon juice**
1   **fresh pineapple, weighing about 2 lb (1 kg), peeled and finely chopped**
1   **lb (500 g) fresh or frozen puff pastry, thawed if frozen**
1   **cup (120 g) pistachios**
3   **ladyfingers**
1   **large egg, lightly beaten**
2   **tablespoons confectioners' (icing) sugar, to dust**

Serves: 10
Preparation: 40 minutes
Cooking: 30 minutes
Level: 2

ORANGE PUFF

Line a 12-inch (30-cm) pie plate with parchment paper. Dampen the paper. • Beat the butter and brown sugar in a small bowl with an electric mixer at high speed until creamy. Spread in the prepared pie plate. Refrigerate for 30 minutes. • Arrange the orange slices on the prepared base, overlapping them slightly. • Preheat the oven to 350°F (180°C/gas 4). • Roll the pastry out on a lightly floured surface to a 12-inch (30-cm) round. Place the pastry over the oranges. Prick all over with a fork. • Bake for 20–30 minutes, or until the edges of the pastry are crisp. • Invert onto a serving plate. Carefully remove the paper and serve. • If the surface is not caramelized, place under the broiler (grill) for a few minutes.

¼ cup (60 g) butter
¼ cup (50 g) firmly packed brown sugar
1 large orange, very thinly sliced
1 lb (500 g) frozen puff pastry, thawed

Serves: 8
Preparation: 15 minutes
Cooking: 20–30 minutes
Level: 1

YEAST CAKES

APPLE CRUMBLE KUCHEN

Dough: Combine the flour, sugar, vanilla sugar, and salt in a large bowl. • Place the milk in a small bowl and stir in the yeast. Set aside for 10 minutes until frothy. • Add the yeast mixture, butter, and egg to the flour and stir with a plastic spatula, or with a mixer fitted with a dough hook at low speed. Mix to a medium soft dough, adding a little more flour if needed. • Knead for 10 minutes, or for 5 minutes with the dough hook, until the dough is smooth and springy and comes away from the sides of the bowl. • Cover with a clean kitchen towel and let rise in a warm place for 1–2 hours, or until doubled in bulk.

Apple Topping: Peel, quarter, and core the apples, then slice thinly. Sprinkle with lemon juice and zest.

Streusel Topping: Put the flour and both sugars in a bowl and rub in the butter until crumbly. Stir in the almonds. • Lightly butter a $10^1/_2$ x $15^1/_2$-inch (26 x 40-cm) jellyroll pan. • Dust your hands with flour, punch the risen dough down, and knead briefly on a lightly floured work surface. • Place the dough in the pan, stretching and pulling to fill it. • Brush the dough with melted butter and arrange the apple slices, close together and overlapping, on top. • Sprinkle with the golden raisins. • Sprinkle the streusel crumble over the top, pressing it down lightly. • Let rise for 1 hour more. • Preheat the oven to 400°F (200°C/gas 6). • Bake for 10 minutes. • Decrease the oven temperature to 350°F (180°C/gas 4) and bake for 10–15 minutes more, or until well risen and golden brown at the edges. • Leave for 10 minutes in the pan before slicing. • Serve warm with whipped cream.

Dough

- 2½ cups (375 g) all-purpose (plain) flour
- 3 tablespoons sugar
- 1 tablespoon vanilla sugar
- ¼ teaspoon salt
- ¾ cup (200 ml) lukewarm (110°F/43°C) milk
- ½ oz (15 g) fresh yeast or 1 (¼-oz/7-g) package active dry yeast
- ¼ cup (60 g) butter, melted
- 1 large egg, beaten

Apple Topping

- 8 large apples
  Finely grated zest and juice of ½ lemon
- 2 tablespoons golden raisins (sultanas)
- 2 tablespoons melted butter

Streusel Topping

- 1⅓ cups (200 g) all-purpose (plain) flour
- ⅓ cup (70 g) sugar
- 2 tablespoons vanilla sugar
- ½ cup (125 g) butter, chilled
- ½ cup (40 g) flaked almonds

Serves: 8–10
Preparation: 45 minutes + 3 hours to rise
Cooking: 20–25 minutes
Level: 2

MARZIPAN PLUM TART

Dough: Combine the flour, sugar, and salt in a large bowl. • Place the milk in a small bowl and stir in the yeast. Set aside for 10 minutes until frothy. • Add the yeast mixture, butter, and egg to the flour and stir with a plastic spatula, or with a mixer fitted with a dough hook at low speed, and mix to a medium soft dough, adding a little more flour if needed. • Knead for 10 minutes, or for 5 minutes with the dough hook, until the dough is smooth and springy and comes away from the sides of the bowl. • Butter an 11-inch (28 cm) springform pan. Line with parchment paper. • Place the dough in the pan. Flour your fingers and stretch it to fit. • Cover with a clean kitchen towel and leave to rise for 1–2 hours, or until doubled in bulk. • Filling: Beat the marzipan, preserves, egg, and rum with an electric mixer on low speed until smooth. • Mix in the almonds. • Carefully spread the marzipan mixture on the risen dough with a round-bladed knife. • Topping: Arrange the plums, overlapping, in circles on top. Sprinkle with the brown sugar. • Leave to rise for 15 minutes. • Preheat the oven to 400°F (200°C/gas 6).• Bake for 25–30 minutes, or until the dough is golden brown at the edges and the plums are soft. • Seve warm or at room temperature.

Dough

1⅓ cups (200 g) all-purpose (plain) flour

4 tablespoons superfine (caster) sugar

¼ teaspoon salt

7 tablespoons lukewarm (110°F/43°C) milk

½ oz (15 g) compressed fresh yeast or 1 (¼-oz/ 7-g) package active dry yeast

2 tablespoons butter, melted

1 large egg, beaten

Filling

7 oz (200 g) marzipan, softened

2 tablespoons plum preserves (jam)

1 large egg

2 tablespoons rum or (plum/apricot) juice

2 tablespoons almonds, finely chopped

Topping

1½ lb (750 g) plums, pitted and quartered

1 tablespoon brown sugar

Serves: 6–8

Preparation: 45 minutes + 2 hours 15 minutes to rise

Cooking: 30 minutes

Level: 2

STRAWBERRY LATTICE CAKE

Dough: Place the milk and yeast in a small bowl. Set aside for 10 minutes until frothy. • Combine the flour, sugar, and salt in a large bowl. • Rub in the butter with your fingertips, or an electric mixer with a dough hook at low speed for 30 seconds, until the butter is evenly dispersed. • Stir in the yeast mixture, eggs, and lemon zest to form a soft dough. • Transfer to a floured work surface and knead by hand until smooth and elastic, about 10 minutes, or beat with a dough hook until smooth and elastic, 5 minutes. • Shape into a ball and place in an oiled bowl. Cover with a clean kitchen towel and let rise in a warm place for 1 hour, or until doubled in bulk. Filling: Place the sliced strawberries, lemon peel, sugar, and water in a stainless steel pan. Simmer over low heat for 8–10 minutes, until the sugar has dissolved. • Butter a 10½ x 15½-inch (25 x 40-cm) jellyroll pan. • Punch the risen dough down and knead on a lightly floured work surface. Press into the pan. • Let rise for 30 minutes. • Preheat the oven to 400°F (200°C/gas 6). • Brush the dough with butter and sprinkle with the bread crumb mixture. Cover with the strawberries. • Bake for 10–15 minutes, or until the edges are golden. • Meringue Topping: Beat the egg whites in a large bowl with an electric mixer until soft peaks form. Gradually add the sugar, vanilla, and lemon juice, beating until stiff peaks form. • Fit a pastry bag with a ½-inch (1 cm) star tip. • Fill the bag and pipe a lattice pattern over the cake. • Return to the oven for 15 minutes, until the meringue is crisp. Let cool in the pan.

Dough
- ½ cup (125 ml) lukewarm (110°F/43°C) milk
- ½ oz (15 g) fresh yeast or 1 (¼-oz/7-g) package active dry yeast
- 2⅓ cups (350 g) all-purpose (plain) flour
- 4 tablespoons sugar
- ½ teaspoon salt
- ¼ cup (50 g) butter, diced
- 1 large egg + 2 large egg yolks, beaten
- 2 teaspoons finely grated lemon zest

Filling
- 4 cups (600 g) strawberries
- 2 strips lemon peel
- 1 cup (200 g) sugar
- 2 tablespoons water
- 2 tablespoons melted butter
- 3 tablespoons fresh bread crumbs, mixed with 1 tablespoon brown sugar

Meringue Topping
- 3 large egg whites
- ¾ cup (150 g) sugar
- ½ teaspoon vanilla extract
- 2 teaspoons lemon juice

Serves 8–10
Preparation: 50 minutes + 90 minutes to rise
Cooking: 25–30 minutes
Level: 2

STOLLEN

Dough: Place the raisins in a small bowl, drizzle with the rum, and leave to soak for 2 hours or overnight. • Place the yeast in a medium bowl with 1 teaspoon of sugar. Add the milk and stir until smooth. Add 1 cup (150 g) of the flour and mix well into a runny paste. This is your yeast starter. • Set the bowl aside in a warm, draft-free place for 15–20 minutes, or until the yeast mixture has doubled in bulk. • In the meantime, combine the remaining sugar, butter, salt, egg, vanilla, lemon zest, spices, and the remaining flour in a large warmed bowl. • When the starter is ready, pour it into the bowl and mix into a soft and rather sticky dough. • Turn out onto a lightly floured work surface, dust your fingers with flour, and knead the dough for 10 minutes, until it is soft and elastic and no longer sticky. Alternatively, use an electric mixer fitted with a dough hook and knead the dough for 1–2 minutes at low speed and then at high speed for 5 minutes, until it comes away clean from the sides of the bowl. • Place in a lightly oiled bowl, cover with a clean kitchen towel or plastic wrap (cling film) and set aside in a warm place for 1 hour, or until it has doubled in bulk. • Dust a work surface with flour, punch the risen dough down, and turn it out onto the work surface. • Scatter the soaked raisins, mixed peel, and almonds on the dough and knead briefly, gradually working the fruit and nuts into it. Try not to squash the raisins, as the juice discolors the dough. • Flatten the dough into a rectangle about 14 x 10 inches (35 x 25 cm) with a rolling pin. • Roll out the

Dough

- 2 cups (350 g) raisins
- ¼ cup (60 ml) rum
- 1 oz (30 g) compressed fresh yeast or 2 (¼-oz/7-g) packages active dry yeast
- ⅓ cup (70 g) sugar
- ⅓ cup (90 ml) lukewarm (110°F/43°C) milk
- 3⅓ cups (500 g) all-purpose (plain) flour
- 1 cup (250 g) butter
- ½ teaspoon salt
- 1 large egg
- 1 teaspoon vanilla extract (essence)
- Finely grated zest of 1 lemon
- ¼ teaspoon ground cardamom
- ¼ teaspoon ground mace
- ¼ teaspoon nutmeg
- 1 cup (100 g) mixed peel
- 1 cup (150 g) almonds, roughly chopped
- 8 oz (250 g) marzipan, softened

Glaze

²⁄₃ **cup (150 g) butter, melted**

4 **tablespoons vanilla-flavored sugar**

²⁄₃ **cup (100 g) confectioners' (icing) sugar**

Serves: 10–15
Preparation: 45 minutes + 2–12 hours to soak + 2 hours 15–20 minutes to rise
Cooking: 45 minutes
Level: 3

marzipan into a rectangle measuring 12 x 6 inches (30 x 15 cm) and place on top of the dough. • Roll the Stollen up lengthways finishing with the fold on top, running down the middle. Pat into a loaf shape. Cut into the fold of the Stollen with a sharp knife to make a 1-inch (2.5-cm) deep ridge. Leave the ends uncut. • Line a cookie sheet with a double layer of baking parchment and lift the Stollen on to it. • Cover with a towel or slip the baking sheet into a plastic carrier bag and return to a warm place to rise for another hour, or until almost doubled in bulk. • Preheat the oven to 400°F (200°C/gas 6). • Place the loaf on a low oven rack and bake for 20 minutes. Decrease the oven temperature to 350°F (180°C/gas 4) and move the Stollen to the center of the oven. Bake for another 20–25 minutes, or until the top is pale golden and the bottom is baked and golden brown too. • <u>Glaze</u>: Take out of the oven and brush with half the butter. Dust with the vanilla sugar and half the confectioners' sugar. • Let cool for 5 minutes, then brush with the remaining butter and confectioners' sugar.

■ ■ ■ *Stollen is a fruit bread from Germany, especially the city of Dresden. The name comes from the Old High German word* stollo, *which means "post," although it is said that the oblong shape with a ridge down the middle represents baby Jesus in swaddling clothes. That's why it is also called* Christstollen. *It can be made with or the without marzipan.*

DANISH PASTRIES

Pastry: Mix $1/2$ teaspoon of sugar, 2 tablespoons of milk, and the yeast together in a small bowl. Set aside for 10 minutes until frothy. • Place the flour, salt, and remaining sugar in a large bowl. • Rub 2 tablespoons of butter into the flour mixture with your fingertips, until it resembles fine bread crumbs. • Add the yeast mixture, 3 tablespoons of milk, and the egg, and mix to a soft dough with a fork. • Knead lightly until smooth, adding a little more milk if necessary, and shape into a ball. • Wrap in plastic wrap (cling film) and chill in the refrigerator for 10 minutes. • Flour a work surface, roll the ball into a flat circle, and then roll out 4 flaps from it to form a star shape. • Shape the remaining butter into a rectangular tile, just big enough to fit in the center of the dough star. Place on the dough and fold the flaps over the top, overlapping them slightly, so that the butter is completely enclosed. • Turn the dough and roll gently away from you into a strip measuring roughly 5 x 15 inches (13 x 37 cm). • Fold the dough in three, bringing the bottom third up to the center and the top third down over it, making it a square. Seal the edges, cover the dough square, and place in the refrigerator to rest for 10 minutes. • Repeat the rolling, folding, and chilling twice more. • Apricot Filling: Chop the apricots roughly and mix with the preserves. • Almond Filling: Process the almonds and sugar until finely ground. • Add the butter and almond extract and pulse briefly. • Stir in

Pastry

3   teaspoons superfine (caster) sugar

$1/3$ cup (90 ml) lukewarm (110°F/43°C) milk

$1/2$ oz (15 g) compressed fresh yeast or 1 ($1/4$-oz/ 7-g) package active dry yeast

$1^2/3$ cups (250 g) all-purpose (plain) flour

$1/3$ teaspoon salt

$1^3/4$ cups (180 g) butter, slightly softened

1   large egg, beaten

Apricot Filling

$1/2$ cup (90 g) dried apricots (soaked overnight and drained)

$1/3$ cup (90 ml) apricot preserves (jam)

1   egg beaten, to brush

Almond Filling

$3/4$ cup (120 g) blanched almonds, toasted

$1/3$ cup (70 g) superfine (caster) sugar

1   tablespoon butter, softened

1/4 teaspoon almond
    extract (essence)
1 large egg, lightly beaten

Glaze

2/3 cup (100 g)
    confectioners' (icing)
    sugar
1 tablespoon freshly
    squeezed lemon juice
1 tablespoon water

Serves: 8–10
Preparation: 1 hour
  + 30 minutes to soak
  + 90 minutes to rise
Cooking: 15 minutes
Level: 3

enough egg to make a firm paste. • Shaping the Pastries: Roll the dough out into a long rectangle to about 1/4 inch (5 mm) thick. Cut into 3-inch (8-cm) squares and place a heaped spoonful of the filling in the center of each square. • For triangles, stick the edges together with water and fold diagonally. • For stars, make 1 1/2-inch (4-cm) cuts at each corner and fold the 4 dough points into the center. Pinch together to seal. • For parcels, bring up the opposite corners of the dough square to the center and press them together with a little water. • For combs, fold the filled pastry square in half and seal the edges with water. Make 1/2-inch (1-cm) slits along the long sealed side. • Brush all the shapes with a little beaten egg. • Butter 2 baking sheets and place the pastries on them, spacing well. • Slip the sheets into a plastic bag and leave in a warm place for 30–60 minutes, until the pastries have almost doubled in bulk. • Preheat the oven to 400°F (200°C/gas 6). • Brush the risen pastries again with the remaining egg and bake for 10–15 minutes, until they are puffy and golden brown. • Transfer to racks with a spatula. • Glaze: Mix the confectioners' sugar, lemon juice, and water in a small saucepan into a paste, and warm over low heat. • Drizzle over the pastries as they cool.

■ ■ ■ *The fillings can be made in advance and kept in the refrigerator for up to a week. The pastries are best on the day they are made.*

POTECA
(SLOVENIAN NUT RING)

Dough: Melt the butter with the milk in a small saucepan over low heat. Remove from the heat and let cool to lukewarm. Stir in the yeast. Set aside for 10 minutes until frothy. • Combine $2^2/_3$ cups (400 g) of flour in a large bowl with the salt and sugar. • Pour in the yeast mixture and egg yolks. Using your fingers, gradually draw the flour into the liquid and mix until the dough comes away from the sides of the bowl, adding more flour if needed. • Transfer to a floured work surface and knead until smooth and elastic, about 10 minutes, or beat with a dough hook until smooth and elastic, 5 minutes. • Shape into a ball and place in an oiled bowl. Cover with a clean kitchen towel and let rise for 1–2 hours, until doubled in bulk. • Filling: Beat the egg whites in a large bowl with an electric mixer on high speed until soft peaks form. Gradually add the sugar and lemon juice and beat until stiff and glossy. • Fold in the walnuts and zest. • Knead the dough for 3–4 minutes. Roll out into a 15 x 25-inch (37 x 63 cm) rectangle. • Spread with the filling, leaving a 2-inch (5-cm) border. • Roll up from one long side and pinch the seam to seal. • Shape into a ring. Wet the ends with a little water and press together to seal. • Butter a baking sheet and carefully transfer the roll to it. • Cover and let rise in a warm place for 30–45 minutes, until nearly doubled in bulk. • Preheat the oven to 400°F (200°C/gas 6). • Glaze: Beat the yolk with the milk and sugar and brush over the dough ring. • Bake for 15 minutes. • Decrease the oven temperature to 350°F (180°C/gas 4) and bake for 30–35 minutes, or until golden brown.

Dough

½ cup (125 g) butter

⅔ cup (150 ml) milk

3   cups (450 g) all-purpose (plain) flour

1   teaspoon salt

½ cup (100 g) sugar

½ oz (15 g) compressed fresh yeast or 1 (¹/₄-oz/ 7-g) package active dry yeast

2   large egg yolks, beaten

Filling

3   large egg whites

½ cup (100 g) superfine (caster) sugar

¼ teaspoon lemon juice

2   cups (200 g) walnuts, finely chopped

    Zest of 1 lemon, finely grated

    Zest of 1 orange, finely grated

Glaze

1   large egg yolk

1½ tablespoons milk

1   tablespoon brown sugar

Serves: 8–10
Preparation: 40 minutes
  + 2 hours to rise
Cooking: 45–50 minutes
Level: 2

KUGELHOPF

Mix the yeast, sugar, and milk in a small bowl. Set aside for 10 minutes until frothy. • Combine the flour, sugar, and salt in a large bowl. Pour in the yeast mixture, melted butter, and vanilla, followed by the eggs. • Mix with a spatula until smooth. Alternatively, use an electric mixer fitted with a dough hook and knead for 1 minute at low speed and then at high speed for 5 minutes. • Add the golden raisins, currants, almonds, peel, zest, and rum or juice. Mix well for 2 minutes. • Cover the bowl with a clean kitchen towel or plastic wrap (cling film) and leave in a warm place for 1–2 hours, until doubled in bulk. • Brush the inside of a $9^1/_2$-inch (24-cm) Kugelhopf mold with butter or oil. Make sure the flutes are well greased. • Briefly knead the risen dough or beat for 30 seconds with the dough hook attachment. • Turn the mixture into the pan and leave to rise again in a warm place for about 40 minutes, until almost level with the rim of the pan. • Preheat the oven to 350°F (180°C/gas 4). • Bake for 50–60 minutes, until golden brown and just starting to shrink from the sides of the pan, or until a skewer inserted into the center comes out clean. • Let cool in the mold for 10 minutes before turning out carefully. Serve warm.

■ ■ ■ *Kugelhopf is baked in a ring-shaped fluted mold, but can be done in any other tube pan. Kugelhopf originated in Austria—the German word* Kugel *means ball or sphere. It was traditionally baked for Sunday breakfast when the village baker had his day off.*

1   oz (30 g) compressed fresh yeast or 2 ($^1/_4$-oz/7-g) packages active dry yeast

1   teaspoon sugar

$^3/_4$ cup (200 ml) lukewarm (110°F/43°C) milk

3   cups (450 g) all-purpose (plain) flour

$^3/_4$ cup (150 g) sugar

$^1/_2$ teaspoon salt

$^3/_4$ cup (200 g) butter, melted and cooled

1   teaspoon vanilla extract (essence)

$^1/_2$ cup (100 g) golden raisins (sultanas)

$^3/_4$ cup (150 g) currants

$^1/_2$ cup (100 g) almonds, coarsely chopped

$^1/_2$ cup (50 g) mixed peel

1   tablespoon finely grated lemon zest

2   tablespoons rum or lemon juice

4   large eggs, beaten

Serves: 8–10
Preparation: 35 minutes
   + 2–3 hours to rise
Cooking: 50–60 minutes
Level: 2

RHUBARB CREAM DELIGHT

Dough: Mix the yeast and milk in a small bowl. Set aside for 10 minutes until frothy. • Combine the flour, both sugars, and salt in a large bowl. • Add the yeast mixture, lemon zest, butter, and eggs. Stir to a medium-soft dough, adding a little more flour if needed. • Transfer to a lightly floured work surface and knead until smooth and elastic, about 10 minutes, or beat with a dough hook until smooth and elastic, 5 minutes. • Cover with a clean kitchen towel and let rise in a warm place for about 90 minutes, until doubled in bulk. • Filling: Slice the strawberries, place in a bowl, and sprinkle with the brown sugar. • Butter a $10^{1}/_{2}$ x $15^{1}/_{2}$-inch (26 x 40 cm) jellyroll pan. • Punch the risen dough down and knead briefly. • Press the dough into the pan. • Brush with the butter and sprinkle with the cookie crumbs. • Spoon the strawberries on top with a slotted spoon, reserving the juices. • Leave to rise for 15 minutes in a warm place. • Preheat the oven to 375°F (190°C/gas 5). • Bake for 10 minutes. • Topping: Beat the egg yolks and sugar in a medium bowl with an electric mixer at high speed until pale and creamy. Mix in the sour cream and reserved strawberry juice. • Beat the egg whites in a separate bowl until stiff then fold into the yolk mixture. • Remove the half-baked cake from the oven and spoon the creamy egg mixture on top. Bake for 20 minutes, or until the dough is swelling, golden at the edges, and golden on top. • Leave in the pan for 15 minutes before cutting into slices. Serve warm.

Dough

- ½ oz (15 g) fresh yeast or 1 ($^{1}/_{4}$-oz/7-g) package active dry yeast
- ½ cup (125 ml) lukewarm (110°F/43°C) milk
- $2^{2}/_{3}$ cups (400 g) all-purpose (plain) flour
- 3 tablespoons sugar
- 1 tablespoon vanilla sugar
- ½ teaspoon salt
- 1 teaspoon finely grated lemon zest
- ¼ cup (50 g) butter, melted
- 2 large eggs

Filling

- 2½ lb (1.25 kg) strawberries
- 5 tablespoons brown sugar
- 2 tablespoons melted butter, for brushing
- 3 amaretti cookies, crushed

Topping

- 3 large eggs, separated
- ⅓ cup (70 g) sugar
- ½ cup (125 ml) sour cream

Serves: 8–10
Preparation: 40 minutes + 1 hour 45 minutes to rise
Cooking: 50–60 minutes
Level: 2

BRIOCHE

Mix the yeast, 1 teaspoon of sugar, and the milk in a small bowl. Set aside for 10 minutes until frothy. • Combine the flour, remaining sugar, and salt in a large bowl. • Make a well in the center and pour in the eggs, milk, and yeast mixture. • Electric Mixer: Knead the dough with an electric mixer fitted with a dough hook for 8–10 minutes, until smooth. • Beat the butter, one piece at a time, into the dough with mixer at low speed. • Mix for 5 minutes, until the dough is smooth and elastic. Mixing by hand: Gradually draw the flour into the eggs and yeast mixture with a plastic spatula. Mix until you have a soft dough. This will take about 15 minutes. • Work small pieces of butter into the dough with your hands, rubbing and squeezing the butter in. • Flour your hands, gather the dough together, and knead on a lightly floured surface for 15 minutes, until smooth and elastic. • Form the smooth dough into a ball, place in an oiled bowl, cover with a clean kitchen towel, and leave to rise at room temperature for 2–3 hours, until doubled in bulk. (The temperature should be about 75°F/24°C, no hotter, as the butter will melt and separate out from the dough.) • Punch the risen dough down, turn out onto a lightly floured work surface and knead for 2–3 minutes. • Return to the bowl and place in the refrigerator for several hours or overnight, ready to bake for breakfast the next day. • Butter a large 1 quart (1 liter) brioche mold. • For a Large Brioche: Divide the dough into two pieces—three quarters

1   oz (30 g) compressed fresh yeast or 2 ($^{1}/_{4}$-oz/ 7-g) packages active dry yeast

2   tablespoons sugar

$^{1}/_{3}$ cup (90 ml) lukewarm (110°F/43°C) milk

3   cups (450 g) all-purpose (plain) flour

1   teaspoon salt

4   large eggs, beaten

$^{3}/_{4}$ cup (200 g) butter, cut into small pieces and softened

Egg Wash

1   large egg yolk, lightly beaten with 1 tablespoon milk

Serves: 12–15
Preparation: 30 minutes + 12–15 hours to rest and rise
Cooking: 40 minutes for large brioche; 8–12 minutes for brioche buns
Level: 3

■ ■ ■ Brioche is a buttery French bread with a soft cake-like texture. It is baked in a deep, round, fluted mold. The traditional Parisian brioche, known as brioche à tête *(brioche with a head) is made by placing a small dough ball on top of a larger one. Brioche Nanterre is made in a rectangular loaf pan with several small dough balls placed around the sides. Small fluted molds (3¼-inches/8-cm in diameter) are used for brioche buns. Serve the brioches warm with fruit compote or chocolate mousse, or slice and serve for breakfast with apricot or raspberry preserves (jam). Brioche dough can be frozen and thawed in the refrigerator before baking.*

and a quarter. • Roll the larger piece into a ball and place in the brioche mold. • Press a deep hole in the center. Roll the smaller piece into an egg shape and press it, pointed end down, into the hole of the large ball. Keep your fingertips lightly floured and gently push the rounded top well down, so it is almost level with the surrounding dough. • <u>For Brioche Buns</u>: Butter 18 small brioche molds or muffin cups. • Divide the dough into 18 portions of three quarters and a quarter. Roll into balls, place one of the larger pieces in each mold, make a hole, and press the smaller ball into it. • Cover and leave to rise for about 90 minutes for a large brioche and 20 minutes for brioche buns. • Preheat the oven to 425°F (220°C/gas 7). • Lightly glaze the brioche top with the egg wash. • Snip 5 little cuts around the edges of the large brioche with sharp scissors dipped in cold water. Do not snip the edges of the brioche buns. • Bake the large brioche for 20 minutes. Decrease the oven temperature to 375°F (190°C/gas 5) and bake for 15–20 more minutes. Cover loosely with foil toward the end of baking if the glaze begins to burn. • The brioche is done when a skewer inserted in the center comes out clean. • Brioche buns only need to bake for 8–12 minutes at the higher temperature, until golden brown on top. • Remove the brioche from the mold immediately and let cool on a rack.

CHOCOLATE CHELSEA BUNS

574

Soak the apricots with the juice in a small bowl and put aside for the filling. • Dough: Mix 2 tablespoons of flour with the yeast, sugar, and milk in a large bowl. Stir and set aside for 15 minutes. • Melt the butter and white chocolate in a small saucepan over low heat and let cool. • Place the remaining flour, salt, and cinnamon in a large bowl and stir in the yeast mixture. Then add the warm butter and chocolate mixture and the egg. • Mix to a fairly soft dough. • Transfer to a lightly floured work surface and knead until smooth and elastic, about 10 minutes, or beat with a dough hook until smooth and elastic, 5 minutes. • Place in an oiled bowl, cover with a kitchen towel, and let rise for about 1 hour, or until doubled in bulk. • Knead lightly on a work surface dusted with flour. • Roll out to a 9 x 12-inch (23 x 30-cm) rectangle. • Brush with butter. • Sprinkle the apricots, currants, mixed peel, and chocolate evenly over the dough, leaving a 1-inch (2.5–cm) border. • Roll up tightly from the shorter side, starting at a long edge. • Seal the edge by dampening with cold water. • Cut into 10 equal-sized slices. • Oil a large baking sheet and place the slices on it cut side up. Cover and let rise for 30 minutes, until doubled in bulk. • Preheat the oven to 375°F (190°C/gas 5). Bake for 25–30 minutes, until risen and golden brown. (Cover with aluminum foil after 20 minutes, if they are browning too quickly.) • Brush with maple syrup while still hot and leave in the pan for 10 minutes. • Separate the buns and serve warm.

Filling

6   dried apricots, finely chopped

1   tablespoon fresh orange juice

3   tablespoons currants

1   tablespoon mixed peel

2½ oz (75 g) dark chocolate, coarsely chopped

1   tablespoon butter, melted for brushing

3   tablespoons maple syrup

Dough

1²⁄₃ cups (250 g) all-purpose (plain) flour

½   oz (15 g) compressed fresh yeast or 1 ($^{1}/_{4}$-oz/7-g) package active dry yeast

1   teaspoon sugar

⅓   cup (90 ml) lukewarm (110°F/43°C) milk

2   tablespoons butter

1   oz (30 g) white chocolate, melted

½   teaspoon salt

½   teaspoon cinnamon

1   large egg, beaten

Serves: 10
Preparation: 15 minutes + 2 hours to rise
Cooking: 30 minutes
Level: 2

KULICH

Place the yeast in a large bowl and mix with the sugar and water to a smooth paste. • Add the milk and 1¹/₂ cups (225 g) of flour. • Stir well, until the mixture resembles a batter. Cover with a clean kitchen towel and leave in a warm place for 1–2 hours, until doubled in bulk. • Place both raisins in a medium bowl with the vodka or rum and leave to soak. • Soak the saffron in the tablespoon of hot water. • Beat the eggs and yolks in a small bowl. • When the yeast mixture is puffed up and there are bubbles on top, add the remaining flour and salt. • Mix first with a plastic spatula and then your hands, until well blended. • Add the beaten egg, a little at a time, then the butter, saffron, spices, and orange zest and continue mixing until all the ingredients have been incorporated and a smooth dough is formed. • Transfer to a lightly floured work surface and knead until smooth and elastic, about 10 minutes, or beat with a dough hook until smooth and elastic, 5 minutes. • Form into a ball and place in an oiled bowl. Cover and leave in a warm place to rise for about 1 hour, or until doubled in bulk. • Punch the dough down and flatten it with a roller or your hand on a work surface. • Sprinkle the soaked fruit, peel, and nuts on the dough and fold it over the top. • Knead gently for 1–2 minutes, until worked in evenly. • Preheat the oven to 375°F (190°C/gas 5). • Line the bottom and sides of a deep pan or cylindrical mold about 6 inches (15 cm) wide and

1 oz (30 g) compressed fresh yeast or 2 (¹/₄-oz/ 7-g) packages active dry yeast

1 teaspoon sugar

2 tablespoons lukewarm (110°F/43°C) water

³/₄ cup (200 ml) lukewarm (110°F/43°C) milk

4 cups (600 g) all-purpose (plain) flour

¹/₃ cup (60 g) golden raisins (sultanas)

¹/₃ cup (60 g) raisins

3 tablespoons vodka or rum

¹/₂ teaspoon saffron

1 tablespoon hot water

¹/₄ teaspoon salt

3 large eggs + 2 large egg yolks

1 cup (225 g) butter, melted

1 cup (200 g) vanilla-flavored superfine (caster) sugar

3 cardamom seeds, finely ground

¹/₂ teaspoon ground mace

Pinch of nutmeg

1 teaspoon orange zest, finely grated

¼ cup (45 g) mixed candied peel, finely chopped

¾ cup (75 g) toasted almonds, coarsely chopped

Pink Frosting

1⅓ cups (200 g) confectioners' (icing) sugar

2 tablespoons red wine

1 tablespoon cold water

1 teaspoon orange zest, finely grated

White Frosting

1⅓ cups (200 g) confectioners' (icing) sugar

2 tablespoons freshly squeezed lemon juice

1 teaspoon lemon zest, finely grated

Serves: 8–10
Preparation: 50 minutes
 + 2–4 hours to rise
Cooking: 50–60 minutes
Level: 3

7 inches (18 cm) tall (You could use a 2 pound/ 1 kg coffee can lined with buttered parchment paper. Allow the paper to come up over the rim of the mold.) • Form the dough into a ball and place in the pan or mold, which should be about a third full. • Cover and leave to rise for 30 minutes, or until the dough almost reaches the top of the mold. • Place on a baking sheet and bake on the bottom oven shelf for 30 minutes. • Decrease the oven temperature to 350°F (180°C/gas 4) and bake for 20–30 more minutes, or until golden brown and a skewer inserted in the center comes out clean. • Cover the top with foil after 20 minutes if it is browning too quickly. • Leave in the pan for 10 minutes to cool before turning out. Stand upright on a rack and cover with a clean kitchen towel. • When completely cooled, decorate the top with pink or white frosting. • <u>Frostings</u>: Combine the frosting ingredients and spoon the frosting over the cake, allowing it to run down the sides. • Kulich is cut horizontally into thin slices and the top replaced to prevent the cake from becoming dry.

■ ■ ■ *In Russia this rich fruit cake is traditionally baked to celebrate Easter and eaten with Pashka, a cream cheese dessert made in a special wooden mold.*

BIRNBROT

Prepare the dough. • <u>Filling</u>: Bring the water to a boil in a small saucepan. Add the pears, prunes, raisins, and lemon juice and simmer over low heat for 10 minutes, stirring frequently, until the fruit is soft. • Drain well and purée in a blender. • Stir the walnuts, brown sugar, lemon zest, pear liqueur or kirsch, and spices into the purée. • Mix well and then stir in the wine, drop by drop, as the purée should be very thick. Coat a 19^1/$_2$ x 9-inch (49 x 23 cm) baking sheet with butter using a pastry brush. Lightly dust a piece of baking parchment, about 18-inches (45 cm) square, with flour. • Punch the risen dough down and turn out onto the paper. • Knead lightly and roll into a square about ^{1}/$_4$ inch (5 mm) thick. • Spread the filling evenly over the dough, leaving a 1-inch (2.5–cm) border. Fold the edges over the filling and roll the dough up, like a jellyroll, using the paper to lift the dough. • Transfer the roll to the baking sheet, cover, and leave to rise in a warm place for 45 minutes. • Preheat the oven to 375°F (190°C/gas 5). • Brush the top of the dough with egg to glaze. • Bake for 45–50 minutes, or until well risen and golden brown on top. Decrease the oven temperature to 350°F (180°C/gas 4) after 20 minutes if it is browning too quickly. Cool on a rack.

■ ■ ■ *This Swiss pear tea bread is made with dried pears. It can also be made with fresh or well-drained canned pears.*

1   recipe Citrus Dough
    (see page 582)

Filling

1   cup (250 ml) water

1^1/$_3$ cups (250 g) dried
    pears, coarsely chopped

^{1}/$_2$ cup (100 g) dried
    prunes, pitted (stoned)
    and coarsely chopped

^{1}/$_3$ cup (60 g) raisins

2   tablespoons freshly
    squeezed lemon juice

^{1}/$_2$ cup (60 g) walnuts,
    coarsely chopped

2   tablespoons light brown
    sugar

1   tablespoon lemon zest,
    finely grated

2   tablespoons pear liqueur
    or kirsch

^{1}/$_4$ teaspoon ground
    nutmeg

^{1}/$_4$ teaspoon cinnamon

2   tablespoons red wine

1   teaspoon butter, melted

1   small egg, beaten

Serves: 8–10
Preparation: 40 minutes
    + 2 hours to rise
Cooking: 50–60 minutes
Level: 2

CREAM CHEESE AND BERRY CAKE

582

Mix the yeast with the milk in a small bowl. Set aside for 10 minutes until frothy. • Combine the flour, salt, both sugars, and both zests in a large bowl. • Add the yeast mixture, butter, and eggs. • Stir to form a medium-soft dough, adding a little more flour if needed. • Transfer to a lightly floured work surface and knead until smooth and elastic, about 10 minutes, or beat with a dough hook until smooth and elastic, 5 minutes. • Cover with a clean kitchen towel and leave to rise in a warm place for about 1 hour, or until doubled in size. • Filling: beat the butter with the sugar and egg yolks in a medium bowl with an electric mixer at medium speed until pale. • Beat in the cream cheese, sour cream, orange juice, and cornstarch. Strip the redcurrants from their stalks and reserve. • Lightly butter a 10½ x 15½-inch (26 x 39 cm) jellyroll pan. • Dust your hands with flour, punch the risen dough down, and take it out of the bowl. Briefly knead it on a lightly floured work surface. • Place the dough in the pan, stretching and pulling it to fill the whole pan. • Leave to rise for another 20–30 minutes, or until puffed up. • Preheat the oven to 375°F (190°C/gas 5). • Brush the risen dough with the butter and sprinkle with the bread crumbs and sugar mix. • Stir the berries into the cream cheese mixture. Spoon onto the dough, smooth the top with a palette knife or the back of the spoon. • Bake for about 20 minutes, or until the edges are golden.

Citrus Dough
- ½ oz (15 g) compressed fresh yeast or 1 (¼-oz/ 7-g) package active dry yeast
- ½ cup (125 ml) lukewarm (110°F/43°C) milk
- 2⅓ cups (350 g) all-purpose (plain) flour
- ¼ teaspoon salt
- 3 tablespoons sugar
- 1 tablespoon vanilla sugar
- 1 tablespoon finely grated lemon zest
- 1 tablespoon finely grated orange zest
- ¼ cup (60 g) butter, melted
- 2 large eggs, beaten

Filling
- 3 tablespoons (45 g) butter, softened
- ½ cup (100 g) sugar
- 2 large egg yolks
- 1½ cups (375 g) cream cheese
- ½ cup (125 ml) sour cream
- 1 tablespoon freshly squeezed orange juice

2 tablespoons cornstarch (cornflour)

3 cups (450 g) redcurrants or blueberries (blackberries)

2 tablespoons butter, melted, for brushing

3 tablespoons fresh bread crumbs mixed with 1 tablespoon light brown sugar, for sprinkling

Meringue Topping

2 large egg whites

$^2/_3$ cup (100 g) superfine (caster) sugar

$^1/_2$ teaspoon freshly squeezed lemon juice

2 tablespoons flaked almonds

Serves: 8–10
Preparation: 40 minutes
    + 90 minutes to rise
Cooking: 25–30 minutes
Level: 2

Meringue Topping: Beat the egg whites in a large bowl with an electric mixer at medium speed until soft peaks form. With the mixer at high speed, gradually add the sugar and lemon juice and beat until stiff. • Remove the cake from the oven and increase the oven temperature to 400°F (200°C/gas 6). • Spread the meringue topping over the cake and sprinkle with the almonds. Return to the oven for another 5–8 minutes, or until the meringue is firm. Leave to cool in the pan for 10 minutes. • Serve warm or at room temperature.

583

SUGAR WHEELS

Dough: Mix the yeast with the milk in a small bowl. Set aside for 10 minutes until frothy. • Combine the flour, salt, and sugar in a large bowl. • Add the yeast mixture, butter, and egg. Mix to form a medium-soft dough, adding a little more flour if needed. • Transfer to a lightly floured work surface and knead until smooth and elastic, about 10 minutes, or beat with a dough hook until smooth and elastic, 5 minutes. • Cover with a clean kitchen towel and leave to rise in a warm place for 60–80 minutes, until doubled in bulk. • Butter a large baking sheet. • Dust your hands with flour, punch the risen dough down, and briefly knead it on a lightly floured work surface. • Roll out the dough into a rectangle, about 10 x 14 inches (25 x 35 cm). Filling: Use a pastry brush to glaze the dough with the melted butter. • Mix the brown sugar and cinnamon and sprinkle evenly over the dough. • Scatter the currants over the top and press the filling in with a rolling pin. • Carefully roll up the dough, starting from a long side, to form a log. • Use a sharp knife to cut the log into 12 slices. • Place cut side up on the baking sheet. • Cover with a clean kitchen towel and leave to rise in a warm place for 30–40 minutes, until the dough has puffed up. • Preheat the oven to 400°F (200°C/gas 6). • Glaze: Just before baking, mix the egg with the milk and glaze the tops with a pastry brush. • Bake for 12–15 minutes, or until golden brown. • Serve warm or leave to cool and lightly dust with confectioners' sugar.

Dough
- ½ oz (15 g) fresh yeast or 1 (¼-oz/7-g) package active dry yeast
- ½ cup (125 ml) lukewarm (110°F/43°C) milk
- 2 cups (300 g) all-purpose (plain) flour
- ¼ teaspoon salt
- 2 tablespoons superfine (caster) sugar
- ¼ cup (60 g) butter, melted
- 1 large egg, beaten

Filling
- ⅓ cup (100 g) butter, melted
- ¼ cup (60 g) firmly packed light brown sugar
- 1 teaspoon cinnamon
- ¾ cup (100 g) currants

Glaze
- 1 small egg, beaten
- 1 tablespoon milk
- Confectioners' sugar, to dust

Serves: 12
Preparation: 45 minutes + 2 hours to rise
Cooking: 12–15 minutes
Level: 2

HAMENTASCHEN

<u>Dough</u>: Mix the yeast with the milk in a small bowl. Set aside for 10 minutes until frothy. • Combine the flour, sugar, and salt in a large bowl. • Make a well in the center and mix in the yeast mixture, butter, and eggs with a spatula or an electric mixer with a dough hook attachment at low speed. • Transfer the dough to a lightly floured work surface and knead until smooth and elastic, about 10 minutes, or beat with a dough hook until smooth and elastic, 5 minutes. • Form into a ball and place in an oiled bowl, turning to coat the ball. Cover the bowl with a clean kitchen towel or plastic wrap (cling film), and let rise in a warm place for 60–90 minutes, or until doubled in bulk. • <u>Poppy-Seed Filling</u>: Heat the milk with the honey in a small saucepan. Stir in the poppy seeds and simmer over low heat for 15 minutes, stirring frequently, until thick. • Add the raisins and butter and simmer for 5 more minutes. Stir in the lemon zest and juice. Thicken with bread crumbs, if needed, and leave to cool. • <u>Fruit Filling</u>: Mix the lackwa, prune purée, or damson cheese with the almonds and orange zest. Add orange juice if it is too thick. • Punch down the risen dough and knead on a lightly floured work surface for 5 minutes. • Butter 2 large baking sheets. Divide the risen dough in half and roll out to 1/4-inch (5-mm) thick. Cut into 4-inch (10-cm) squares with a sharp knife or cookie cutter. • Place a heaped tablespoon of poppy-seed filling on each square and fold the dough over into a triangle. Transfer to the baking

Dough

1/2 oz (15 g) compressed fresh yeast or 1 (1/4-oz/ 7-g) package active dry yeast

1/2 cup (125 ml) lukewarm (110°F/43°C) milk

2 2/3 cups (400 g) all-purpose (plain) flour

1/3 cup (75 g) sugar

1/2 teaspoon salt

1/2 cup (125 g) butter, melted

2 small eggs

Poppy Seed Filling

1/2 cup (125 ml) milk

5 tablespoons honey

1 1/4 cups (150 g) poppy seeds

4 tablespoons raisins

1 tablespoon butter

1 teaspoon finely grated lemon zest

1 tablespoon freshly squeezed lemon juice

3 teaspoons fresh bread crumbs, to thicken (optional)

Fruit Filling

1 cup lackwa (prune butter), prune purée, or damson cheese

3 tablespoons ground almonds

1 tablespoon orange zest, finely grated

2 teaspoons freshly squeezed orange juice, to thin (optional)

Glaze

1 small egg, beaten

1 tablespoon milk

Serves: 12–15
Preparation: 1 hour
+ 2 hours to rise
Cooking: 25 minutes
Level: 2

sheet. Do the same with the other half of the dough, and fill with fruit filling. • Cover the baking sheets and let rise in a warm place for about 30 minutes, or until the pastries look puffy. • Preheat the oven to 375°F (190°C/gas 5). • <u>Glaze</u>: Just before baking, mix the egg with the milk and glaze the tops of the pastries with a pastry brush. • Bake for 20–25 minutes, or until golden brown. • Leave on the sheets for
10 minutes, then transfer with a palette knife to a rack to cool.

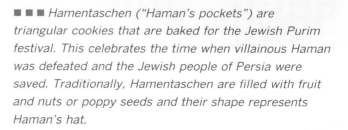

■ ■ ■ *Hamentaschen ("Haman's pockets") are triangular cookies that are baked for the Jewish Purim festival. This celebrates the time when villainous Haman was defeated and the Jewish people of Persia were saved. Traditionally, Hamentaschen are filled with fruit and nuts or poppy seeds and their shape represents Haman's hat.*

CINNAMON SPIRALS

Dough: Mix the yeast with the milk in a small bowl. Set aside for 10 minutes until frothy. • Combine the flour, sugar, and salt in a large bowl. • Add the yeast mixture, butter, and egg yolks. Mix to a medium-soft dough, adding a little more flour if needed. • Transfer to a lightly floured work surface and knead until smooth and elastic, about 10 minutes, or beat with a dough hook until smooth and elastic, 5 minutes. • Form into a ball, place in an oiled bowl, and cover with a clean kitchen towel. Leave to rise in a warm place for 60–80 minutes, or until doubled in bulk. • Butter a large baking sheet or line with baking parchment. • Dust your hands with flour, punch the risen dough down, and lightly knead for 1–2 minutes. • Divide the dough in two and roll into 15 x 12-inch (37 x 30 cm) rectangles, about $1/4$ inch (5 mm) thick. • Brush generously with melted butter and sprinkle with a layer of cinnamon sugar. Roll up one long side of the dough to the center, then roll up the other side, so that they meet in the middle. Press the edges together and join them. • Cut into 1-inch- (2.5-cm)-thick slices. Sprinkle the cut side with superfine sugar. • Flatten the slices with a palette knife. • Place on the prepared sheet, sugared side up. • Leave to rise in a warm place for 15–20 minutes. • Preheat the oven to 375°F (190°C/gas 5). • Gently dab the spirals with melted butter, using your finger or a pastry brush. Bake for 15–20 minutes, until pale brown. Transfer to a rack to cool.

Dough

½ oz (15 g) compressed fresh yeast or 1 ($1/4$-oz/ 7-g) package active dry yeast

½ cup (125 ml) lukewarm (110°F/43°C) milk

$2^{2}/_3$ cups (400 g) all-purpose (plain) flour

¼ cup (60 g) superfine (caster) sugar

¼ teaspoon salt

⅓ cup (90 g) unsalted butter, melted

2 egg yolks, lightly beaten

Filling

⅓ cup (100 g) butter, melted

6 tablespoons cinnamon sugar (or 5 tablespoons superfine (caster) sugar mixed with 1 tablespoon ground cinnamon)

3 tablespoons superfine (caster) sugar, to sprinkle

1 tablespoon melted butter, for brushing

Serves: 12
Preparation: 1 hour
  + 2–3 hours to rise
Cooking: 15–20 minutes
Level: 2

SWEET BEE-STING

Dough: Mix the yeast with the milk in a small bowl. Set aside for 10 minutes until frothy. • Combine the flour, salt, both sugars, and the zest in a large bow. • Add the yeast mixture, eggs, and butter. Stir with a spatula or your hands to form a medium-soft dough, adding a little more flour if needed. • Transfer to a lightly floured work surface and knead until smooth and elastic, about 10 minutes, or beat with a dough hook until smooth and elastic, 5 minutes. • Place in an oiled bowl. Cover the bowl with a clean kitchen towel and leave to rise in a warm place for 60–80 minutes, or until doubled in bulk. • Topping: Melt the butter in a small saucepan over low heat. Stir in the sugar, vanilla sugar or extract, honey, and cream. Bring to a boil, stirring all the time. Take the pan off the heat and mix in the almonds. Stir the mixture every now and then while it is cooling. • Filling: Prepare the pastry cream. Cover the surface with plastic wrap (cling film) to stop a film from forming, and chill in the refrigerator until needed. • Butter and line a $10^{1}/_2$ x $15^{1}/_2$-inch (39 x 29 cm) jellyroll pan with baking parchment. • Dust your hands with flour, punch the risen dough down, and take it out of the bowl. • Briefly knead on a lightly floured work surface then roll out. • Place the dough in the prepared jellyroll pan, stretching and spreading with your fingers so that it covers the bottom of the pan evenly. • Spread the topping over the top evenly. • Leave to rise

Dough

- $^1/_2$ oz (15 g) compressed fresh yeast or 1 ($^1/_4$-oz/ 7-g) package active dry yeast
- $^3/_4$ cup (180 ml) lukewarm (110°F/43°C) milk
- $2^2/_3$ cups (400 g) all-purpose (plain) flour
- $^1/_4$ cup (60 g) superfine (caster) sugar
- $^1/_4$ teaspoon salt
- 2 tablespoons vanilla sugar
- 1 teaspoon lemon zest, finely grated
- 2 eggs, lightly beaten
- $^1/_3$ cup (90 g) butter, melted

Topping

- $^2/_3$ cup (150 g) butter
- $^1/_3$ cup (70 g) sugar
- 1 packet vanilla sugar or 1 teaspoon vanilla extract
- 1 tablespoon honey
- 3 tablespoons light (single) cream
- 1 cup (150 g) blanched almonds, coarsely chopped

Filling

1   recipe Vanilla Pastry
    Cream (see page 526)

Serves: 12–15
Preparation: 1 hour
  + 2–3 hours to rise
Cooking: 15–20 minutes
Level: 3

again in a warm place for 15–30 minutes, until visibly puffed up. • Preheat the oven to 375°F (190°C/gas 5). • Bake for 15–20 minutes, or until golden brown. Leave to cool in the pan on a rack. • Once completely cooled, cut into squares or 6-inch (15-cm) wide strips and then cut the strips in half horizontally. • Spread the pastry cream on the bottom half and sandwich together with the almond top half. Cut into smaller squares for serving.

■ ■ ■ *This is a traditional German almond cake with a vanilla custard filling. You could also fill it with vanilla-flavored buttercream.*

APPLE TURNOVERS

Dough: Mix the yeast with the milk in a small bowl. Set aside for 10 minutes until frothy. • Combine the flour, salt, sugar, vanilla sugar, and zest in a large bowl. • Make a well in the center of the flour mixture and add the yeast mixture, egg, and butter. • Stir with a plastic spatula or your hands to form a medium-soft dough, adding a little more flour if needed. • Transfer to a lightly floured work surface and knead until smooth and elastic, about 10 minutes, or beat with a dough hook until smooth and elastic, 5 minutes. • Dust with flour and cover with a clean kitchen towel. Leave to rise in a warm place for 60–80 minutes, or until doubled in bulk. • Filling: Melt the butter in a medium saucepan over low heat, add the sugar, and stir until it dissolves. Add the apples, golden raisins, and cinnamon and simmer until the apples start to soften. Set aside to cool. • Line a large baking sheet with parchment paper. • Dust your hands with flour, punch the risen dough down, and take it out of the bowl. • Briefly knead it on a lightly floured work surface then roll out to 1/4-inch (5-mm) thick. • Cut out 5-inch (13 cm) rounds with a cutter or saucer. • Put a heaped tablespoon of the apple filling on one half of the dough round and fold into a half-moon shape. Pinch the edges to seal. • Brush the tops with milk and sprinkle some turnovers with almonds. • Place on the baking sheet, spacing well. • Leave in a warm

Dough

1/2 oz (15 g) compressed fresh yeast or 1 (1/4-oz/ 7-g) package active dry yeast

3/4 cup (200 ml) lukewarm (110°F/43°C) milk

2½ cups (375 g) all-purpose (plain) flour

1/4 teaspoon salt

3 tablespoons sugar

1 tablespoon vanilla sugar

1 teaspoon lemon zest, finely grated

1 large egg, lightly beaten

1/4 cup (60 g) butter, melted

Filling

1 tablespoon butter

3 tablespoons sugar

3 large eating apples (Gala or Cox), peeled, cored, and finely chopped

3 tablespoons golden raisins (sultanas)

1/4 tablespoon ground cinnamon

Topping

2 tablespoons milk

2 tablespoons flaked
   almonds, optional

⅔ cup (100 g)
   confectioners' (icing)
   sugar

1 tablespoon freshly
   squeezed lemon juice

1 teaspoon butter, melted

Serves: 8–10
Preparation: 40 minutes
   + 2 hours to rise
Cooking: 15–20 minutes
Level: 2

place for about 20 minutes, or until well risen and puffy. • Preheat the oven to 375°F (190°C/gas 5). Bake for 15 minutes, or until golden brown. • <u>Glaze</u>: Mix the sugar with the lemon juice in a small bowl until smooth then stir in the butter. Drizzle the glaze over the turnovers as soon as they come out of the oven. Leave to cool before serving.

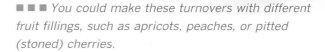

■ ■ ■ *You could make these turnovers with different fruit fillings, such as apricots, peaches, or pitted (stoned) cherries.*

TRIPLE TWIST

Dough: Mix the yeast with the milk in a small bowl. Set aside for 10 minutes until frothy. • Mix the flour, sugar, and salt in a large bowl. Add the yeast mixture, crème fraîche, butter, and vanilla extract. • Mix with a plastic spatula, gradually working in the flour. • Transfer to a lightly floured work surface and knead until smooth and elastic, about 10 minutes, or beat with a dough hook until smooth and elastic, 5 minutes. • Form into a ball, place in an oiled bowl, and cover. Leave to rise for 2 hours, or until doubled in bulk. • Flavorings: Soak the fruit in the rum. • Cut the marzipan into small pieces and mix with the almonds. • Combine the apricots, pecans, and sugar. • Dust the risen dough with flour, punch down, and knead briefly on a floured surface. Cut into 3 equal pieces. Flatten the dough with your hand and knead one of the flavorings into each one, dusting with a little more flour. • When the flavorings have been incorporated, form each one into a ball. Flour your hands and roll the dough balls into 3 strips of even length. Braid (plait) into a loaf. (You could make 2 small loaves, in which case divide the balls into 6 strips and braid.) • Line a baking sheet with parchment paper and place the loaf on it. • Cover with a towel and leave for 30–60 minutes, until doubled in bulk. • Preheat the oven to 375°F (190°C/gas 5). • Brush the loaf (or loaves) with egg and bake for 40–50 minutes, until golden brown. (Bake small loaves for 30–35 minutes.) Cool for 30 minutes on a rack before serving.

Dough

1 oz (30 g) fresh yeast or 2 ($^{1}/_{4}$-oz/7-g) package active dry yeast

$^{2}/_{3}$ cup (150 ml) lukewarm (110°F/43°C) milk

3 cups (500 g) all-purpose (plain) flour

$^{1}/_{3}$ cup (70 g) superfine (caster) sugar

$^{1}/_{2}$ teaspoon salt

$^{2}/_{3}$ cup (150 g) crème fraîche

$^{1}/_{3}$ cup (90 g) butter

1 teaspoon vanilla extract

Flavorings

$^{1}/_{2}$ cup (100 g) raisins

$^{1}/_{4}$ cup (50 g) currants or dried banana, chopped

2 tablespoons rum

3 ounces (90 g) marzipan, softened

$^{2}/_{3}$ cup (100 g) almonds, toasted and chopped

1$^{1}/_{2}$ oz (40 g) dried apricots, diced

$^{1}/_{3}$ cup (40 g) pecans, toasted and chopped

2 tablespoons brown sugar

1 small egg, beaten

Serves: 8–10

Preparation: 35 minutes + 2–3 hours to rise

Cooking: 40–50 minutes large twist; 35 minutes small loaves

Level: 2

HONEY AND NUT RING

Combine the sugar and cream in a small bowl and stir in the yeast. Set aside for 10 minutes until frothy. • Beat the butter in a large bowl with an electric mixer until pale. • Add the honey and beat until combined. • Beat in the eggs, one at a time, adding a teaspoon of flour after each addition. Gradually beat in 2 cups (300 g) of flour and the salt followed by the yeast mixture and milk. • Beat with a dough hook or stir with a plastic spatula until well blended and the dough is smooth and elastic. Add the remaining flour if the dough is still very sticky. • Work in the nuts and zest. • Cover the bowl with a clean kitchen towel and let rise in a warm place for 1–2 hours, until doubled in bulk. • Butter a 10-inch (25 cm) ring mold with a pastry brush. Sprinkle with the toasted nuts. • When the dough has risen, stir once to expel air. Place in the pan. • Cover and let rise again for 1–2 hours, or until almost doubled in bulk. • Preheat the oven to 375°F (190°C/gas 5). • Bake for 30 minutes, or until the top is golden brown and a skewer inserted into the center comes out clean. Let cool in the pan for 10 minutes before turning out on a rack. • Glaze: Beat all the ingredients together until smooth. • Place the cake on a serving plate and spoon the glaze over the top. • Serve warm.

1   teaspoon sugar

¼   cup (60 ml) light (single) cream

½   oz (15 g) compressed fresh yeast or 1 (¼-oz/ 7-g) package active dry yeast

½   cup (125 g) butter

2   tablespoons honey

3   large eggs

2⅓ cups (350 g) all-purpose (plain) flour

¼   teaspoon salt

⅓   cup (90 ml) lukewarm (110°F/43°C) milk

½   cup (60 g) almonds or hazelnuts, toasted and roughly chopped

Finely grated zest of 1 orange

Glaze

1   cup (150 g) confectioners' (icing) sugar

3   tablespoons fresh orange juice

2   teaspoons orange zest, finely grated

2   teaspoons Cointreau

Serves: 10–12
Preparation: 35 minutes + 2–3 hours to rise
Cooking: 30 minutes
Level: 2

PEAR BREAKFAST CAKE

<u>Cake</u>: Set out a 13 x 9-inch (33 x 23-cm) baking pan. • Stir together the yeast, honey, and water. Set aside for 10 minutes until frothy. • Combine 1½ cups (225 g) of flour and salt in a large bowl. Stir in the yeast mixture. • Cover with a clean kitchen towel and let rise in a warm place for 30 minutes. • Soak the raisins in enough warm water to cover for 10 minutes. Drain well and pat dry with paper towels. • Stir the batter and add the raisins, walnuts, and cinnamon. • Gradually stir in the remaining flour a little at a time until a smooth dough is formed. • Transfer to a lightly floured work surface and knead until smooth and elastic, about 10 minutes, or beat with a dough hook until smooth and elastic, 5 minutes. Add more flour if needed. (The dough should be soft but not sticky.) • Shape into a ball and place in a clean bowl. Cover with a kitchen towel and let rise in a warm place for about 1 hour, or until doubled in bulk. • Punch down the dough. Place in the pan, spreading it out. Cover and let rise for 15 minutes more. • <u>Topping</u>: Stir the flour, cinnamon, honey, brown sugar, and walnuts in a medium bowl. Arrange the pear slices on top of the dough. Sprinkle with the topping mixture. • Cover and let rise in a warm place for 30 minutes. • Preheat the oven to 350°F (180°C/gas 4). • Bake for 25–30 minutes, or until golden brown. • Serve warm.

Cake

1 oz (30 g) compressed fresh yeast or 2 (¼-oz/ 7-g) package active dry yeast

⅓ cup (90 ml) honey

1 cup (250 ml) lukewarm (100°F/43°C) water

3 cups (450 g) whole-wheat (wholemeal) flour

¼ teaspoon salt

¾ cup raisins

½ cup walnuts, coarsely chopped

1½ teaspoons ground cinnamon

Topping

½ cup (75 g) whole-wheat (wholemeal) flour

½ teaspoon ground cinnamon

¼ cup (60 g) honey

¼ cup (50 g) firmly packed dark brown sugar

2 tablespoons walnuts, coarsely chopped

2 large pears, peeled, cored, and thinly sliced

Serves: 8–10
Preparation: 1 hour
 + 2 hours to rise
Cooking: 25–30 minutes
Level: 2

TRENTINO CAKE

Butter a deep 10-inch (26-cm) round cake pan. • Stir together the yeast and milk. Set aside for 10 minutes. • Place 1⅓ cups (200 g) of flour in a large bowl and make a well in the center. Mix in the yeast mixture to form a smooth batter. • Cover with a clean kitchen towel and let rest for 1 hour, or until doubled in bulk. • Stir 1¼ cups (175 g) of flour into the batter. Gradually mix in enough of the remaining flour to form a soft dough. • Transfer to a lightly floured work surface and knead until smooth and elastic, about 10 minutes, or beat with a dough hook until smooth and elastic, 5 minutes. • Cover with a clean kitchen towel and let rise for 1 hour, or until doubled in bulk. • Beat the butter with an electric mixer at medium speed until creamy. Gradually add the egg yolks and superfine sugar. Knead the butter mixture, half of the remaining flour, and salt into the dough on a lightly floured work surface. Knead for 5 minutes then shape into a ball. • Return to the bowl. Cover with a towel and let rise for 1 hour, or until doubled in bulk. • Mix the golden raisins, lemon peel, coriander seeds, pine nuts, and rum in a large bowl. Cover and soak for 15 minutes. • Mix the orange zest and remaining flour into the soaked fruit. • Knead the fruit mixture into the dough on a lightly floured surface until well blended. Shape the dough into a long rope and join the two ends to form a ring. • Transfer to the prepared pan, cover with a kitchen towel, and let rise for 1 hour. • Preheat the oven to 375°F (190°C/gas 5). • Brush with the beaten egg and sprinkle with the nuts. • Bake for 60–70 minutes, or until golden. Cool completely in the pan.

1 oz (30 g) compressed fresh yeast or 2 (¼-oz/7-g) package active dry yeast

1 cup (250 ml) lukewarm (110°F/43°C) milk

4 cups (600 g) all-purpose (plain) flour

½ cup (125 g) butter, softened

3 large egg yolks + 1 large egg, lightly beaten

1 cup (200 g) superfine (caster) sugar

¼ teaspoon salt

1 cup (180 g) golden raisins (sultanas)

1½ cups (250 g) candied (glacé) lemon peel

1 teaspoon coriander seeds, crushed

⅔ cup (120 g) pine nuts

½ cup (125 ml) dark rum

2 tablespoons finely grated orange zest

1 cup (120 g) mixed nuts, finely chopped

Serves: 10–12
Preparation: 1 hour
  + 4 hours to rise
Cooking: 60–70 minutes
Level: 2

SWEET POPPY LOAF

Butter and flour a large baking sheet. • Stir the yeast and milk in a small bowl. Set aside for 10 minutes until frothy. • Place the flour, sugar, and salt in a large bowl and make a well in the center. Stir in the yeast mixture, egg yolks, oil, and anise extract. • Transfer to a lightly floured work surface and knead by hand until smooth and elastic, about 10 minutes, or beat with a dough hook until smooth and elastic, 5 minutes. • Cover with a clean kitchen towel and let rise in a warm place until doubled in bulk, about 1 hour. • Soak the raisins in the anisette for 15 minutes. • Punch the dough down and roll out on a lightly floured work surface to about $1/4$-inch (5-mm) thick. • Drain the raisins. Do not squeeze out all the liqueur; it will add to the flavor of the bread. • Sprinkle the raisins over the dough and roll it up. • Beat the remaining egg and brush it over the surface of the rolled dough. Sprinkle with the poppy seeds. • Place the roll on the baking sheet. Cover with a clean kitchen towel and set aside in a warm place to rise for about 90 minutes. • Preheat the oven to 350°F (180°C/gas 4). • Bake for 35–45 minutes, or until golden brown. • Cool the loaf on a rack. Serve lightly buttered slices at room temperature.

½ oz (15 g) compressed fresh yeast or 1 ($1/4$-oz/ 7-g) package active dry yeast

¾ cup (180 ml) lukewarm (110°F/43°C) milk

3⅔ cups (550 g) all-purpose (plain) flour

½ cup (100 g) sugar

½ teaspoon salt

3 large egg yolks + 1 large egg

¼ cup (60 ml) vegetable oil

1 teaspoon anise extract (essence)

1 cup (180 g) raisins

1 cup (250 ml) anisette

½ cup (90 g) poppy seeds

Butter, to serve

Serves: 8–10
Preparation: 30 minutes + 2 hours 30 minutes to rise
Cooking: 35–45 minutes
Level: 2

CANDIED FRUIT AND PINE NUT BUNS

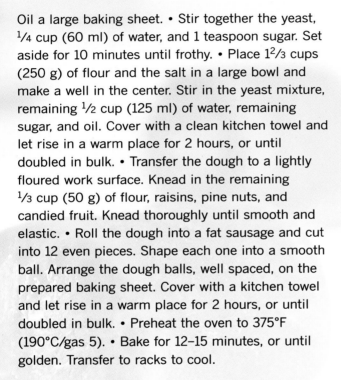

Oil a large baking sheet. • Stir together the yeast, 1/4 cup (60 ml) of water, and 1 teaspoon sugar. Set aside for 10 minutes until frothy. • Place 1²/₃ cups (250 g) of flour and the salt in a large bowl and make a well in the center. Stir in the yeast mixture, remaining 1/2 cup (125 ml) of water, remaining sugar, and oil. Cover with a clean kitchen towel and let rise in a warm place for 2 hours, or until doubled in bulk. • Transfer the dough to a lightly floured work surface. Knead in the remaining 1/3 cup (50 g) of flour, raisins, pine nuts, and candied fruit. Knead thoroughly until smooth and elastic. • Roll the dough into a fat sausage and cut into 12 even pieces. Shape each one into a smooth ball. Arrange the dough balls, well spaced, on the prepared baking sheet. Cover with a kitchen towel and let rise in a warm place for 2 hours, or until doubled in bulk. • Preheat the oven to 375°F (190°C/gas 5). • Bake for 12–15 minutes, or until golden. Transfer to racks to cool.

- ½ oz (15 g) compressed fresh yeast or 1 (¹/₄-oz/ 7-g) package active dry yeast
- ³/₄ cup (180 ml) lukewarm water (110°F/43°C)
- ¼ cup (50 g) sugar
- 2 cups (300 g) all-purpose (plain) flour
- ¼ teaspoon salt
- 2 tablespoons extra-virgin olive oil
- ½ cup (90 g) golden raisins (sultanas), plumped in warm water for 15 minutes, well drained
- 3 tablespoons pine nuts
- 2 tablespoons chopped mixed candied (glacé) orange and lemon peel

Serves: 12
Preparation: 30 minutes
+ 4 hours to rise
Cooking: 12–15 minutes
Level: 2

RUM BABA CAKES

Baba Cakes: Butter twelve 2 x 3-inch (5 x 7.5-cm) baba molds. • Stir together the yeast, water, and 1 teaspoon sugar. Set aside for 10 minutes until frothy. • Beat the eggs and remaining sugar in a large bowl with an electric mixer at high speed until pale and thick. • Stir in the oil, butter, and yeast mixture. • Stir in the flour and salt. • Transfer to a lightly floured work surface and knead by hand until smooth and elastic, about 10 minutes, or beat with a dough hook until smooth and elastic, 5 minutes. • Roll the dough into a fat sausage and cut into 12 even pieces. Place in the prepared molds. Cover with plastic wrap (cling film) and let rise in a warm place until the dough has risen to just below the top of each mold, about 1 hour. • Preheat the oven to 350°F (180°C/gas 4). • Bake for 12–15 minutes, or until lightly browned. • Rum Syrup: Stir the water and sugar in a saucepan over medium heat until the sugar has dissolved and the mixture comes to a boil. Simmer for 10 minutes, or until syrupy and thick. • Stir in the rum and lemon. Set aside to cool. • Cool the babas in the molds for 15 minutes. Soak in the rum syrup and let drain on racks.

Baba Cakes

½ oz (15 g) compressed fresh yeast or 1 (¼-oz/ 7-g) package active dry yeast

¼ cup (60 ml) lukewarm water (110°F/43°C)

2 tablespoons sugar

5 large eggs

½ cup (125 ml) extra-virgin olive oil

¼ cup (60 g) butter, melted and cooled

2⅓ cups (350 g) all-purpose (plain) flour

¼ teaspoon salt

Rum Syrup

2 cups (500 ml) water

1½ cups (300 g) sugar

½ cup (125 ml) rum

1 lemon, sliced

Serves: 12
Preparation: 30 minutes
 + 1 hour to rise
Cooking: 12–15 minutes
Level: 2

CHERRY DOUGHNUTS

Stir the yeast and milk together in a small bowl. Set aside for 10 minutes until frothy. • Stir the flour, yeast mixture, sugar, salt, and eggs in a large bowl. • Transfer to a lightly floured work surface and knead by hand until smooth and elastic, about 10 minutes, or beat with a dough hook until smooth and elastic, 5 minutes. • Beat the butter in a medium bowl with an electric mixer at medium speed until creamy. Work the butter into the dough and continue kneading until well mixed. Set aside to rest in a large bowl for about 1 hour, or until doubled in bulk. • Roll the dough out on a lightly floured work surface to about $1/2$-inch (1-cm) thick. Using 3-inch (7.5-cm) pastry cutters, cut out disks. • Brush half the disks with the jelly. Place the remaining halves on top and seal the edges well. • Heat the oil in a deep-fryer or deep saucepan to 365°F (190°C). If you don't have a thermometer, test the oil temperature by dropping a small piece of bread into the hot oil. If the bread immediately bubbles to the surface and begins to turn golden, the oil is ready. • Fry the doughnuts in small batches until golden brown all over. Drain on paper towels. • Dust with the confectioners' sugar and serve hot or warm.

1   oz (30 g) compressed fresh yeast or 2 ($1/4$-oz/7-g) package active dry yeast

1   cup (250 ml) lukewarm (110°F/43°C)

$4^1/_3$ cups (650 g) all-purpose (plain) flour

$3/4$ cup (150 g) sugar

$1/2$ teaspoon salt

2   large eggs

$1/2$ cup (125 g) butter, softened

4   tablespoons cherry preserves (jelly)

4   cups (1 liter) vegetable oil, to fry

Confectioners' sugar, to dust

Serves: 10–12
Preparation: 40 minutes + 1 hour to rise
Cooking: 45 minutes
Level: 3

FLORENTINE CARNIVAL CAKE

Butter a 9 x 13 inch (23 x 33 cm) baking pan. Line with parchment paper. Butter the paper. • Stir together the yeast and $1/2$ cup (125 ml) of water. Set aside for 10 minutes until frothy. • Mix the flour and sugar in a large bowl and make a well in the center. • Add the yeast mixture and stir until the flour has all been absorbed, adding enough of the remaining water to obtain a smooth dough. • Transfer to a lightly floured work surface and knead by hand until smooth and elastic, about 10 minutes, or beat with a dough hook until smooth and elastic, 5 minutes. • Shape into a ball and place in a clean bowl. Cover with a clean kitchen towel and let rise in a warm place for about 1 hour. • Knead the dough again, gradually working in the eggs, butter, orange zest, and salt. • Place the dough in the prepared pan, spreading it evenly. Let rise for 2 hours more, or until doubled in bulk. • Preheat the oven to 350°F (180°C/gas 4). • Bake for 25–35 minutes, or until a toothpick inserted into the center comes out clean. • Cool the cake in the pan for 15 minutes. Turn out onto a rack to cool completely. Dust with confectioners' sugar just before serving.

1	oz (30 g) compressed fresh yeast or 2 ($1/4$-oz/7-g) package active dry yeast
1	cup (250 ml) lukewarm (110°F/43°C) water
3	cups (450 g) all-purpose (plain) flour
1	cup (200 g) sugar
4	large egg yolks
$1/3$	cup (90 g) butter, melted
2	tablespoons finely grated orange zest
$1/4$	teaspoon salt
	Confectioners' sugar, to dust

Serves: 10–12
Preparation: 25 minutes + 3 hours to rise
Cooking: 25–35 minutes
Level: 2

■ ■ ■ *In Florence this cake is traditionally eaten on the Thursday before Lent. If there is any left the day after, cut the cake horizontally and fill with whipped cream.*

TUSCAN HARVEST BREAD

Butter a large baking sheet. Line with parchment paper. • Stir together the yeast and water in a small bowl. Set aside for 10 minutes until frothy. • Combine the flour, sugar, and salt in a large bowl and make a well in the center. Stir in the yeast mixture until the flour has all been absorbed, adding enough extra water to obtain a smooth dough. • Transfer to a lightly floured work surface and knead by hand until smooth and elastic, about 10 minutes, or beat with a dough hook until smooth and elastic, 5 minutes. • Shape into a ball. Cover with a clean kitchen towel and set aside to rise in a warm place for about 1 hour, or until doubled in bulk. • Divide the dough in two. Roll out the dough into two sheets about 1-inch (2.5 cm) thick. Place a dough sheet on the prepared baking sheet. Cover with half the grapes and sprinkle with half the sugar. Top with the remaining dough sheet and seal the edges. • Spread the remaining grapes over the top, pressing them down into the dough. Sprinkle with the remaining sugar and set aside to rise for 1 hour. • Preheat the oven to 350°F (180°C/gas 4). • Bake for 40–50 minutes, or until lightly browned. • Let cool on a rack.

1 oz (30 g) compressed fresh yeast or 2 (^{1}/4-oz/ 7-g) package active dry yeast

^{2}/3 cup (150 ml) lukewarm (110°F/43°C) water + extra, as required

3 cups (450 g) all-purpose (plain) flour

¼ cup (50 g) sugar

¼ teaspoon salt

Topping

1 lb (500 g) black grapes (preferably seedless), lightly crushed

^{3}/4 cup (150 g) sugar

Serves: 10–12
Preparation: 25 minutes + 3 hours to rise
Cooking: 40–50 minutes
Level: 2

■ ■ ■ *This recipe for sweet focaccia comes from Tuscany, where it is made every year throughout the grape harvest with the small black grapes used to make the local Chianti wines.*

LEMON CURD BREAKFAST CAKE

Stir together the yeast, water, and 1 teaspoon sugar. Set aside for 10 minutes until frothy. • Beat the sour cream, remaining sugar, lemon zest, and salt with an electric mixer at high speed in a large bowl until well blended. • Place the flour in a large bowl and make a well in the center. Stir in the yeast mixture and the beaten eggs. Use a large rubber spatula to gradually fold the flour into the sour cream mixture. • Beat in the butter, making a firm, slightly sticky dough. • Transfer to a lightly floured work surface and knead by hand until smooth and elastic, about 10 minutes, or beat with a dough hook until smooth and elastic, 5 minutes. • Shape into a ball and place in a bowl. Cover with a clean kitchen towel and let rise in a warm place for about 1 hour, or until doubled in bulk. • Line a baking sheet with parchment paper. • Punch the dough down and roll out on a lightly floured work surface to an 18 x 12-inch (46 x 30-cm) rectangle. Spread with the lemon curd, leaving a 1-inch (2.5-cm) border on all sides. Carefully roll up the dough from a short side. • Use a sharp knife to cut into 1½-inch (4-cm) thick slices. Arrange in a round ¼-inch (5 mm) apart on the prepared sheet. Cover with plastic wrap (cling film) and let rise in a warm place for 30 minutes. • Preheat the oven to 375°F (190°C/gas 5). • Beat the remaining egg and brush over the rolls. Sprinkle with the almonds. • Bake for 25–35 minutes, or until browned. • Serve hot or at room temperature.

½ oz (15 g) compressed fresh yeast or 1 (¼-oz/ 7-g) package active dry yeast

¼ cup (60 ml) lukewarm water (105°–115°F)

⅓ cup (70 g) granulated sugar

½ cup (125 ml) sour cream

1 tablespoon finely grated lemon zest

¼ teaspoon salt

2⅔ cups (400 g) all-purpose (plain) flour

2 large eggs, lightly beaten + 1 large egg

⅓ cup (90 g) butter, softened

1 cup (250 ml) lemon curd

¼ cup slivered almonds

Serves: 6–8
Preparation: 30 minutes + 90 minutes to rise
Cooking: 25–35 minutes
Level: 2

SWEDISH BREAKFAST CAKE

Preheat the oven to 350°F (180°C gas 4). • Butter a 10-inch (26-cm) springform pan. Sprinkle with the bread crumbs. • Stir the yeast, milk, and 1 teaspoon sugar in a small bowl. Set aside for 10 minutes until frothy. • Combine the flour, 1 tablespoon sugar, vanilla, and salt in a large bowl. Add the egg yolks. Stir in the yeast mixture until a smooth dough is formed. • Transfer to a lightly floured work surface and knead by hand until smooth and elastic, about 10 minutes, or beat with a dough hook until smooth and elastic, 5 minutes. • Break off a piece slightly larger than an egg and knead for a few seconds. • Knead the remaining dough for a few seconds. • Shape each piece of dough into a ball and place in two separate bowls. Cover with a clean kitchen towel and let rise in a warm place until doubled in bulk, about 30 minutes. • Roll out the smaller dough ball on a lightly floured surface to 1/8 inch (3 mm) thick. Fit the dough into the prepared pan. • Roll out the larger dough ball into a 16 x 7-inch (40 x 18-cm) rectangle. • Brush with the melted butter and sprinkle with the remaining sugar and raisins. • From a long side, roll up the dough jelly-roll fashion. Cut into 1 1/2-inch (4-cm) thick slices. Arrange the slices evenly on the dough base. • Cover with a kitchen towel and let rest in a warm place until the slices have expanded to fill the pan, about 1 hour. • Brush with the beaten egg. • Bake for 30–35 minutes, or until golden brown. • Cool the cake in the pan for 10 minutes. Loosen and remove the pan sides and bottom and let cool completely.

2 tablespoons fine dry bread crumbs

1/2 oz (15 g) compressed fresh yeast or 1 (1/4-oz/ 7-g) package active dry yeast

1/2 cup (125 ml) lukewarm milk (110°F/43°C)

1/2 cup (100 g) sugar

1 2/3 cups (250 g) all-purpose (plain) flour

1/2 teaspoon vanilla extract (essence)

1/4 teaspoon salt

4 large egg yolks + 1 large egg, lightly beaten

1/2 cup (125 g) butter, melted

1 cup (180 g) golden raisins (sultanas)

Serves: 6–8
Preparation: 30 minutes
+ 90 minutes to rise
Cooking: 30–35 minutes
Level: 2

SAVORIES

SCONES

Line a baking sheet with parchment paper. Preheat the oven to 350°F (180°C/gas 4). • Combine the flour, sugar, baking powder, and salt in a medium bowl. • Rub the butter into the flour with your fingertips until it resembles bread crumbs. • Lightly beat the egg in a small bowl with a fork and add half the milk. Keep the remaining milk to hand. • Pour the egg-milk mixture into the flour and mix it in quickly and lightly with a round-bladed knife. Add the remaining milk gradually—you might not need all of it—until the dough comes together, but don't mix it for too long. The dough should be soft, but not too sticky to pick up. • Lightly dust a work surface and pat the dough out to a about 1 inch (2.5 cm) thick. • Flour a 2$\frac{1}{2}$-inch (6 cm) pastry cutter and cut out 8 rounds. • Place 2 inches (5 cm) apart on the prepared sheet. • Glaze: Beat the egg yolk with the milk in a small bowl. Brush over the tops of the scones. Sprinkle with a little sugar. • Bake for 15–20 minutes, until risen and golden. • Cool on a rack. • Halve and serve with raspberry or strawberry preserves and cream.

Dough

1$\frac{1}{2}$ cups (225 g) all-purpose (plain) flour

1 tablespoon superfine (caster) sugar

1 teaspoon baking powder

$\frac{1}{4}$ teaspoon salt

$\frac{1}{4}$ cup (50 g) unsalted butter, cubed

$\frac{1}{3}$ cup (90 ml) cold milk

1 large egg

Glaze

1 egg yolk

1 tablespoon milk

1 teaspoon superfine (caster) sugar, to sprinkle

Raspberry or strawberry preserves (jam), to serve

Whipped cream, to serve

Serves: 4–6
Preparation: 20 minutes
Cooking: 15–20 minutes
Level: 1

■ ■ ■ *Freshly baked scones spread with butter or clotted cream and jam are a British teatime treat. They are served in tearooms throughout the country. The trick for getting a moist light scone is to be quick when making it.*

GOAT CHEESE PARCELS

Preheat the oven to 400°F (200°C/gas 6). Line a baking sheet with parchment paper. • Cut the pastry into quarters and roll out into four 7-inch (18 cm) squares. • Cut the goat cheese into four thick slices. • Place each slice in the middle of a pastry square. Mix together 2 tablespoons of Parmesan, the anchovy fillets, capers, garlic, and oil in a small bowl. • Spoon equal amounts of the mixture over the goat cheese slices. • Brush the edges of the pastry with beaten egg. • To wrap up the parcels, gather up the four corners of the pastry like a money pouch, snugly enclosing the cheese. Pinch the edges to seal the parcels. • Place the parcels on the prepared baking sheet. Brush with the remaining egg and sprinkle with the remaining Parmesan. • Bake for 15–20 minutes, until the parcels are puffed and golden brown. • Serve hot or at room temperature.

630

1 **13-oz (375-g) pack ready-rolled puff pastry**

8 **oz (225 g) soft goat cheese**

4 **tablespoons freshly grated Parmesan cheese**

5 **anchovy fillets in oil, drained and finely chopped**

2 **teaspoons salt-cured capers, rinsed**

1 **large clove garlic, crushed**

1 **teaspoon extra-virgin olive oil**

1 **medium egg, beaten**

Serves: 4
Preparation: 20 minutes
Cooking: 15–20 minutes
Level: 1

PEA TARTLETS

Unroll the pastry on a lightly floured work surface and roll out to a $\frac{1}{8}$-inch (3 mm) thick. • Cut around a 6-inch (15-cm) saucer to make 6 circles. • Press the pastry circles into six 4-inch (10 cm) wide and 1-inch (2.5 cm) deep tartlet pans. Prick the bases with a fork and chill in the refrigerator for 30 minutes. • Preheat the oven to 400°F (200°C/gas 6). • Line each tartlet with parchment paper and baking beans. Place on a baking sheet and bake for 10 minutes. • Remove the parchment and beans from the pastry shells. • Decrease the oven temperature to 300°F (150°C/gas 2) and leave the oven door open so it cools down more quickly while you are preparing the filling. • Boil the peas in a little salted water for 2 minutes, or until tender. Drain well. • Combine the peas, egg yolks, cheese, and crème fraîche in a food processor and pulse briefly. • Stir in the parsley, and season with pepper and nutmeg. • Spoon into the pastry cases. • Bake for 20 minutes, or until the filling is just set. Serve warm or at room temperature.

8 oz (250 g) ready-rolled shortcrust pastry, thawed if frozen

6 oz (180 g) frozen peas, thawed

2 large egg yolks

4 tablespoons freshly grated Parmesan or Pecorino cheese

½ cup (125 g) crème fraîche

3 tablespoons flat-leaf parsley, finely chopped

Pinch of freshly ground black pepper

Pinch of freshly grated nutmeg

Serves: 6
Preparation: 20 minutes
  + 30 minutes to chill
Cooking: 30–35 minutes
Level: 1

632

■ ■ ■ *You can make these tartlets very quickly with fresh or frozen ready-rolled short pastry and frozen peas. Alternatively, you can make your own short-crust pastry.*

SPICY THAI ROLLS

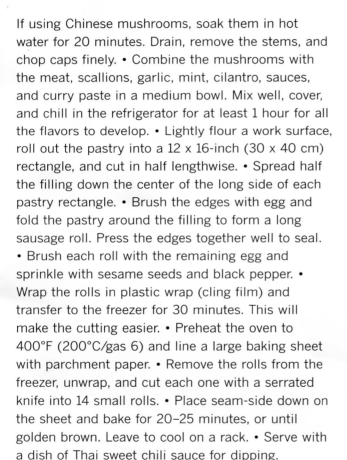

If using Chinese mushrooms, soak them in hot water for 20 minutes. Drain, remove the stems, and chop caps finely. • Combine the mushrooms with the meat, scallions, garlic, mint, cilantro, sauces, and curry paste in a medium bowl. Mix well, cover, and chill in the refrigerator for at least 1 hour for all the flavors to develop. • Lightly flour a work surface, roll out the pastry into a 12 x 16-inch (30 x 40 cm) rectangle, and cut in half lengthwise. • Spread half the filling down the center of the long side of each pastry rectangle. • Brush the edges with egg and fold the pastry around the filling to form a long sausage roll. Press the edges together well to seal. • Brush each roll with the remaining egg and sprinkle with sesame seeds and black pepper. • Wrap the rolls in plastic wrap (cling film) and transfer to the freezer for 30 minutes. This will make the cutting easier. • Preheat the oven to 400°F (200°C/gas 6) and line a large baking sheet with parchment paper. • Remove the rolls from the freezer, unwrap, and cut each one with a serrated knife into 14 small rolls. • Place seam-side down on the sheet and bake for 20–25 minutes, or until golden brown. Leave to cool on a rack. • Serve with a dish of Thai sweet chili sauce for dipping.

4 dried Chinese mushrooms or 4 oz (125 g) field mushrooms, finely chopped

15 oz (450 g) finely ground pork or chicken

3 large scallions (spring onions), finely chopped

1 clove garlic, finely chopped

1 tablespoon finely chopped fresh mint

1 tablespoon finely chopped fresh cilantro (coriander)

1 tablespoon Thai fish sauce

1 tablespoon soy sauce

4 teaspoons Thai green curry paste

1 13-oz (375-g) pack frozen puff pastry, thawed

1 egg, beaten for brushing

3 tablespoons sesame seeds, for sprinkling

1 teaspoon freshly ground black pepper

Thai Sweet Chili Sauce, to serve

Serves: 8–10
Preparation: 30 minutes
  + 90 minutes to chill
Cooking: 20–25 minutes
Level: 1

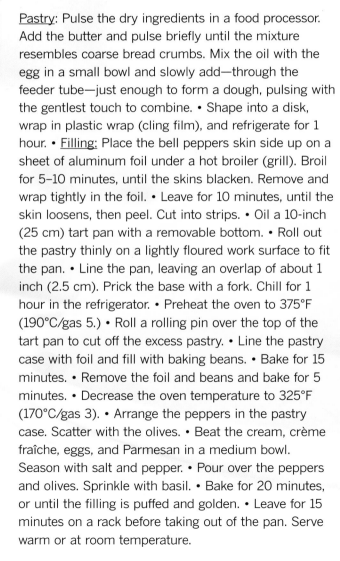
PEPPER AND OLIVE TART

Pastry: Pulse the dry ingredients in a food processor. Add the butter and pulse briefly until the mixture resembles coarse bread crumbs. Mix the oil with the egg in a small bowl and slowly add—through the feeder tube—just enough to form a dough, pulsing with the gentlest touch to combine. • Shape into a disk, wrap in plastic wrap (cling film), and refrigerate for 1 hour. • Filling: Place the bell peppers skin side up on a sheet of aluminum foil under a hot broiler (grill). Broil for 5–10 minutes, until the skins blacken. Remove and wrap tightly in the foil. • Leave for 10 minutes, until the skin loosens, then peel. Cut into strips. • Oil a 10-inch (25 cm) tart pan with a removable bottom. • Roll out the pastry thinly on a lightly floured work surface to fit the pan. • Line the pan, leaving an overlap of about 1 inch (2.5 cm). Prick the base with a fork. Chill for 1 hour in the refrigerator. • Preheat the oven to 375°F (190°C/gas 5.) • Roll a rolling pin over the top of the tart pan to cut off the excess pastry. • Line the pastry case with foil and fill with baking beans. • Bake for 15 minutes. • Remove the foil and beans and bake for 5 minutes. • Decrease the oven temperature to 325°F (170°C/gas 3). • Arrange the peppers in the pastry case. Scatter with the olives. • Beat the cream, crème fraîche, eggs, and Parmesan in a medium bowl. Season with salt and pepper. • Pour over the peppers and olives. Sprinkle with basil. • Bake for 20 minutes, or until the filling is puffed and golden. • Leave for 15 minutes on a rack before taking out of the pan. Serve warm or at room temperature.

Pastry

1½ cups (225 g) all-purpose (plain) flour

½ teaspoon salt

2 tablespoons freshly grated Parmesan cheese

1⅔ cups (150 g) butter, chilled and diced

1 tablespoon extra-virgin olive oil

1 large egg, beaten

Filling

1 red bell pepper (capsicum), cut in half lengthways, seeded

1 green bell pepper (capsicum), cut in half lengthways, seeded

10 black olives, pitted and halved

1 cup (250 ml) heavy (double) cream

4 tablespoons crème fraîche

2 large eggs

3 tablespoons freshly grated Parmesan cheese

Salt and black pepper

Handful of basil leaves, finely chopped

Serves: 6
Preparation: 30 minutes
   + 2 hours to chill
Cooking: 45 minutes
Level: 2

SWEET POTATO AND CARAMELIZED ONION TARTLETS

Pastry: Combine the flour and salt in a medium bowl. Cut the butter in with a pastry blender until the mixture resembles medium crumbs. Stir in the cheese and add the egg yolk and enough water to bind. • Mix to a firm dough and knead lightly. • Form into a disk and wrap in plastic wrap (cling film). • Chill in the refrigerator for 30 minutes. • Preheat the oven to 400°F (200°C/gas 6). • Brush six 4 x 1-inch (10 x 2.5-cm) flan pans with removable bottoms. • Roll out the pastry on a floured work surface and line the pans. • Chill for 15 minutes in the refrigerator. • Line the pastry cases with parchment paper, fill with baking beans, and bake for 10 minutes. Remove the paper and beans and leave to cool slightly. Decrease the oven to 350°F (180°C/ gas 4). • Filling: Heat the butter in a non-stick frying pan and add the onion with a pinch of salt. Fry over low heat for 10 minutes, until golden and caramelized. • Cook the sweet potatoes in boiling water for 10–12 minutes, until tender. • Drain thoroughly and mash with the crème fraîche and $\frac{1}{4}$ teaspoon salt until smooth. • Beat the eggs and milk in a medium bowl with a wire whisk. Stir in half the cheese and the parsley. Mix in the onions and sweet potatoes, and season to taste with salt and pepper. • Divide the mixture evenly among the pastry cases and sprinkle the remaining cheese over the tops. • Bake for 20 minutes, or until golden and just set in the middle. Leave to cool for 10 minutes before removing from the pans.

Pastry

1¼ cups (180 g) all-purpose (plain) flour

¼ teaspoon salt

⅓ cup (90 g) butter, chilled

4 tablespoons freshly grated Gruyere cheese

1 large egg yolk

2 tablespoons cold water

Filling

2 tablespoons butter

3 medium onions, sliced

1 lb (500 g) sweet potatoes, peeled and cubed

2 tablespoons crème fraîche (or cream)

3 large eggs

1 cup (250 ml) milk

4 oz (125 g) freshly grated mature Cheddar or other tasty cheese

1 tablespoon finely chopped fresh parsley

Salt and freshly ground black pepper

1 tablespoon butter, to brush

Serves: 6
Preparation: 25 minutes
  + 45 minutes to chill
Cooking: 1 hour
Level: 2

MINI TARTLETS AND PASTRY BOATS FOR CANAPÉS

Combine the flour and salt in a medium bowl. Add the butter, egg, and sugar. Rub in the ingredients with your fingertips, gradually drawing in the flour. • When the mixture has come together, add the milk. • Lightly knead on a floured work surface into a smooth dough. Wrap in plastic wrap (cling film) and chill for 2–3 hours. • Preheat the oven to 400°F (200°C/gas 6). Oil or butter 20 fluted tartlet pans, about $1^{1}/_{2}$ inches (4 cm) in diameter, or barquette molds, about 3 x $1^{1}/_{4}$ inches (8 x 3 cm). • Roll out the dough between 2 sheets of plastic wrap to a $^{1}/_{8}$ inch (3 mm) thick. Cut out circles with a pastry cutter, slightly larger than the pans, re-rolling the dough as necessary. Line the pans with dough. • Prick the bases with a fork. • Cover the tartlets with aluminum foil and fill with baking beans. • Bake for 8 minutes. • Remove the foil and beans and bake for 3–5 more minutes, until golden. • Transfer to a rack and let cool completely. • Mushroom Filling: Melt 2 tablespoons of butter in a small saucepan and add the mushrooms and lemon juice. Simmer over low heat for 8–10 minutes, until the mushrooms are tender. • Heat the remaining butter in a separate saucepan over low heat and stir in the flour. Gradually add the milk, stirring constantly for about 6–8 minutes, until thickened. Stir in the parsley and season with salt and freshly ground pepper. Leave to cool a little, then spoon into the tartlets. Garnish with parsley. • Herb and Cheese Filling: Beat the cheese in a bowl until smooth. Mix

$1^{2}/_{3}$ cups (250 g) all-purpose (plain) flour

$^{1}/_{2}$ teaspoon salt

$^{2}/_{3}$ cup (150 g) butter, diced and slightly softened

1 large egg, beaten

Pinch of sugar

1 tablespoon cold milk

Mushroom Filling

$^{1}/_{4}$ cup (60 g) butter

4 oz (125 g) button mushrooms, sliced

2 tablespoons freshly squeezed lemon juice

1 tablespoon all-purpose (plain) flour

1 cup (250 ml) milk

1 tablespoon finely chopped fresh parsley

Salt and black pepper

Herb and Cheese filling

8 oz (250 g) cream cheese or ricotta cheese

1 tablespoon finely chopped chives

1 garlic clove, crushed

1 tablespoon finely chopped fresh parsley

1 tablespoon finely chopped fresh dill

1 teaspoon finely chopped fresh mint

Salt and black pepper

Goat Cheese Filling

- 5 oz (150 g) goat cheese
- ½ cup (125 g) cottage cheese
- 2 scallions (spring onions), finely chopped
- 1 tablespoon finely chopped fresh parsley
- 1 tablespoon finely chopped fresh dill
- Pimento strips, to decorate

Minted Bean Filling

- 12 oz (350 g) fresh fava (broad) beans
- 8 oz (250 g) ricotta cheese
- 3 tablespoons finely chopped fresh mint
- 1 tablespoon olive oil
- Zest and juice of 1 lemon
- Salt and black pepper
- 1 tablespoon freshly grated pecorino cheese

Crab Filling

- 1 red bell pepper (capsicum)
- 5 oz (150 g) white crab meat, flaked
- ½ teaspoon lemon juice
- 1 tablespoon mayonnaise
- Salt and pepper

Serves: 8–10
Preparation: 30 minutes + 2–3 hours to chill
Cooking: 8 minutes
Level: 1

in the herbs and season to taste. Chill until needed. • Spoon into the tartlets. Garnish with herb sprigs. • Goat Cheese Filling: Combine all the ingredients, except the pimento strips, in the bowl of a food processor, and blend until smooth and creamy. Chill until needed. Fill the pastry cases and garnish with pimento strips. • Minted Bean Filling: Bring a small saucepan of water to a boil, add a pinch of salt, and cook the beans for 3–5 minutes, until tender. • Drain and refresh under cold water. • Peel off the skins, if tough. • Blend the beans in a food processor with the cheese, mint leaves, oil, and lemon zest and juice. • Season with salt and freshly ground pepper. • Spoon into the pastry cases. Sprinkle with pecorino and garnish with mint. • Crab Filling: Halve the bell pepper and remove the seeds. Place skin side up on a sheet of aluminum foil under a hot broiler (grill). Broil for 5–10 minutes, until the skin blisters and blackens. Wrap tightly in the foil and leave until the skin loosens. Peel and chop finely or mash. Mix with the other ingredients. Fill each pastry case.

■ ■ ■ *The recipe makes enough pastry for about 20–25 tartlets. Each filling recipe is enough to fill 20–25 tartlets. These little tarts make great party food. Fill the pastry cases no more than 2 hours before serving, as the bases will become soggy and unappetizing if left any longer.*

SPINACH QUICHE

Pastry: Combine the flour and salt in a bowl and cut in the butter with a pastry blender until it resembles fine bread crumbs. Mix in the egg yolk and just enough water to bring the dough together. • Shape into a ball and wrap in plastic wrap (cling film). Chill in the refrigerator for 1 hour. • Preheat the oven to 375°F (190°C/gas 5). • Oil a 9-inch (23 cm) fluted tart pan with a removable bottom. • Roll out the pastry to 1/4 inch (5 mm) thick. Line the base and sides of the pan. Line the pastry with foil and fill with baking beans. • Bake for 15 minutes. Remove the foil and beans and brush with the egg white. This will act as a seal and prevent leaks. • Bake for 8–10 more minutes, until lightly golden. • Decrease the oven temperature to 350°F (180°C/gas 4). • Filling: Sauté the bacon in a non-stick frying pan until crisp. Drain on kitchen paper. • Place the spinach in a large saucepan with a pinch of salt and 1 tablespoon of water, cover, and cook for 4 minutes, until the spinach has wilted. • Drain, and when cool enough to handle, squeeze out excess water with your hands. Chop coarsely with a sharp knife. • Whisk the cream cheese with the eggs and egg yolk in a large bowl. Whisk in the cream, Parmesan, and garlic. Season with salt, pepper, and nutmeg.• Stir in the spinach. • Spread the bacon over the pastry base. Pour the filling on top. • Put the feta and tomatoes in a small bowl and coat with oil. Sprinkle over the quiche. • Bake for 35–40 minutes, until just set, golden, and lightly puffed. Serve hot.

Pastry

- 1½ cups (225 g) all-purpose (plain) flour
- 1/4 teaspoon salt
- 2/3 cup (150 g) butter, chilled and diced
- 1 large egg, separated
- 2 tablespoons cold water

Filling

- 8 thin slices rindless bacon or pancetta, chopped
- 1 lb (500 g) baby spinach
- 5 oz (150 g) cream cheese
- 2 large eggs + 1 large yolk
- 1²/₃ cups (400 ml) heavy (double) cream
- 1 tablespoon freshly grated Parmesan cheese
- 1 garlic clove, crushed
- Salt and freshly ground black pepper
- Generous grating of nutmeg
- 1/3 cup (100 g) feta cheese, cut into small cubes
- 10 cherry tomatoes, halved
- 1 teaspoon sunflower oil

Serves: 6
Preparation: 35 minutes + 1 hour to chill
Cooking: 80 minutes
Level: 2

MINI LEEK AND POTATO STRUDELS

Boil the potatoes for 10–15 minutes, until tender. Slice 1/4-inch (5 mm) thick and place in a bowl. • Melt the butter in a large frying pan and sauté the onions, leeks, and garlic until softened, about 5 minutes. • Add the mushrooms and sauté for 2 minutes. • Add the sesame seeds and sauté for 1 minute. • Combine with the potatoes in the bowl and season with salt and pepper. • Add the eggs, cheese, and chives. Mix well. • <u>To Assemble</u>: Phyllo pastry usually comes in blocks of 8 x 12-inch (20 x 30 cm) sheets. Cut the block in half across its width, so it measures 6 x 8 inches (15 x 20 cm). • Place one rectangle of phyllo dough on a clean work surface, so that the length stretches away from you. Working from the short side, brush the sheet with melted butter. Place another sheet on top of the first and brush with more butter. • Sprinkle with a little of the almonds. • Place 2–3 teaspoons of the leek mixture along the short edge nearest to you, leaving about 1 inch (2.5 cm) free at the bottom and sides. • Turn the bottom edge up to cover the mixture, and fold the side edges over. • Brush the pastry again with melted butter and roll it up loosely like a jelly roll. • Repeat with the remaining pastry sheets, until you run out of filling. • Butter a large baking sheet. Preheat the oven to 375°F (190°C/gas 5). • Place the rolls seam-side down on the sheet, at least 1 inch (2.5 cm) apart. • Brush generously with butter. • Bake for 20–30 minutes, until golden and crisp. • Serve hot or at room temperature.

1½ lb (750 g) small new potatoes, unpeeled

¼ cup (60 g) butter

2 scallions (spring onions), finely chopped

2 small leeks, finely sliced

1 garlic clove, peeled and crushed

5 oz (150 g) small mushrooms, finely diced

1 tablespoon sesame seeds

Salt and freshly ground black pepper

2 large eggs, beaten

2 tablespoons freshly grated pecorino cheese

1 bunch chives, finely chopped

Block of 20 sheets phyllo pastry

½ cup (125 g) melted butter

1 cup (120 g) ground almonds

Serves: 10
Preparation: 1 hour
Cooking: 20–30 minutes
Level: 2

GREEK ZUCCHINI AND HERB TRIANGLES

648

Place the zucchini in a colander, sprinkle with salt, and mix well. Let stand for 15 minutes. Squeeze the zucchini in a clean kitchen towel to get rid of excess water. • Crumble the feta into a large bowl. Add the zucchini, eggs, onions, garlic, nuts, herbs, lemon juice and zest, and paprika. Mix well. • Mix the oil and butter in a small bowl. • Brush a baking sheet with some of the melted butter. • Unroll the phyllo pastry on a flat surface. (Always cover the block with a damp tea towel to keep it from drying out.) The sheets usually measure 8 x 12 inches (20 x 30 cm). Layer 3 sheets per portion. Brush each sheet with the butter and oil mix. Cut in half lengthways and brush the top sheet with more butter. Working from the short side, place 2 tablespoons of the filling into the corner nearest to you. Fold the other corner over, enclosing the filling to make a triangle. Seal the edge and continue folding up the pastry strip in triangles until you reach the other end. Fold the remaining pastry onto the triangle. Brush with more butter and oil mix and seal well. • Place on the baking sheet and repeat with the remaining phyllo sheets until the filling runs out. • Preheat the oven to 350°F (180°C/gas 4). • Brush the outside of each triangle with more butter mixture. • Bake for 15–20 minutes, until golden brown and crispy. Serve warm or at room temperature.

4 medium zucchinis (courgettes) (about 12 oz/350 g), trimmed and coarsely grated

¾ teaspoon fine sea salt

4 oz (125 g) feta cheese

2 medium eggs, beaten

3 scallions (spring onions), finely chopped

1 clove garlic, finely sliced

1 tablespoon pine nuts, toasted

4 tablespoons finely chopped fresh parsley

4 tablespoons finely chopped fresh mint

4 tablespoons finely chopped fresh dill

Zest and juice of half a lemon

¼ teaspoon sweet paprika

3 tablespoons extra-virgin olive oil

3 tablespoons butter, melted

1 packet frozen phyllo pastry (thawed)

Serves: 6–8
Preparation: 40–50 minutes
Cooking: 15–20 minutes
Level: 2

SALMON PHYLLO PARCELS

Preheat the oven to 375°F (190°C/gas 5). • Combine the cooked and smoked salmon, pepper, tomato, mustard, dill, and onion in a bowl and mix well. Season with salt and freshly ground pepper.
• Cut 2 sheets of phyllo pastry into 2-inch (5-cm) squares. Place one on top of the other and brush with olive oil. Place a heaped teaspoon of the salmon filling in the middle of each square. Fold the pastry over the top and wrap to form a parcel. Brush with a little more oil. Repeat with the remaining pastry and filling. • Line a baking sheet with parchment paper and place the parcels on the sheet. Bake for 5–7 minutes, until golden brown.
• Serve hot or warm.

650

3½ oz (100 g) cooked salmon, diced

3½ oz (100 g) smoked salmon, diced

1 small red pepper (capsicum), finely chopped

1 plum tomato, skinned, seeded, and finely chopped

1 teaspoon grain mustard

2 tablespoons finely chopped fresh dill

2 scallions (spring onions), finely sliced

Salt and freshly ground black pepper

1 packet frozen phyllo pastry

Extra-virgin olive oil, for brushing

Serves: 6–8
Preparation: 10 minutes
Cooking: 5–7 minutes
Level: 1

CORNISH PASTIES

Pastry: Combine the flour and salt in a large bowl. Cut in the butter and shortening with a pastry blender or rub them in with your fingertips until the mixture resembles fine bread crumbs. • Stir in enough of the cold water to just bind the dough. • Turn onto a lightly floured work surface and knead briefly to make a soft dough. • Wrap in plastic wrap (cling film) and chill for at least 30 minutes in the refrigerator. • Filling: Preheat the oven to 350°F (180°C/gas 4). Lightly grease a baking sheet. • Combine all the cut-up vegetables and meat in a bowl. Season well with salt and pepper. • Divide the pastry into 4 equal pieces. • Dust a work surface with flour and roll out each piece to a circle about the size of a dinner plate. Use a plate as a guide and cut around it. • Arrange a quarter of the filling mixture along the center of the pastry circle. Dampen the edges of the pastry with water. Bring up the edges to the center, so the pastry covers the filling. Pinch the edges with your fingers to make a crimped seam across the top of the pasty. • Place on the prepared baking sheet. Make a small slit on top to let out steam. • Brush with the egg to glaze. Repeat with the remaining pastry and filling. • Bake for 50–60 minutes, until the pasties are golden, the undersides have turned brown, and the filling is cooked through. Serve hot or cold.

Pastry

3 cups (450 g) all-purpose (plain) flour

¼ teaspoon salt

½ cup (125 g) butter, chilled and diced

4 oz (125 g) vegetable shortening

⅓ cup (90 ml) cold water

Filling

2 large potatoes, peeled and cut into ½-inch (1 cm) cubes

1 small swede (rutabaga) or carrot (about 5 oz/ 150 g), peeled and cut into ½-inch (1 cm) cubes

1 lb (500 g) braising steak, finely sliced or cut into ½-inch (1 cm) cubes

1 large onion, finely chopped

Salt and freshly ground pepper

1 small egg, beaten

Serves: 4
Preparation: 1 hour
+ 30 minutes to chill
Cooking: 35 minutes
Level: 2

HAM AND ONION SPIRALS

654

Dough: Place the yeast and sugar in a small bowl with the milk. Set aside for 10 minutes until frothy. • Combine the flour and salt in a large bowl. • Use a wooden spoon to gradually stir in the yeast mixture and eggs. • Transfer to a lightly floured work surface and knead by hand, gradually working in the butter as you work, until smooth and elastic, about 10 minutes. Alternatively, gradually add the butter while beating with a dough hook until smooth and elastic, 5 minutes. • Shape into a ball, cover with a cloth and set aside in a warm place to rise for 1 hour, or until doubled in bulk. • Filling: Sauté the pancetta in a large frying pan over medium heat until crisp. • Add the butter, onion, and garlic. Simmer over low heat for 10 minutes, until tender. Stir in the thyme, and season with salt and pepper. • Dust your hands with flour, punch the risen dough down, and briefly knead on a floured work surface. • Roll out to ¼ inch (5 mm) thick and cut into two 8 x 12-inch (20 x 30-cm) rectangles. • Spread the filling evenly over the dough. • Working from the short side, roll up each rectangle into a log. Cut into ³⁄₄-inch (2-cm) slices. • Line a baking sheet with parchment paper and transfer the spirals to the sheet, placing them at least 1 inch (2.5 cm) apart. • Cover and let rise in a warm place for 15–30 minutes. • Preheat the oven to 375°F (190°C/gas 5). • Just before baking, whisk the yolk with the milk and brush the spirals. • Bake for 20–25 minutes, or until golden brown. • Serve warm or at room temperature.

Dough

½ oz (15 g) compressed fresh yeast or 1 (¹/₄-oz/ (7-g) package active dry yeast

1 teaspoon sugar

²⁄₃ cup (150 ml) lukewarm (110°F/43°C) milk

3 cups (500 g) all-purpose (plain) flour

1½ teaspoons salt

2 large eggs, beaten

²⁄₃ cup (150 g) butter, diced and softened

Filling

8 oz (250 g) pancetta (or bacon), cut into small pieces

1 tablespoon butter

1 lb (500 g) onions, finely chopped

2 garlic cloves, finely sliced

1 teaspoon finely chopped fresh thyme

Salt and black pepper

1 large egg yolk

2 tablespoons milk

Serves: 12–15
Preparation: 50 minutes + 90 minutes to rise
Cooking: 40 minutes
Level: 2

SOUR CREAM AND MUSHROOM PIROSHKI

Sour Cream Pastry: Combine the flour, baking powder, and salt in a large bowl. Add the butter, sour cream, egg, and sugar. Mix with a fork until combined. • Turn out onto a floured work surface and knead briefly into a smooth stiff dough. Form into a ball, warp in plastic wrap (cling film) and chill in the refrigerator for 45 minutes. • Filling: Preheat the oven to 400°F (200°C/gas 6). • Melt the butter in a medium frying pan, add the onion and simmer over low heat for about 10 minutes, until golden. • Increase the heat, add the mushrooms, and cook for 5 minutes until soft, stirring often. • Stir in the salt and cayenne and cook for 1 more minute. • Transfer to a bowl and mix with the eggs. Stir in the sour cream, bread crumbs, and dill. • Roll out the pastry on a lightly floured surface to 1/4-inch (5 mm) thick and cut into 3-inch (8 cm) circles. • Use 2–3 teaspoons of the filling for each. Fold the pastry over the filling and pinch the edges together. • Brush with the beaten egg. • Lightly oil a baking sheet or line with parchment paper. • Place the piroshki on the sheet and bake for 15–20 minutes, or until browned.

■■■Piroshki, Russian for small pies, comes from the word pir, meaning "feast," Pirog (a large pie) and piroshki can be made from a variety of doughs —yeast, short, or flaky pastry—and are filled with meat, cabbage, mushrooms, or any leftovers. Serve hot or cold with soup, especially borsch, or alone as an appetizer.

Sour Cream Pastry

2½ cups (375 g) all-purpose (plain) flour

1 teaspoon baking powder

½ teaspoon salt

¼ cup (60 g) butter, diced

1¼ cups (300 ml) sour cream

1 large egg, beaten

1 teaspoon sugar

Filling

3 tablespoons butter

1 large onion, finely chopped

12 oz (350 g) mushrooms, chopped

1 teaspoon salt

¼ teaspoon cayenne pepper

2 hard-boiled eggs, chopped

2 tablespoons sour cream or crème fraîche

3 tablespoons fresh bread crumbs

2 tablespoons finely chopped fresh dill

1 egg, lightly beaten

Serves: 6–8

Preparation: 40 minutes + 45 minutes to chill

Cooking: 40 minutes

Level: 2

VIENNA LOAF

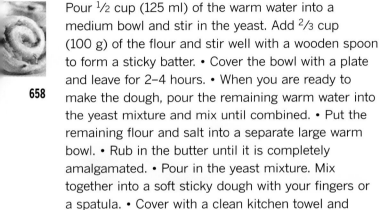

Pour ½ cup (125 ml) of the warm water into a medium bowl and stir in the yeast. Add ⅔ cup (100 g) of the flour and stir well with a wooden spoon to form a sticky batter. • Cover the bowl with a plate and leave for 2–4 hours. • When you are ready to make the dough, pour the remaining warm water into the yeast mixture and mix until combined. • Put the remaining flour and salt into a separate large warm bowl. • Rub in the butter until it is completely amalgamated. • Pour in the yeast mixture. Mix together into a soft sticky dough with your fingers or a spatula. • Cover with a clean kitchen towel and leave for 15 minutes. This will help the flour to absorb moisture. • Pour 1 teaspoon of oil on your work surface and rub it out into a circle about 12 inches (30 cm) in diameter. Oil your hands with ½ teaspoon of oil. Rub the oil over the dough, so you can scoop it up without it sticking. • Knead the dough on the oiled surface for 10 seconds, return to the bowl, and cover. • Repeat these brief kneads 3 times over 45 minutes. • Lightly flour a surface, place the dough on it, and pat into an oval about 8 inches (20 cm) long. • Butter a baking sheet and place the loaf on it. Cover and let rise for 50 minutes, until doubled in bulk. • Preheat the oven to 425°F (220°C/gas 7). Place a small metal dish of hot water on the bottom shelf. • Dust the loaf with flour and make a ½-inch (1-cm) deep cut along the top with a serrated knife. • Bake for 20 minutes. • Decrease the heat to 400°F (200°C/gas 6) and bake for 15–20 minutes, or until golden brown.

¾ cup (200 ml) lukewarm (110°F/43°C) water

½ oz (15 g) compressed fresh yeast or 1 (¼-oz/ (7-g) package active dry yeast

2 cups (300 g) all-purpose (plain) flour

1 teaspoon fine sea salt

1 tablespoon butter

2 teaspoons sunflower oil

Serves: 6
Preparation: 1 hour 15 minutes + 3–5 hours to rise
Cooking: 35–40 minutes
Level: 2

PAIN AU LARDON (BACON ROLLS)

660

Place the yeast in a small bowl with $\frac{1}{2}$ cup (125 ml) of water. Set aside for 10 minutes, until frothy.
• Combine both flours, salt, sugar, and pepper in a large bowl. • Stir in the oil, the yeast mixture, and enough of the remaining water to obtain a firm dough. • Transfer to a lightly floured work surface and knead by hand until smooth and elastic, about 10 minutes, or beat with a dough hook until smooth and elastic, 5 minutes. • Shape into a ball, place in an oiled bowl, cover with a cloth and set aside in a warm place to rise for 2 hour, or until doubled in bulk. • Meanwhile, grill the bacon until crisp, and cut into small pieces. • Turn out the dough onto a floured work surface, knock it back to expel the air, and knead briefly, working in the bacon pieces. • Divide the dough into 12 equal pieces. Knead each roll with the palm of your hand on the work surface, rolling and folding. Shape into rounds or pull into long rolls. • Oil a large baking sheet and place the rolls on it, spacing them well apart. • Make small crosses $\frac{1}{4}$ inch (5 mm) deep in the top of round rolls, and make incisions in the top of long rolls.
• Cover the rolls with a clean kitchen towel to stop them from drying out, and leave in a warm place for 30–60 minutes to rise. • Preheat the oven to 400°F (200°C/gas 6). Place a small metal dish of water at the bottom to create a steamy baking environment.
• Bake for 15–20 minutes, or until golden brown. • Brush the hot rolls with a slightly moistened brush, for a shiny finish. Allow to cool before cutting.

1 oz (30 g) compressed fresh yeast or 2 ($\frac{1}{4}$-oz/ 7-g) packages active dry yeast

1$\frac{1}{3}$ cups (300 ml) lukewarm (110°F/43°C) water

1 cup (150 g) whole-wheat (wholemeal) flour

2$\frac{1}{3}$ cups (350 g) all-purpose (plain) flour

1 teaspoon salt

1 teaspoon sugar

$\frac{1}{2}$ teaspoon ground pepper

2 tablespoons warm extra-virgin olive oil

4 oz (125 g) bacon or pancetta, sliced

Serves: 6–8
Preparation: 25 minutes
  + 3 hours to rise
Cooking: 25 minutes
Level: 2

CHOUX PUFF PARTY SAVORIES

Prepare the pastry. • Preheat the oven to 400°F (200°C/gas 6). Line 2 baking sheets with parchment paper. • Pipe or spoon the pastry onto the sheets while still warm. Use a pastry bag with a plain 1/2-inch (1 cm) nozzle or a teaspoon to make rounds the size of small walnuts. • Bake for 10–20 minutes, until golden. • Make a slit in the side of each puff with a knife. • Leave to cool in the turned-off oven with the door ajar. • Cheese Filling: Melt the butter in a small pan over low heat and stir in the flour. Cook for 3 minutes, stirring continuously. • Gradually add the milk, stirring for 4–5 minutes, until the mixture is smooth and thick. • Remove from the heat and stir in the egg yolk, cream, and cheese. Season with salt, pepper, and cayenne. Pour into a bowl and keep at room temperature. • Tapenade Filling: Put the olives, anchovy, tuna, capers, mustard, and 1/2 teaspoon of lemon juice in a food processor and pulse to a thick purée. • Gradually trickle in the olive oil, as for mayonnaise. • Add more lemon juice to taste, keeping the filling thick enough for piping. Season with black pepper. • Roasted Pepper Filling: Halve the bell pepper and remove the seeds. Place skin side up on a sheet of aluminum foil under a hot broiler (grill). Broil for 5–10 minutes, until the skin blisters and blackens. Wrap tightly in the foil and leave for 10 minutes. Peel and purée in a food processor with the cheeses. • Add oil and brandy, until the consistency is right for piping. Stir in basil, and season with salt and pepper. • Pipe the fillings into the choux puffs.

1 recipe Choux Pastry (see page 526)

Cheese Filling
1 tablespoon butter
1 tablespoon flour
1 cup (250 ml) milk
1 large egg yolk
1 tablespoon heavy cream
4 tablespoons freshly grated pecorino cheese
Salt and pepper
Pinch cayenne pepper

Tapenade Filling
12 pitted black olives
4 anchovy filets, drained
1 tablespoon tinned tuna fish, drained and flaked
1 heaped tablespoon bottled capers, drained
1/2 teaspoon dry mustard
1 teaspoon lemon juice
2 tablespoons olive oil

Roasted Pepper Filling
2 red peppers (capsicums)
5 oz (150 g) goat cheese
8 oz (200 g) cream cheese
1 tablespoon olive oil
1 tablespoon basil

Serves: 10–15
Preparation: 1 hour
Cooking: 45 minutes
Level: 2

PROVENÇAL BLACK OLIVE BREAD

664

Place the yeast in a small bowl with ½ cup (125 ml) of water. Set aside for 10 minutes, until frothy. • Combine the flour and salt in a large bowl and stir in the yeast mixture, oil, and enough of the remaining water to obtain a soft dough. • Transfer to a lightly floured work surface and knead by hand until smooth and elastic, about 10 minutes, or beat with a dough hook until smooth and elastic, 5 minutes. • Form into a ball and place in a lightly oiled bowl. Cover with a clean kitchen towel and leave in a warm place for 2 hours, until well risen. • Oil a pizza pan or small baking sheet. • Turn out the risen dough, punch it down to expel the air, and knead again for 1 minute. Knead in the thyme, if using. • Pat the dough into an oval shape and place on the sheet. • Cut 4 slits, 1 inch (2.5 cm) deep, like the veins of a leaf, on each side of the loaf. Gently press the olives into the dough and sprinkle the top with sea salt. • Cover with a clean kitchen towel and let rise again in a warm place for 90 minutes. • Preheat the oven to 425°F (220°C/gas 7). Place a small metal dish of water in the bottom to create a steamy baking environment. • When the loaf has risen, push the slits apart a little, so they don't close up during baking. • Bake for 20–25 minutes, or until golden brown. To test if the bread is cooked, tip the loaf out of the tin (using oven gloves), and tap the underside. It should sound hollow like a drum. If it sounds heavy, return to the oven for 5 more minutes. • Leave to cool on a rack.

1　oz (30 g) compressed fresh yeast or 2 (¼-oz/ 7-g) packages active dry yeast

1⅓ cups (300 ml) lukewarm (110°F/43°C) water

4⅓ cups (650 g) all-purpose (plain) flour

2　teaspoons salt

2　tablespoons extra-virgin olive oil

1　teaspoon finely chopped fresh thyme, optional

15 black olives, pitted

1　teaspoon coarse sea salt, for sprinkling

Serves: 12
Preparation: 30 minutes
　3 hours 30 minutes
　to rise
Cooking: 20–25 minutes
Level: 2

GRUYERE GALETTES

Preheat the oven to 300°F (150°C/gas 2). Line a large baking sheet with parchment paper. • Place the butter in a mixing bowl and beat with an electric mixer at medium speed until soft and smooth. Add the flour, salt, and cheese, and mix at slow speed until combined. Don't be too vigorous. • Flour your hands and shape the dough into a ball. • Flour the work surface and roll the dough out to $\frac{1}{2}$-inch (1 cm) thick. Cut out rounds with a 2-inch (5-cm) pastry cutter. • Place on the baking sheet and prick the galettes with a fork twice over. • Bake for 8 minutes. • Increase the heat to 400°F (200°C/gas 6) and bake for 5–6 more minutes, until golden brown at the edges. • Cool on the sheet for 5 minutes. Transfer to a rack with a spatula and leave to cool completely.

1 cup (225 g) butter, softened

$1\frac{1}{3}$ cups (200 g) all-purpose (plain) flour

$\frac{1}{2}$ teaspoon salt

4 oz (125 g) freshly grated Gruyere cheese

Serves: 6–8
Preparation: 25 minutes
Cooking: 15 minutes
Level: 1

BLACK OLIVE BITES

Combine the flour, baking powder, salt, sugar, and butter in a large bowl. • Add $1/3$ cup (90 ml) of the milk and the Parmesan. Knead with an electric mixer fitted with a dough hook (or your hands) into a smooth dough. • Add the olives and the remaining milk, if crumbly. • Flour your hands and shape into a ball. Divide the ball in half. • Place each half on a sheet plastic wrap (cling film) large enough to fully enclose it. • Roll each dough half into a log, about 2 inches (5 cm) in diameter inside the wrap. • Seal the ends and place the logs in the freezer for 45 minutes. • Preheat the oven to 350°F (180°C/gas 4). • Line 2 baking sheets with parchment paper. • Unwrap the chilled logs of dough. Cut into $1/4$-inch (5 mm) thick slices with a sharp knife. • Place the slices $1^1/2$ inches (4 cm) apart on the sheets. • Bake for 10–12 minutes, or until the edges are firm and golden and the bottoms are lightly browned. Cool completely on a rack.

2   cups (300 g) all-purpose (plain) flour
1   teaspoon baking powder
$1/2$ teaspoon salt
$1/4$ teaspoon sugar
$2/3$ cup (150 g) butter, chilled and diced
$1/2$ cup (125 ml) milk
$2^1/2$ oz (75 g) freshly grated Parmesan cheese
1   cup (100 g) pitted black olives, finely chopped

Serves: 10–12
Preparation: 25 minutes + 45 minutes to chill
Cooking: 12 minutes
Level: 1

■ ■ ■ *These crisp little savories are perfect to serve with a pre-dinner drink or as a snack with a cool handle of beer.*

APPLE AND STILTON STRUDEL

670

Preheat the oven to 350°F (180°C/gas 4). • Butter a large baking sheet. • Sprinkle the apples with the lemon juice in a large bowl. Add the lemon zest, Stilton, walnuts, thyme, nutmeg, and black pepper. • Lay the sheets of dough out flat and cover with a damp kitchen towel. (This will stop them from drying out.) Carefully fold two sheets of dough to fit on the baking sheet. Brush with some melted butter and sprinkle with bread crumbs. Top with another two sheets and repeat until all the phyllo is used up, finishing with a little butter and some bread crumbs. • Spread with the apple and cheese mixture and roll. Brush with the remaining butter and sprinkle with the remaining bread crumbs.
• Bake for 30–35 minutes, or until lightly browned.
• Serve warm.

1 lb (500 g) apples, peeled, cored, and coarsely chopped

Finely grated zest and freshly squeezed juice of 1 lemon

8 oz (250 g) Stilton cheese, crumbled

$\frac{1}{4}$ cup (30 g) walnuts, coarsely chopped

10 sprigs fresh thyme

Freshly grated nutmeg

Freshly ground black pepper

10 sheets phyllo dough, thawed if frozen

$\frac{1}{2}$ cup (125 g) butter, melted

$\frac{1}{2}$ cup (75 g) fine dry bread crumbs

Serves: 6–8
Preparation: 30 minutes
Cooking: 30–35 minutes
Level: 2

CHERRY TOMATO QUICHE

Quick Quiche Crust: Place the flour and salt in the bowl of a food processor with a metal blade. Add the butter and 2 tablespoons of water. Pulse until just amalgamated, adding more water if too crumbly. • Remove from the processor and press into a ball. Wrap in plastic wrap (cling film) and refrigerate for 30 minutes. • Preheat the oven to 350°F (180°C/gas 4). • Butter a 10-inch (25-cm) springform pan or pie plate. • Filling: Cut the cherry tomatoes in half and gently squeeze out as many seeds as possible. • Beat the eggs, cream, ricotta, and Parmesan in a large bowl. Season with salt and pepper. • Stir in the basil and oregano. • Roll the pastry out on a lightly floured work surface to 1/4-inch (5 mm) thick. • Line the prepared pan with the pastry. • Pour the egg and cheese mixture into the crust. • Add the tomatoes one by one, cut side down, pressing them into the filling slightly. • Bake for about 45 minutes, or until the pastry is golden brown and the filling has set. • Serve hot or at room temperature.

Quick Quiche Crust

1²⁄₃ cups (250 g) all-purpose (plain) flour

1/4 teaspoon salt

1/2 cup (125 g) cold butter, cut up

3 tablespoons cold water

Filling

15 cherry tomatoes

4 large eggs

1/2 cup (125 ml) heavy (double) cream

1/2 cup (125 g) ricotta cheese, drained

6 tablespoons freshly grated Parmesan cheese

Salt and freshly ground black pepper

6 leaves fresh basil, finely chopped

1/2 teaspoon dried oregano

Serves: 6
Preparation: 30 minutes + 30 minutes to chill the dough
Cooking: 45 minutes
Level: 1

BABY SQUASH QUICHE

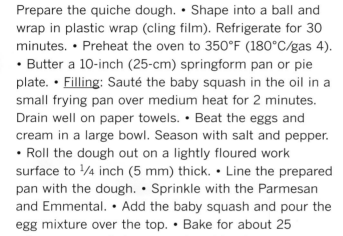

Prepare the quiche dough. • Shape into a ball and wrap in plastic wrap (cling film). Refrigerate for 30 minutes. • Preheat the oven to 350°F (180°C/gas 4). • Butter a 10-inch (25-cm) springform pan or pie plate. • <u>Filling</u>: Sauté the baby squash in the oil in a small frying pan over medium heat for 2 minutes. Drain well on paper towels. • Beat the eggs and cream in a large bowl. Season with salt and pepper. • Roll the dough out on a lightly floured work surface to ¼ inch (5 mm) thick. • Line the prepared pan with the dough. • Sprinkle with the Parmesan and Emmental. • Add the baby squash and pour the egg mixture over the top. • Bake for about 25 minutes, or until the pastry is golden brown and the filling has set. Let cool slightly. • Serve warm.

1 recipe Quick Quiche Crust (see page 672)

Filling

8 ounces (250 g) mixed baby squash, diced

2 tablespoons extra-virgin olive oil

5 large eggs

1 cup (250 ml) heavy (double) cream

Salt and freshly ground black pepper

1¼ cups (150 g) freshly grated Parmesan cheese

1¼ cups (150 g) freshly grated Emmental cheese

Serves: 6
Preparation: 30 minutes
+ 30 minutes to chill the dough
Cooking: 30 minutes
Level: 1

POTATO AND TOMATO QUICHE

Preheat the oven to 400°F (200°C/gas 6). • Butter an 8-inch (20-cm) springform pan or pie plate. • Peel the potatoes and cut into 1/4-inch (5-mm) slices. Steam the potato slices for 10 minutes, or until tender. • Beat the eggs, cream, Parmesan, and oregano in a large bowl. Season with salt and pepper. • Roll the pastry out on a lightly floured work surface to 1/8 inch (3 mm) thick. • Line the prepared pan with the pastry. Arrange the potatoes and tomato on the pastry base. • Pour in the egg mixture. • Bake for 15 minutes. Lower the oven temperature to 350°F (180°C/gas 4). Bake for 15 minutes more, or until the pastry is golden brown and the filling has set. • Serve warm or at room temperature.

2   potatoes

2   large eggs

1/2   cup (125 ml) heavy (double) cream

1   tablespoon freshly grated Parmesan cheese

1/2   teaspoon dried oregano

Salt and freshly ground black pepper

8   oz (250 g) fresh or frozen puff pastry, thawed if frozen

1   large firm-ripe tomato, thinly sliced

Serves: 4–6
Preparation: 30 minutes
Cooking: 45 minutes
Level: 1

ZUCCHINI AND HAM PIE

Sauté the garlic in the oil in a large frying pan until pale gold. • Discard the garlic. Add the zucchini and crumble in the stock cube. Cook over low heat for 1 minute. • Pour in the milk and simmer over medium heat for 5 minutes, or until the zucchinis are tender and the milk has been absorbed. • Add the potato and cream. • Preheat the oven to 350°F (180°C/gas 4). • Butter a 9-inch (23-cm) springform pan or pie plate. • Roll the pastry out on a lightly floured work surface to $1/8$ inch (3 mm) thick. Line the base and sides of the prepared pan with the pastry. • Arrange the ham in the pastry case and top with the zucchini mixture. Add the cheese. • Cut out decorative shapes from the remaining pastry and arrange them on top of the pie. • Bake for about 35 minutes, or until the pastry is golden brown and the filling has set. • Serve warm.

678

1   clove garlic, lightly crushed but whole

2   tablespoons extra-virgin olive oil

2   zucchini (courgettes), coarsely grated

½   vegetable bouillon cube

¼   cup (60 ml) milk

1   boiled potato, cubed

3   tablespoons heavy (double) cream

8   oz (250 g) fresh or frozen puff pastry, thawed if frozen

4   slices of ham

2   oz (60 g) Fontina or Cheddar cheese, cut in small cubes

Serves: 4–6
Preparation: 30 minutes
Cooking: 45 minutes
Level: 1

ONION QUICHE

Preheat the oven to 350°F (180°C/gas 4). • Roll the pastry out on a lightly floured work surface to $1/8$ inch (3 mm) thick. • Line the base and sides of a 10-inch (25-cm) springform pan or deep pie plate with the pastry. • Sauté the onions in the oil in a large frying pan over medium heat until softened, 5–7 minutes. • Beat the eggs, cream, and cheese in a large bowl. Season with salt and pepper. • Add the onions and mix well. • Pour the onion mixture into the pastry case. • Bake for 15 minutes. • Increase the oven temperature to 400°F (200°C/gas 6). Bake for about 15 minutes more, or until the pastry is golden brown and the filling has set. • Serve warm or at room temperature.

8 oz (250 g) puff pastry, thawed if frozen

12 medium white onions, thinly sliced

2 tablespoons extra-virgin olive oil

5 large eggs

1 cup (250 ml) heavy (double) cream

$1\frac{3}{4}$ cups (215 g) freshly grated Emmental cheese

Salt and freshly ground black pepper

Serves: 6
Preparation: 30 minutes
Cooking: 35 minutes
Level: 1

PUMPKIN BREAD WITH HERBS

Combine the yeast and sugar in a small bowl with the milk. Set aside for 10 minutes or until frothy.
• Combine the flour and salt in a large bowl. • Beat the egg in a small bowl until frothy. Season with pepper and beat in the sage, rosemary, nutmeg, and butter. • Use a wooden spoon to gradually stir the milk and yeast mixture into the flour. Add the egg mixture and stir well. Stir in the pumpkin. The dough should be fairly soft but kneadable.
• Transfer to a lightly floured work surface and knead by hand until smooth and elastic, about 10 minutes, or beat with a dough hook until smooth and elastic, 5 minutes. • Shape into a ball and place in an oiled bowl. Cover with a clean kitchen towel and place in a warm place to rise for 1 hour, or until doubled in bulk. • Preheat the oven to 350°F (180°C/gas 4). • Oil a 9 x 5-inch (23 x 13-cm) loaf pan. • Punch the dough down and knead briefly. • Place the dough in the pan and bake for about 45 minutes, or until well-risen and golden brown.

1 oz (30 g) compressed fresh yeast or 2 (1/4-oz/7-g) packages active dry yeast

1 teaspoon sugar

1/2 cup (125 ml) lukewarm (100°F/43°c) milk

3 cups (450 g) all-purpose (plain) flour

1 teaspoon salt

1 large egg

Freshly ground white pepper to taste

2 teaspoons finely chopped sage

2 teaspoons finely chopped rosemary

1/2 teaspoon ground nutmeg

3 tablespoons melted butter

1 cup (250 g) canned pumpkin purée

Serves: 6–8
Preparation: 45 minutes + 1 hour to rise
Cooking: 45 minutes
Level: 2

POTATO BREAD

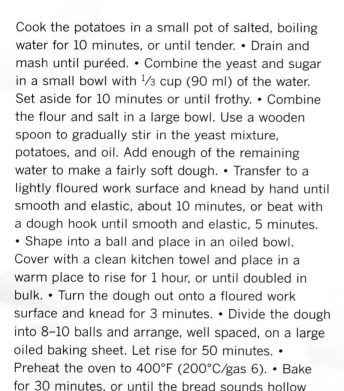

Cook the potatoes in a small pot of salted, boiling water for 10 minutes, or until tender. • Drain and mash until puréed. • Combine the yeast and sugar in a small bowl with $1/3$ cup (90 ml) of the water. Set aside for 10 minutes or until frothy. • Combine the flour and salt in a large bowl. Use a wooden spoon to gradually stir in the yeast mixture, potatoes, and oil. Add enough of the remaining water to make a fairly soft dough. • Transfer to a lightly floured work surface and knead by hand until smooth and elastic, about 10 minutes, or beat with a dough hook until smooth and elastic, 5 minutes. • Shape into a ball and place in an oiled bowl. Cover with a clean kitchen towel and place in a warm place to rise for 1 hour, or until doubled in bulk. • Turn the dough out onto a floured work surface and knead for 3 minutes. • Divide the dough into 8–10 balls and arrange, well spaced, on a large oiled baking sheet. Let rise for 50 minutes. • Preheat the oven to 400°F (200°C/gas 6). • Bake for 30 minutes, or until the bread sounds hollow when tapped on the bottom.

5 oz (150 g) potatoes, peeled and diced

1 oz (30 g) compressed fresh yeast or 2 ($1/4$-oz/7-g) packages active dry yeast

1 teaspoon sugar

$3/4$ cup (200 ml) lukewarm (100°F/43°C) water

$3^1/3$ cups (500 g) all-purpose (plain) flour

2 teaspoons salt

2 tablespoons extra-virgin olive oil

Serves: 8–10
Preparation: 45 minutes
  + 1 hour 50 minutes
  to rise
Cooking: 40 minutes
Level: 2

PIQUANT ONION PINWHEELS

Combine the yeast and sugar in a small bowl with 1/3 cup (90 ml) of water. Set aside for 10 minutes or until frothy. • Combine the flour and salt in a large bowl. • Use a wooden spoon to gradually stir in the yeast mixture, 1 tablespoon of butter, and the egg. Add enough of the remaining water to make a soft dough. • Transfer to a lightly floured work surface and knead by hand until smooth and elastic, about 10 minutes, or beat with a dough hook until smooth and elastic, 5 minutes. • Shape into a ball, cover with a cloth and set aside in a warm place to rise for 1 hour, or until doubled in bulk. • Sauté the onions in the remaining butter in a large frying pan until softened, about 5 minutes. Season with the red pepper flakes. • Turn the dough out onto a floured work surface and roll into a rectangle about 1/4 inch (5 mm) thick. • Spread with the onions. Roll the dough up carefully and cut into slices about 1/2 inch (1 cm) thick. Arrange, well-spaced, on a greased baking sheet and let rise for 30 minutes. • Preheat the oven to 350°F (180°C/gas 4). • Bake for about 20 minutes, or until golden brown. • Serve warm or at room temperature.

½ oz (15 g) compressed fresh yeast or 1 (¼-oz/ 7-g) package active dry yeast

1 tablespoon sugar

1 cup (250 ml) lukewarm (110°F/43°C) water

2 cups (300 g) all-purpose (plain) flour

1 teaspoon salt

5 tablespoons butter

1 large egg, lightly beaten

4 large onions, finely sliced

½ teaspoon red pepper flakes

Serves: 8–10
Preparation: 45 minutes
+ 90 minutes to rise
Cooking: 20 minutes
Level: 2

SPICY CORN MUFFINS

Preheat the oven to 400°F (200°C/gas 6). • Butter a 12-cup muffin pan. • Combine the flour, cornmeal, sugar, salt, baking powder, cumin, cayenne, pepper, and Parmesan in a large bowl. Mix well with a fork. • Heat two tablespoons of oil in a large frying pan over medium heat. Sauté the onion, bell pepper, corn, and jalapeño until softened, 5–7 minutes. • Remove from the heat. Stir in the cilantro. Cool to room temperature. • Combine the eggs, milk, and remaining olive oil in a small bowl. • Make a well in the flour mixture. Pour in the milk mixture all at once, and use a spatula to scrape all the ingredients from the frying pan into the well. Stir to combine. The mixture will be lumpy. • Spoon the batter into the prepared pans. • Bake for 20–25 minutes, or until the muffins are puffed, golden brown on top, and a toothpick inserted in the center comes out clean. • Cool on a wire rack for 10 minutes. Serve warm.

688

1 cup (150 g) all-purpose (plain) flour

1 cup (150 g) cornmeal

2 tablespoons sugar

½ teaspoon salt

1 tablespoon baking powder

¼ teaspoon ground cumin

⅛ teaspoon cayenne

¼ teaspoon freshly ground black pepper

½ cup (125 ml) finely grated Parmesan cheese

5 tablespoons extra-virgin olive oil

1 small onion, diced

½ small red bell pepper (capsicum)

1 cup (250 ml) canned corn (sweet corn), drained

1 large jalapeño chile, seeds removed, diced

3 tablespoons finely chopped fresh cilantro (coriander)

2 large eggs, lightly beaten

¾ cup (180 ml) milk

Serves: 6–8
Preparation: 20 minutes
Cooking: 20–25 minutes
Level: 1

SPINACH AND FETA CHEESE MUFFINS

Preheat the oven to 350°F (180°C/gas 4). • Butter a 12-cup muffin pan. • Cook the spinach in a little lightly salted water over medium heat until tender, about 5 minutes. Drain well, squeezing out excess moisture. Chop finely. • Combine the flour, baking powder, and salt in a medium bowl. • Beat the eggs, oil, and yogurt in a large bowl with an electric mixer on medium speed until smooth. • With mixer on low, gradually add the dry ingredients, beating until just combined. • Stir in the spinach and feta by hand. • Spoon the batter into the prepared pans. • Bake until well risen and springy to the touch, about 20 minutes. • Let cool slightly before turning out onto a wire rack.

8　oz (250 g) fresh or frozen spinach

2⅓ cups (350 g) all-purpose (plain) flour

3　teaspoons baking powder

½　teaspoon salt

2　large eggs

¼　cup (60 ml) extra-virgin olive oil

1　cup (250 ml) plain yogurt

8　oz (250 g) Feta cheese, cut into small cubes

Serves: 6–8
Preparation: 20 minutes
Cooking: 30 minutes
Level: 1

BACON AND HAZELNUT MUFFINS

Preheat the oven to 375°F (190°C/gas 5). • Butter a 12-cup muffin pan. • Sauté the bacon in a large frying pan over medium heat until lightly browned, 3–4 minutes. • Add the onion and hazelnuts and sauté until the onion is tender, 3–4 minutes. • Combine the flour, baking powder, and salt in a medium bowl. • Beat the eggs, butter, yogurt, and milk in a large bowl with an electric mixer on medium speed. • With mixer on low speed, add the bacon mixture and dry ingredients, beating until just combined. • Spoon the batter into the prepared pans. • Bake until well risen and springy to the touch, about 20 minutes. • Let cool slightly before turning out onto a wire rack.

8 oz (250 g) bacon, finely chopped

1 small onion, finely chopped

½ cup (50 g) finely chopped hazelnuts

1½ cups (225 g) all-purpose (plain) flour

3 teaspoons baking powder

½ teaspoon salt

2 large eggs

⅓ cup (90 g) butter, melted

½ cup (125 ml) plain yogurt

¾ cup (200 ml) milk

Serves: 6–8
Preparation: 15 minutes
Cooking: 30 minutes
Level: 1

HAM AND PEA MUFFINS

694

Preheat the oven to 350°F (180°C/gas 4). • Butter a 12-cup muffin pan. • Combine the flour, baking powder, salt, and pepper in a bowl. Stir in the Parmesan. • Beat the eggs, butter, and milk in a large bowl with an electric mixer on medium speed. • With mixer on low speed, add the peas, corn, ham and dry ingredients, beating until just combined. • Spoon the batter into the prepared pan. • Bake until well risen and springy to the touch, about 20 minutes. • Let cool slightly before turning out onto a wire rack.

2 cups (300 g) all-purpose (plain) flour

2 teaspoons baking powder

½ teaspoon salt

½ teaspoon freshly ground black pepper

6 tablespoons freshly grated Parmesan cheese

2 large eggs

¼ cup (60 g) butter, melted

⅔ cup (150 ml) milk

⅓ cup (50 g) cooked peas

⅓ cup (50 g) canned corn (sweetcorn)

⅔ cup (90 g) ham, diced

Serves: 6–8
Preparation: 20 minutes
Cooking: 20 minutes
Level: 1

PARMESAN MUFFINS WITH THYME

Preheat the oven to 350°F (180°C/gas 4). • Butter a 12-cup muffin pan. • Combine the flour, baking powder, and salt in a medium bowl. Stir in the Parmesan. • Beat the eggs, oil, yogurt, and thyme in a large bowl with an electric mixer on medium speed until smooth. • With mixer on low, gradually add the dry ingredients, beating until just combined. • Spoon the batter into the prepared pan. • Bake until well risen and springy to the touch, about 20 minutes. • Let cool slightly before turning out onto a wire rack.

1²⁄₃ cups (250 g) all-purpose (plain) flour

2½ teaspoons baking powder

½ teaspoon salt

²⁄₃ cup (100 g) freshly grated Parmesan cheese

2 large eggs

2 tablespoons extra-virgin olive oil

1 cup (250 ml) plain yogurt

1 tablespoon finely chopped fresh thyme

Serves: 6–8
Preparation: 15 minutes
Cooking: 20 minutes
Level: 1

INDEX

Butter Cakes

Cookies, Bars, and Brownies

Layer Cakes

Pastries

Pies and Tarts

SAVORIES

SMALL CAKES

Yeast Cakes